A DREAMER OF PICTURES

A DREAMER OF PICTURES

NEIL YOUNG
THE MAN AND HIS MUSIC

DAVID DOWNING

DA CAPO PRESS • New York

First published in the United States of America 1995
Da Capo Press, 233 Spring Street, New York, NY 10013

First published in Great Britain 1994
Bloomsbury Publishing Plc, 2 Soho Square, London W1V 5DE

PICTURE SOURCES

Richie Aaron/Redferns: page 7 *top*
Greg Allen/Retna: page 14 *top*
Glen A. Baker Archives/Redferns: page 1
A. J. Barratt/Retna: page 15
Dave Ellis/Redferns: page 4
Barry Levine/Redferns: page 2 *bottom*
LFI: pages 2 *top*, 3, 5 *top*, 8, 10, 16
Neal Preston/LFI: page 5 *bottom*
Rex Features: pages 6, 7 *bottom*, 9, 11, 12, 13, 14 *bottom*

ISBN 0-306-80611-8

10 9 8 7 6 5 4 3 2 1

Typeset by Hewer Text Composition Services, Edinburgh
Printed in Great Britain by Cox & Wyman, Reading

Library of Congress Cataloging-in-Publication Data

Downing, David.
       A dreamer of pictures : Neil Young, the man and his music / David Downing
          p.   cm.
       Originally published: London : Bloomsbury, 1994.
       Includes index.
       ISBN 0-306-80611-8
       1. Young, Neil. 2. Rock musicians--Canada--Biography. I. Title.
ML420.Y75D68   1995
782.42166'092--dc20
[B]   94-29686
                                                                 CIP
                                                                 MN

FOR NANCY

CONTENTS

1

'ALL MY CHANGES WERE THERE'

Neil Young was born in Toronto General Hospital on 12th November 1945, the second son of Scott and Edna Young. His parents had met about eight years earlier in Winnipeg, that city halfway between oceans which serves as the gateway to the Canadian prairies.

The black-haired, brown-eyed Edna, whom everyone knew as 'Rassy', was the daughter of American-born parents. Her mother was of French descent, her father a plantation Virginian of the old school, who had been moved to Manitoba by his employers before World War I, only to fall in love with the prairies. Rassy was her father's favourite, and seems to have acquired from him both a love of the great outdoors and an outspokenness which took few hostages.

Scott Young's ancestors had been Canadians for at least three generations, but this apparent solidity concealed a background more eccentric than Rassy's, with one grandfather a rich, fiddle-playing prairie farmer, the other a revivalist preacher-cum-horse-trainer. His parents had parted company when Scott was a young adolescent, and life thereafter with his mother appears to have been economically constrained, to say the least. He left school at sixteen, got his first job as a cashier for a tobacco wholesaler, and started a lifelong habit of writing stories. By the age of eighteen he was working as a copy boy at the *Winnipeg Free Press*, the first step in what would prove a reasonably illustrious career, as both writer and journalist.

When second son Neil arrived – first son Bob had been born in 1942 – the Youngs were living on Brooke Avenue in north Toronto and Scott was an assistant editor at *Maclean's* magazine. He was already providing a supplement to the family income through freelance short-story writing, and over the next couple of years his success and reputation in this field steadily grew. He decided to quit his regular job and write stories full time. There was no longer any need to live in Toronto, and in 1948 they sold the house and rented a summer property in the lake country

1

of central Ontario. It was there that the three-year-old Neil had his first brush with death, falling into a lake and having to be rescued from drowning by an older girl, the then famous child radio actress Beryl Braithwaite.

The Youngs rented another house over the winter, then bought one, a large redbrick dwelling with apple-treed garden in a small village about sixty miles north-east of Toronto. Omemee, with its fishing river and swimming hole and water mill, would be home to the family for the next six years, and despite the parents' obviously tempestuous relationship there seems no reason to believe that these weren't, in the main, happy years for their second son. The 'town in north Ontario' in his song 'Helpless' could be nowhere else, with its yellow moons, blue windows and 'big birds flying across the sky'. To anyone who has ever travelled through this part of the world, those lines evoke the quiet, the vastness and the beauty of a largely unspoilt natural landscape – something permanent in a world full of changes, something to hold on to.

The family hadn't been in Omemee two years when the global polio epidemic provided the young Neil with a second opportunity to confront his own mortality. The chances of his dying or being partially paralysed were considerable – another child in the village did indeed die – but he came through apparently unscathed, though a weakness throughout the left side of his body may have had its roots in the illness. The mental scars may well have been worse: six days' complete isolation would have been traumatic for any five-year-old, let alone one who was in severe pain. According to his father, the boy's first words when his parents came to collect him were: 'I didn't die, did I.'

He convalesced for several months, first in Omemee, then in Florida where the family rented a house for several months in the winter and spring of 1952. Then it was back home to the fishing pole, the toboggan, turtles in the sandbox, paddling in the river and, of course, school. Neil, it seems, lacked the necessary deference to be an ideal pupil, and his sense of humour was not always shared by his teachers.

Having two intelligent and knowledgeable parents must have helped make up for anything he might have missed in school. The house was full of reading material, and some of Canada's best-known intellectuals passed through the Youngs' living room. There was no shortage of inspiration should Neil have been leaning towards an artistic career, but at the same time he could hardly have helped noticing that writing was not the securest form of existence. His father was relatively successful, but short-story writing tended to be a constant struggle to stay ahead of the overdraft. Some of Neil's later career decisions might well have sprung from an early insight into how short an artist's commercial shelf-life could be.

As for the deeper matter of emotional security, it is usually difficult enough to know with any certainty how one has been affected by one's own parents' relationship, let alone to work out how other people might have been affected by theirs. Scott and Rassy Young appear to have been a demonstrative couple, and it seems reasonable to assume that just as, later, they found it hard not to act out their anger and resentment towards each other, so at this time they found it easy to act out their mutual love. While Bob and Neil were learning from their parents' example that few things are certain and most things insecure, they may also have been given a priceless insight into the love that can make such uncertainty worthwhile.

Who knows? When Neil was eight his father, away in the north on an assignment, wrote to Rassy asking for a divorce; after a brief separation, the family reunited in Toronto for what Scott called 'a year of tears and recriminations and reunions and separations again'.

They bought a bungalow in Pickering, just east of Toronto, determined on making the most of this second start. During the next three years Neil discovered his business sense, first selling wild raspberries by the roadside, then starting an egg business with chickens he bred himself in an incubator. By the summer of 1957 he was making about twenty dollars a week – a not insignificant sum for an eleven-year-old in those days.

He was also discovering rock'n'roll. The whole family, like most of the rest of North America, had sat open-mouthed in front of Elvis Presley's first TV show early in 1956. Something had changed – nobody knew quite what – and like millions of other kids Neil was soon falling asleep with the radio tuned in to the local rock station, in his case Toronto's 1050-CHUM. Elvis was King, of course, but there were hundreds of other new stars vying for a generation's attention, covering the whole spectrum of new music, from the blackest rhythm'n'blues to the whitest country, from the Coasters to the Everly Brothers and back again.

When Scott went to work for Toronto's *Globe and Mail* in 1958 the family moved back to the city, and the chickens had to go. Neil started a paper round to replace his lost income, and no doubt enjoyed a better reception on his radio. Just before Christmas in 1958 he was given a plastic ukelele by his parents, and began learning how to play chords. A banjo would follow, and then a guitar, but in the meantime his home life was again to take a dramatic turn for the worse.

His parents' new start came to a juddering end when Scott met and fell in love with his next wife, Astrid, on one of his many trips away. The break was neither quick nor clean, and according to Scott, everybody concerned suffered 'a year or more' of 'bitter acrimony' before the final split was announced. Scott took the two boys to a restaurant to try and explain what had happened, and afterwards, out on the street, Neil apparently reached over and gave his father a sympathetic pat on the shoulder. If boys entering adolescence are good at anything, it's covering up their feelings.

Not long after this parting scene, Rassy packed the two boys and their belongings into a small Ford, said goodbye to Toronto and to Scott, and started out for Winnipeg, where she intended to make another new start. *En route* she promised the fourteen-year-old Neil that he could play his guitar all he wanted as long as he stopped biting his nails.

Bob, now seventeen, would soon return to his friends and father in Toronto, but Rassy and her second son were to live together in Winnipeg for the next four years, while Neil finished school and graduated into a professional musician of uncertain prospects.

The two of them settled into an apartment in the city's working-class Fort Rouge district. Though Rassy was obviously not yet reconciled to the end of her marriage – in some ways, it seems, she never would be – she found a much warmer welcome in Winnipeg than her son did. She was coming home, to family and old friends, and Scott's alimony payments ensured that she was not going to starve. Winnipeg society offered the outdoor sporting life she loved, and she was soon a member of both the curling and the golf clubs. As an added bonus she found herself invited onto the regular panel of a local TV show called *Any Questions?* Rassy might have lost Scott but, once given new opportunities to shine, was not the type of woman to sit around moping.

For her son, initially at least, it must have been much harder. With every friend he'd ever made now a thousand miles away, he enrolled in grade 9 at yet another new school – Earl Grey Junior High – bearing the dual stigma of divorced parents and a nonconformist spirit. Since Winnipeg is one of North America's more conservative cities, and adolescent boys the most conformist species on earth, he probably suffered a little on both counts. And once his lack of interest in team sports had become apparent, any last chance of becoming popular with his fellow students should surely have vanished.

In his autobiographical song 'Don't Be Denied' Young does tell of being bullied, just for being different. But any such initial unpopularity doesn't appear to have lasted long. Two characteristics, it seems, pulled him through. One was his sense of humour: at times wicked, often wry, and usually targeted at figures of authority. The other was his already intense interest in popular music, which was itself bidding fair to be considered the third great adolescent obsession, alongside sports and spots. A few jock types might still have thought of him as a weird wimp from a dubious home, but most of his schoolmates, whether boys or girls, seem to have found Young fun to be with.

He lost no time in getting his first group started. Fixing an electric pick-up to his trusty acoustic guitar, he formed the Jades with schoolfriends John Daniel, David Gregg and Jim Atkin. They specialised in playing versions of instrumental hits like the Ventures' 'Walk Don't Run' and the Fireballs' 'Fried Eggs', but threw in a few vocal songs as well, with Daniel at the microphone. He also played lead guitar; Young, still busy learning his instrument, took rhythm. After practising for a few weeks they played their one and only gig, a canteen dance at the Earl Grey Community Club.

They weren't too bad, apparently, but the band's life was brought to an early end when John Daniel, finding himself double-booked to play both music and hockey, was forced by Young to choose between them, once and for all. He chose hockey. 'There really wasn't anything more important in my life than playing music,' Young said later, 'and you had to really want to do it and you had to make music first in your life.' Daniel wouldn't be the last partner of Young's to face such single-minded determination, or such an ultimatum.

Winnipeg, at this time, was fertile soil for someone fixated on making teenage music. The Community Club where the Jades had played their only gig was one of several, all of them built – in response to Winnipeg's long winter – as multipurpose leisure and meeting venues. There were ice rinks for skating and hockey, coffee bars for youngsters to hang out in, and meeting halls where the frequent dances were held. A steady supply of music was required for the latter, and at first this was mostly supplied by teenage DJs, including Young himself, who would simply turn up with an armful of treasured 45s. But with the sixties under way the desire for live music swiftly grew, and the number of local bands willing to fulfil that desire grew with it.

One such was the Esquires, which Young joined in the spring of 1961, only to be swiftly dismissed for his lack of proficiency on the guitar. For the moment his dream was running ahead of his talent, but he was nothing if not determined. Rassy had just bought him a second-hand electric guitar, and he seems to have spent most of the hours school allowed – and quite a few it didn't – practising.

Sometimes he did so alone, sometimes with Ken Koblun, another schoolmate with a passion for music. The two of them also shared an unusual family background (Koblun had foster parents), gangling height, and the sense of being outsiders in a world made in the image of well-co-ordinated athletes. Their friendship survived the transition to different high schools in the summer of 1961, and became the basis of the Stardusters, formed around the end of that year. The band played one dance at Young's Kelvin High School in February 1962, but thereafter drifted into oblivion.

Young probably wished his school would do the same. English apart, he seems to have shown little interest in his studies, and his report cards deteriorated accordingly. In the summer of 1962 he failed grade 10, exasperating his mother and angering his faraway father.

Rassy and Neil moved during this summer, taking over part of an attractive house on Grosvenor Avenue in the more up-market district of Crescentwood. Young vowed to do better at school, and like others before him no doubt felt vague twinges of guilt on those first few occasions he picked up his guitar rather than a book. That autumn he and Ken Koblun formed another group, the Classics, with four other friends. With Young on lead, Koblun on bass, a piano player, drummer, rhythm guitarist and vocalist, the Classics played a selection of current hits – less than well. 'We had trouble getting gigs because we weren't good enough,' Young remembered years later. After six gigs they were history.

A new band was already being born. Young and Koblun had met a drummer (Jack Harper) who knew another guitarist (Allan Bates), and over the 1962 Christmas holidays the four of them tried playing together in Harper's basement. They thought they sounded good, and Young thought up a name for them – the Squires. They planned to concentrate, like Young's earlier groups, almost exclusively on instrumentals, but

Young's intentions for the Squires went beyond the mere aping of other groups' hits. Over the preceding year he had started composing instrumentals of his own, mostly in the style of his and his friends' current idol.

The guitarist who evoked the most worship among Winnipeg's teenage pretenders wasn't Chuck Berry or James Burton or Scotty Moore, but, appropriately enough given Canada's colonial past, an Englishman in horn-rimmed glasses by the name of Hank B. Marvin. The lead guitarist of Cliff Richard's backing group the Shadows, Marvin had invented a tremolo-heavy style of playing which emphasised the lyrical potential of the electric guitar. The Shadows' instrumental records – made without Richard – were melodic, even beautiful. Where contemporaries like Duane Eddy, Link Wray or the Ventures were mostly content to express no more than restless energy, the Shadows conjured emotions out of mystery, evoked worlds other than the industrial one most of their listeners inhabited. In Britain they were in the middle of a long string of huge hits, which had begun in 1960 with 'Apache' and continued on through such glorious slices of suburban romanticism as 'Wonderful Land', 'Atlantis' and 'Kontiki'. They were virtually unknown in the US, but in Winnipeg, at the centre of Canada, they would have been greeted as gods.

Neil and the Squires were certainly avid disciples. The first professional gig of their two-and-a-half-year career was at the Riverview Community Club on 1st February 1963. Jack Harper had by this time already left – another victim of the peculiarly prevalent belief in the importance of school and sports – and been replaced by Ken Smyth.

Replacing the group's inadequate equipment was more problematic. Both Young and Koblun needed new instruments, and the Squires' home-made amps didn't have the power to fill the larger halls they were asked to play. Young had some luck with the guitar, picking up a second-hand orange Gretsch from someone who couldn't keep up the instalment payments, but the new amp they needed would cost around six hundred dollars. He wrote asking his father, who offered help if and when the school report cards improved.

His mother proved more amenable. She was there, she could see how committed her son was to music, and she had probably all but lost hope of his report cards improving. She witnessed Neil's determination and she believed in his talent. 'To me,' she claimed later, 'his music always had a sort of forlorn and desolate undertone . . . at times I would wonder why his face would light up with a sort of joy when he'd play something he'd composed that was so sad it brought tears to my eyes.'

She not only bought them a new amp with her savings, but also became the Squires' unofficial booking agent and general protector. Anyone who tried to mess with the band, be they timid school officials, complaining neighbours, landlords or apologetic cops, found they were outclassed in gutsiness, charm or both.

Thus protected, the band began to build a following among Winnipeg's community clubs, so much so that a local radio DJ was able to get them an audition in the station's two-track recording studio. They impressed the recording engineer, and were asked back first to rehearse and then to record, on 23rd July 1963, two instrumentals which Young had written: 'The Sultan' and 'Aurora'. In late September the single would be released locally on V Records and would, not surprisingly, get a lot of airplay on its parent radio station.

From the perspective of the 1990s it's hard to imagine how the record sounded in 1963, to know whether listeners experienced it as just one more instrumental in an established tradition, or were hit by the difference. When one listens today to the widely available, wonderfully messy bootlegs, it's easier to hear these songs as the halfway house they were. On one level, they sound like the Shadows revisited, melodic guitar instrumentals titled to evoke the mysterious, but on another, one can detect almost an overabundance of passion in the playing. There is nothing distant about the Squires' performance, no cool step backwards. In both 'The Sultan' and 'Aurora', ancestral echoes of the later journey 'from Hank to Hendrix' are already audible.

In the summer of 1963, as he holidayed with friends at Falcon Lake, the seventeen-year-old Young was in most respects an ordinary North American teenager of the time. He had a good relationship with his mother, friendly as well as loving, and the only obvious by-product of Rassy's frequent TV- or sport-related absences was the healthy development of Neil's ability to look after himself. He didn't see his father often, and what meetings there were seem to have been somewhat awkward, but the emotional tie had not been broken or left to fade. The Youngs appear to have managed the problems of a 'broken family' better than most.

Neil met his first real sweetheart, Pam Smith, on the beach at Falcon Lake that summer. In later years she remembered a 'wonderful laugh' which he didn't use that often, his fondness for nature, and an intensity that was rare among her acquaintances. Indeed, if there was one thing that made Young stand out at this time it was an unusual degree of single-mindedness. He *knew* what he wanted his future to be. Music was already his life, the guitar rarely more than an arm's reach away. At school he was just going through the motions.

One thing that threatened everything, and the knowledge of which perhaps accounted in part for Young's intensity, was that he had epilepsy. He had not as yet had a major seizure, but there had been several symptoms over the last few years, and he was careful to tell Pam Smith that summer what to do should the need arise. It can't have been an easy weight to carry for a young man with his ambitions.

Still, it was not something he could plan his future career around. The Squires carried on gigging in Winnipeg, expanding their base of operations out beyond the familiar circle of clean-cut community clubs, and into less salubrious venues like the Cellar downtown. Towards the end of 1963 they played their first dates outside the city, in the small towns of Portage la Prairie and Dauphin. For the latter gig they received the princely sum of $125. The Squires might not be getting anywhere fast, but they did seem to be getting somewhere.

The Squires' sound, however, was about to follow much of North American rock'n'roll into obsolescence. For the past year Britain had been experiencing a music revolution, as a plethora of groups – led by the Beatles – had taken hold of the current (mostly American) pop music, given it a booster injection of black rhythm'n'blues, and then shot it through with their own native wit and energy. As 1964 dawned, America finally succumbed to the shock of the new, and from Newfoundland to San Diego it was hard to hear anything above the sound of bandwagons being jumped on. In Winnipeg, anyone with any pretensions to being hip was trying to write songs like 'Do You Want to Know a Secret?' and learning how to play 'She Loves You'.

The Squires were no exception, and since they lacked a natural singer, Young stepped into the breach. His first vocal performance in public, featuring the songs 'Money' and 'It Won't Be Long', took place in the school cafeteria. 'People told me I couldn't sing,' he admitted later, 'but I just kept at it.' As with the guitar, he practised and practised.

He was also doing a lot of listening, and not just to British groups. Another music, this time American, was also on the rise – urban folk music. Peter, Paul and Mary's Top Ten success in the summer of 1963, with the then virtually unknown Bob Dylan's 'Blowin' in the Wind', was only the tip of an iceberg. Large numbers of the West's 'bulge generation', reared in material plenty and spiritual squalor, were now arriving on campus thirsty for political change and a culture that reflected that need. All around North America folk clubs were either springing up or dusting themselves down to satisfy the new demand.

One such was the 4-D in Winnipeg, where Young became something of a regular during 1964, meeting many of the luminaries of the Canadian folk scene, newcomers Joni Mitchell and Jesse Colin Young among them. The rock'n'roll scene and the folk scene rarely overlapped in 1963–4, and it is probably safe to assume that at this stage Young simply liked both musics without harbouring any desire to merge them into one. That would come gradually, almost accidentally, over the next eighteen months. For the moment, he and the Squires were content to keep one foot in each camp, playing the community clubs for money, the 4-D for food.

The group's musical schizophrenia was more demonstrably illustrated when in April 1964 they had a chance to do some more recording. At least three of the songs they taped at CKRC radio studios were Young compositions, but that was about all they had in common. 'Ain't It the Truth', which would be revived by the Bluenotes almost a quarter of a century later (with a live version appearing on *Lucky Thirteen*), was a strutting rhythm'n'blues number for young males on heat. 'I Wonder', an attempt at the British group sound pitched somewhere between the Searchers and the Dave Clark Five, would turn up twice in the future, first as 'Don't Pity Me Babe' on the 1965 Elektra demo, then as 'Don't Cry No Tears' on *Zuma*. 'Mustang' was a would-be Shadows instrumental. As yet no one could accuse Young of any great originality.

Another instrumental, intended as the follow-up to 'The Sultan', was never even recorded. The song was apparently inspired by the assassination of President Kennedy, with Young tying the symbol of peace to the rhythm of pop through its title, 'White Flower'. In doing so he offered at least some recognition of what was happening in the wide world beyond Winnipeg, where cultures and musics all seemed set on collision course.

In the meantime, the pursuit of too many musical directions – or, to put it another way, the absence of any one direction – was probably a contributing factor in the rifts that split the group in the summer of 1964. They'd been together a year and a half; they had mastered the popular instrumental sound of 1962–3, and then the British sound of 1964. It had been fun – still was fun – but it was hard to believe there was any real future in it.

At least, that's what Allan Bates and Ken Smyth appear to have decided that summer, when they turned down a demand by Young to play a particular gig. The latter was outraged that they could miss such an opportunity – or any opportunity – to further their musical careers. He and Ken Koblun had already resolved, provided that parental approval was forthcoming, to quit school and shoot for the big-time, and they wanted partners who were just as determined as they were. Bates and Smyth were fired, and the search for their replacements began.

As for school, neither of Young's parents seems to have been too happy with Neil's decision to quit, but Scott was far away and Rassy bowed to the inevitable. After all, maybe pigs could fly and her son would become a star. By October he was not only out of school, but also the proud possessor of a means of transporting the group – a 1948 Buick hearse, which he christened Mortimer Hearst, or Mort for short. Its first long haul was to Fort William, four hundred miles away to the east on Lake Superior, where Young had managed to get the group a week's booking at the Flamingo Club.

Winnipeg, he'd decided, had done all it could for him. Not for the last time in his career, Young seems to have felt trapped by others' expectations of his music. Once people knew what to expect from him, he thought, they could never be brought to accept anything else, and if Winnipeg thought it had the Squires completely sussed, then Young would take the band to Fort William, whose worthy denizens would have no such preconceptions to overcome.

They arrived in mid-October, now a trio and boasting a new name: Neil Young and the Squires. What Ken Koblun thought of this isn't known; perhaps he reasoned that Young, as the writer, singer and lead guitarist, deserved the billing.

The third member was Bill Edmundson, the new drummer. A potential fourth, Jeff Wuckert – who had played piano with them throughout September – had failed to get his parents' permission for the trip, and there was no time to start looking for a replacement. It didn't apparently matter: the threesome performed capably enough at the Flamingo to secure another, two-week engagement at the same club in November, and a few other gigs besides at the Fort William incarnation of the 4-D.

11

The music they were playing on this trip was more blues-influenced than before, partly as a result of Jeff Wuckert's recent involvement, but also because Young was becoming more interested both in that area of music and in making a bigger noise. A berserk 'Farmer John' was one of the group's staples at this time, as well as Young-penned numbers like 'Hello Lonely Woman' and 'Find Another Shoulder' which wouldn't be heard again until the Bluenotes tours of 1987–8. Although it might be an exaggeration to say that at this stage he was discovering his own electric-guitar style, there is no doubt that Young was stretching the boundaries of what he was prepared to try. He now had enough basic technique for self-expression to become possible.

He wasn't, however, deserting the softer side. 'Sugar Mountain' – and songs don't come any softer – was written by Young in his Fort William hotel room during this visit, allegedly on the depressing occasion of his nineteenth birthday. And when invited by another admiring radio DJ, Ray Dee, to make a demo in a recording studio, Young chose 'I'll Love You Forever', a song he'd written about meeting Pam Smith on the beach at Falcon Lake, and a couple of other, equally melodic songs. Going berserk on 'Farmer John' might be fun, but by this time Young was beginning to realise that he had to sell himself on record as an original, not as a rehasher of other people's songs. These particular songs, though, were apparently not original enough: none of the Canadian record companies Dee sent them to expressed any interest.

Meanwhile the band had returned to Winnipeg, having earned more than a thousand dollars during their two-month stay in Fort William. It was hardly a fortune, but it wasn't such a bad start to a professional career. Young was encouraged, more single-minded than ever, and determined that the rest of the band should be too. Koblun made the grade, but Edmundson, more interested in love and marriage than in his musical future, didn't. He was fired, and over the next few months of mid-Canadian winter the Squires consisted of Young, Koblun and whomever they could persuade to join them. One young guitarist, Doug Campbell, impressed Young enormously, but when spring arrived, and the time came to head east for Fort William again, he proved unwilling. Once more the Squires set off as a trio, this time with Bob Clark on drums.

They arrived in the lakeside town on a Sunday evening, with only a few minutes to spare before their performance, which was scheduled to fill a slot between two sets by the Company, a travelling offshoot of the Au Go Go Singers folk troupe. The Company's unofficial leader, a young blond Southerner by the name of Stephen Stills, was one of those watching from the wings as Young and his band unveiled their latest style: folk songs with rock instrumentation.

Folk rock, or simple *rock* as it came to be called, involved nothing more complex than putting rock'n'roll's heavy bass and drum rhythm underneath folk's simple changes and lyrical complexity. As the marriage of a music that moved to a music that served as a vehicle for extramusical intelligence, folk rock was a genre whose time had come. After all, why would young people settle for either gut music or brain music if they could have gut-brain music?

In early 1965 it was being invented all over the place. Lennon was putting insightful lyrics to pop music; Dylan was plugging in his guitar at the Newport Folk Festival. Gene Clark and Roger McGuinn were writing Dylanish pop songs and Beatlesish folk songs and finding that they all sounded like Byrds songs. And in distant Fort William, Neil Young was bringing together the musics he loved, creating rock arrangements for classic folk songs like 'Tom Dooley', 'Oh Susannah' and 'Cottonfields'.

Stephen Stills's childhood and youth were not exactly settled. His family came from southern Illinois, he himself was born in Dallas, and before reaching adolescence he'd also lived in New Orleans, Florida and the Central American republic of Costa Rica. His father, a builder, was evidently something of a rolling stone by inclination.

How all this movement affected young Stephen is hard to say. On the one hand, it doubtless gave him a wider experience of life than was offered to most white American boys. On the other, it may have meant that it was hard for him to develop deep friendships, and that he was too dependent on his own judgement.

His first of many musical instruments was a set of drums, and like Young he seems from his early teens to have been committed to a life in music. Around the age of seventeen he left school and started singing, with a friend named Chris Farns, in a New Orleans club called the Bayou Room. Eventually thrown out for drunkenness – an early indication that his talent was not blessed with an accompanying self-control – Stills considered going to college but somehow ended up, in 1964, in New York's Greenwich Village. There he managed to make some sort of living playing those venues where performers passed the hat.

It was a good point in space and time for a young musician to be. The new Lovin' Spoonful and Paul Butterfield Blues Band were much in evidence, and the place was full of young minstrels hoping to be sucked into the slipstream of Dylan's success. Stills played in a trio with future Monkee Peter Torkelson and John Hopkins, then worked in a duo with Chris Farns again, before the addition of several new faces and adoption of the name the New Choctawguins. Farns left and the group transmuted into the Au Go Go Singers, one of whose new members was Richie Furay. By the spring of 1965, stranded by the march of musical progress, this folk aggregation had disbanded, leaving a few of its erstwhile members to form a smaller group, the Company. The latter's decision to do a tour of Canadian coffee-houses appears to have been motivated chiefly by the realisation that they had nothing better to do.

Now here Stills was, in a coffee-house a thousand miles from civilisation, listening to a group he'd never heard of before, who had apparently invented folk rock. To say he was impressed would be an understatement.

It turned out to be a mutual-appreciation society. Young liked Stills's guitar work and loved his voice. After introducing themselves that first night the two young men spent a lot of time together, talking music and, in Stills's words, 'running around in his hearse and drinking good strong Canadian beer and being young and having a good time'. Young has never been slow to decide whether he likes someone, and probably the two of them quickly recognised a kindred spirit in each other. Certainly their pasts bore certain similarities – comfortable but nomadic home lives, constant new starts in friendships with boys of the same age, an obsessive involvement in music, a natural intensity. There were differences too, but these would surface later, when the two musicians were bound together in competitive situations. For the moment, as they roamed loose and inebriated through Fort William and its environs on the northern shore of Lake Superior, there was little to get uptight about, only music to share, and hopes for the future.

They probably made no specific plans to meet up again, but both seem to have sensed the possibility and the musical potential. For the moment there was vague talk of Young coming to New York, and of Stills fixing him up with permission to work in the US. Like travellers swapping addresses, they put down a marker on the future which might or might not be called in.

*   *   *

14

While Stills and the Company moved on to the next gig in their itinerary, Young and the Squires stayed on in Fort William for two months longer, filling in their regular spot at the 4-D coffee-house and doing one-off school or church dance gigs. It was enjoyable, but also, as the weeks went by, less and less challenging. In money terms they were, at best, breaking even.

It all ended suddenly, spontaneously and accidentally. After one Saturday-afternoon gig at the 4-D, Terry Erikson, who'd become almost a regular member of the group over the preceding months, announced that he'd been offered a gig in Sudbury, Ontario, some six hundred miles to the east, the following week. All he needed was a band. How did the others feel about it?

Koblun had already disappeared for the day, but Young, Erikson and three other available musicians decided on the spur of the moment to take off in Mort. Four hundred miles and thirty-six hours later, the hearse was out for the count in a Blind River repair shop and the five travellers were stranded in the middle of nowhere, with only Erikson's motorcycle for transport. The other three set out to hitch back west while Young and Erikson waited in vain for the hearse to be fixed. Once it had become apparent that it was beyond repair, they headed on to North Bay, hoping for help from Erikson's father. When this wasn't forthcoming it seemed a natural step to ride the last two hundred miles south to Toronto, where they would find not only Young's father, but also the artistic and commercial heart of the Canadian music scene.

Scott took them in, showing, for all his distance towards Neil, a tolerance that many fathers would have found unsustainable, and the youngsters started to explore the musical scene. That week of their arrival the Byrds' 'Mr Tambourine Man' was holding the number 1 spot on the *Billboard* chart – folk rock had clearly arrived. A week later they were elbowed aside by the Rolling Stones, whose 'Satisfaction' offered proof that you could take the 'folk' back out again without sacrificing the new articulacy. A few weeks more and Dylan's 'Like a Rolling Stone' would provide the third foundation stone on which most of the following decade's music would be built.

Two of the Squires, it seemed to Young and Erikson themselves, had arrived in the right place at the right time. Martin Onrot, a young manager whose name Young had been given, was equally enthusiastic. The other two members of the group were summoned and duly arrived, complaining bitterly about their earlier abandonment in Fort William.

The four of them then got down to work with a new name that Martin Onrot had dreamed up – Four to Go.

Any enthusiasm they'd brought with them soon evaporated. Onrot, perhaps influenced by the early Byrds, was convinced that folk harmonies over a rock beat was the wave of the future, and his insistence on everyone singing soon led to Bob Clark's departure. Not long after, the group's continuing failure to get their first gig in the big city persuaded Terry Erikson to follow suit. Replacements were found and Four to Go soldiered on, with Young maintaining a disciplined schedule of daily rehearsals while Onrot toured the clubs in search of an owner prepared to gamble on something slightly different. Since he had no income, Young was forced to borrow from his father, and then to take a job for several weeks in Coles bookstore.

In the meantime Toronto continued to live up to its conservative reputation, and Onrot found no takers. The music scene here, unlike that in Winnipeg or Fort William, was large enough to contain sub-scenes and, for all the signs of change in the charts, Toronto's venues were rigidly divided along genre lines: the more raucous, male-oriented rock'n'roll clubs on Yonge Street and the coffee-houses of the Yorkville folk ghetto. The Ronnie Hawkinses and the Joni Mitchells did not hang out together.

By late October, Four to Go had simply run out of faith in its collective future. Koblun found it easier than Young to get work on his own, but that was hardly surprising: he was content to be a freelance bassist for the myriad folkies, while Young still wanted to be the next big thing. He seems to have spent most of November writing and worrying.

A brief respite came with the offer of a Vermont ski-resort gig, and the reunited band travelled east with more enthusiasm than the date warranted. After the first performance, in which a drunk managed to break one of Young's strings, the manager made it plain they weren't playing the sort of music he wanted. As far as Young was concerned, any discontent was mutual, and he quit. Rather than waste the trip altogether, he and Koblun decided to take a detour on the way home, via New York. Koblun had a girl he wanted to see, and Young had the address Stills had given him in April. Once again his luck was apparently out: the apartment was still home to a musician, but it wasn't Stills.

Richie Furay had grown up in small-town Ohio. He had acquired his first guitar at the age of eight and then swiftly lost interest. College and the new folk boom had revitalised his enthusiasm, and inspired by his favourite Kingston Trio albums, Furay had formed a folk trio with two fellow students. After two years of playing around campus, during a school trip in 1964 they made a New York club début, and did well enough to secure a two-week gig that summer.

During the engagement Furay met Stills, also fronting a folkish ensemble, and the two of them decided to merge groups. In their six-month life the Au Go Go Singers made a record, starred in an off-Broadway show and toured, before the usual artistic and financial disillusionments led to an amicable disintegration. Early in the spring of 1965, while Stills led the Company on its tour of Canada, Furay moved temporarily to Massachusetts in search of a living wage. When Stills came back that summer and suggested – perhaps with Young also in mind – a new collaboration, Furay turned him down. Stills decided to try his luck in California, but Furay stayed on at the New York address Young had been given in Fort William, and it was he whom the Canadian found at home that autumn.

Like Stills and Young in the spring, Furay and Young got on well, swapping music and stories. Furay found Young 'a real interesting guy', and liked one of his songs, 'Nowadays Clancy Can't Even Sing', enough to have Young teach it to him. As for Young, he'd left another marker on the future, although this time he was probably not aware of having done so.

Though doubtless buoyed by Furay's appreciation, Young was probably more depressed at having missed Stills. Perhaps this was one of the reasons for his decision, on his return to Toronto, to trade in the much-loved Gretsch for an acoustic twelve-string. Or maybe it was a simple act of desperation. With the new guitar he managed to get a few gigs around the Yorkville coffee-houses, making friends without influencing anyone very much. One review, which called his songs 'all cliché', must have hurt.

But, as Leonard Cohen once observed, 'Even damnation is poisoned with rainbows.' Someone – even Young can't remember who – arranged for him to record some demos of his songs at Elektra in New York. There was no red-carpet welcome: Young was simply led to the tape library where a single microphone had been set up for him to sing and play into. He did seven songs, all written by him.

The tape has since been widely bootlegged, and offers an interesting, if decidedly partial, view of Young as a writer and performer at this time.

17

By virtue of the situation, these sound like folk songs, and there's not much doubt that Young's most innovative work so far had been with an electric band. Here, the acoustic-guitar work is competent, and there's no attempt to demonstrate anything more. Young's voice is lighter, airier, than it would later become, but there's no doubting its plaintive quality, or how effective it promised to prove with better lyrics.

The songs all wear any number of influences on their sleeves. 'Sugar Mountain' sounds as if it could have been an early Tom Paxton song, while 'Run Around Babe' seems ready-made for Donovan, and 'When It Falls It Falls All over You' wouldn't have been out of place in *The Paul Simon Songbook*. 'Don't Pity Me Babe' has the original melody from 'I Wonder', with new lyrics and a rhythm highly reminiscent of the Byrds' 'Feel a Whole Lot Better'.

Like all the popular youthful troubadours of the time Young was cramming his songs with poetic images, and constantly in danger of undermining their earnestness by being too obviously clever. There's precious little in the way of direct self-expression in these songs: the singer is too busy rearranging the world in his own image. 'Run Around Babe' sees him losing his mind, but being oh so understanding about why his girlfriend has left him this way; 'I Ain't Got the Blues' starts off with wry self-deprecation, but the arrogance that's never far from the surface breaks through in the end – 'I ain't got the blues but something more true.' All the songs carry this same potent male adolescent mix of arrogance, uncertainty and absurdity, yet Young is somehow never more believable than when, on 'Don't Pity Me Babe', he asserts, 'I know I'm all right, oh yeah, I'm all right.'

One song, 'Nowadays Clancy Can't Even Sing', clearly stands out. A slightly Gaelic feel to the melody and rhythm distances the music from the usual troubadour fare, and the lyrics, though wordy and far from straightforward, clearly come as much from the heart as from the mind. The song revolves around two realisations: that Young is his own worst enemy, with one side of his character forever getting in the way of the other; and that such problems pale into insignificance when compared with those of Clancy, who 'can't even sing'. Clancy was actually someone Young had known at Kelvin High, a sufferer from multiple sclerosis, but no such inside knowledge was necessary for an appreciation of the song's emotional power. Here, at least, was evidence of an original songwriter.

* * *

Back in Toronto, no doubt nursing the hope that the tape he'd made would lead to more, Young met another kindred spirit. Bruce Palmer had first picked up a guitar in a record store when he was ten, and liked the way it felt. His father, being an orchestra leader, presumably encouraged these musical leanings, though he may have later regretted the type of music his son chose to play.

Palmer took up the bass out of love rather than necessity, having been inspired by a youthful sighting of the then still rare electric bass. Unlike many bass players of his generation, who had adopted the instrument simply because it was the last empty slot in a group's line-up, he had a real feel for the bass guitar, and it showed.

Though still only nineteen, he had already been part of one good Toronto group, Jack London and the Sparrow, and was now involved in another, the Mynah Birds – so named because their bankroller owned both a shop that sold the birds and a club named after them. When Palmer first met the gangling Young on Yorkville Avenue, complete with amp perched on his head, the Mynah Birds had just lost their lead guitarist. Palmer must have liked Young and his playing, because not many men with acoustic twelve-strings get offered the lead-guitar job in rhythm'n'blues bands.

Young certainly needed no second bidding. It was music, it was paid work. He liked Palmer and soon developed a friendship with the band's lead singer, Ricky Matthews, who seemed set on becoming a – if not *the* – black Mick Jagger. The Mynah Birds had already made one single, had an influential backer in retail entrepreneur John Eaton, and looked set for a shot at the big-time.

As it happened they would be together only for another six weeks, but for Young even this short period was valuable enough. Musically the band would never bear much of his individual stamp, but it was another chance to play rhythm'n'blues material, this time with the added piquancy of playing it on an amped-up acoustic twelve-string.

More significantly, perhaps, for the first time in a long while Young was not in charge; he was just a journeyman musician, working mostly on other people's material. How well he would have coped with such a subordinate role in the long term is debatable, but in the event the situation did not arise, and for a few weeks, at the end of several frustrating months, it must have felt good to step back and let someone else take the strain.

Toronto in general, and the Mynah Birds in particular, also offered something else that was new to Young. 'Ricky introduced me to amphetamines and that changed my life,' he said later. 'When I had arrived in Toronto there was a whole new culture that I was introduced to. I had done nothing like that up to then.' The Mynah Birds' few gigs seem to have been almost as notable for the hopped-up antics of the band as for their music.

They can't have been bad, though, because even with John Eaton pulling strings, it seems doubtful that a successful, predominantly black company like Motown would have been prepared to offer a merely mediocre, predominantly white band a recording contract. With $25,000 up front, and a seven-year contract the size of a telephone directory to sign, Young must have thought he'd finally got a foot in the door of major success. The recording sessions in Detroit, held around the end of February 1965, started off well and got better, as the supremely professional Motown music-makers got to work on making the most of the Mynah Birds' unique sound.

And then, out of the blue, it transpired that Ricky Matthews was AWOL from the US Navy. It was still only 1965, the Vietnam War had only just moved into second gear with the first bombing of the North, and draft-dodging and desertion hadn't yet become as American as apple pie. Ricky was taken into custody, Motown pulled the studio plugs, and the band discovered that their manager had used the $25,000 to overdose himself. They made their way forlornly back to Toronto, with Young as yet unaware of the favour Motown had done him in releasing him from his contract.

Years later, after making the most of his second chance to become a Motown star, Ricky Matthews – now Rick James – claimed that he and Young had shared a last sad afternoon together in Detroit, promising each other that one day they would work together again. 'I had really gotten close to the cat,' Matthews said, adding that Young 'was never very healthy – he got bad epileptic fits sometimes – but he had balls like you wouldn't believe'.

Winter in Toronto wasn't exactly the ideal setting for a man lacking either good health or money, and Young had begun to despair of making a professional breakthrough in Canada. Palmer was equally disenchanted, and equally willing to try somewhere else. The question was where. South of the border, certainly: the great Canadian dream was to get out of Canada. Down south there were bigger concentrations of like-minded people, and more chance of finding a large enough audience for something different.

They decided against New York, perhaps because they felt – rightly, as it turned out – that California would be the primary centre for rock innovation over the next few years, perhaps because they looked out of their Toronto window at the snow and yearned for some sunshine. Or maybe they just felt like driving across a continent in a hearse.

There were problems. They couldn't just cross the border and find employment as musicians. A green card was required if they were to work in the US, and to get one they would need the sort of stature they couldn't achieve except by already being there. Such a Catch-22 could only be circumvented illegally.

So, it seemed, could the other main problem – a complete lack of funds or transportation. What they did have in their possession, however, was the Mynah Birds' equipment, which actually belonged to John Eaton. They pawned it, and Young found a 1953 Pontiac hearse in a used-car lot. One other guy and three girls (some memories say two) signed up for the trip, the guitars and dope were loaded aboard, and one day in mid-March 1966 the hearse set off for the promised land.

They drove into the US at Sault Ste Marie, claiming they were Winnipeggers using the short cut home along the south shore of Lake Superior. Once clear of the border they turned south towards St Louis, and a day or so later they were heading west on Route 66, following in the footsteps of Okies, TV shows and the Rolling Stones. Young was getting increasingly uptight about the others' inability to drive the hearse with the care it deserved, and anxious at the prospect of a second Blind River in a strange country, and was taking on too many hours of driving and maybe too many artificial stimulants to compensate.

In Albuquerque, New Mexico, his body had its revenge: he collapsed with some sort of nervous exhaustion, and was flat on his back for several days. By the time he was ready to move on, defections had reduced the party to three: Young, Palmer and one of the girls. On April Fools' Day 1966 they pulled into Los Angeles, the city of the fallen angels.

2

BEFORE THE GOLDRUSH

After failing to persuade Richie Furay to join him in a New York folk-rock band, Stephen Stills had decided to head west. Pausing in New Orleans to collect his mother and sister – his parents' marriage had just broken up – he arrived in San Francisco sometime in the autumn of 1965, and found himself in the midst of what looked suspiciously like a cultural revolution. Two years before the 1967 'summer of love' brought the San Francisco scene to prominence – and simultaneously sentenced it to death – the times really did seem to be a-changin'.

Stills met members of two new and innovative groups – Jefferson Airplane and the Grateful Dead – and seems to have half fallen in love with the lead singer of another, the Great Society's Grace Slick. Too nervous to ask if she'd consider playing with him, and having some songs to sell, he went down to Los Angeles, where there were still people old-fashioned enough to be recording material they hadn't written themselves.

Here he had an immediate stroke of good fortune, selling 'Sit Down I Think I Love You' to a music publisher. The Mojo Men would take this song into the Top Forty over a year later, and Buffalo Springfield would include a version on their first album. In the meantime, Stills could at least afford to eat.

He made demo tapes of other songs, started a friendship with future manager Barry Friedman, tried collaborating with Van Dyke Parks, and joined folkie Ron Long in a short-lived duo called Buffalo Fish. Friend Peter Torkelson arrived from New York and turned the Fish into a trio. In September, Stills heard about auditions for a new pop group, whose lovable antics, lovable music and moptop surrealism would offer network TV audiences cut-price thirty-minute slices of ersatz Beatles movies.

He was one of the 433 auditionees who didn't get to be a Monkee. The length of the odds would seem reason enough for failure, but over the years incipient baldness, a gap in his teeth and an unwillingness to sing other people's material have been offered as alternative explanations.

Rejection may have been sweetened by his friend's acceptance. Changing his name to Tork – the studio probably decided teenagers wouldn't want so many syllables to cope with – Peter Torkelson was anointed as one of the four Monkees, and seemed to spend much of the next decade apologising for such an elevation. Stills had probably had a lucky escape, though it's unlikely he felt he had at the time. His continuing search for willing musical partners showed no signs of paying off. Weeks went by, and months.

Then a letter arrived from Richie Furay in Massachusetts, circuitously, via his father in El Salvador and his mother in San Francisco. Furay was now tired enough of his day job at Pratt and Whitney to consider a move west, and wrote asking Stills about the prospects in LA. 'Come on out,' Stills told him. 'I got a group and all I need is you.'

This was not so much an exaggeration as an outright lie. The best interpretation anyone could put on it was that two musicians were closer to a group than one. But at least Furay was someone Stills knew he could work with, and who seemed equally prepared to work with the difficult Stills.

Once Stills had come clean as to the composition of the 'group' – 'It was frustrating but typical,' Furay would comment later – the two of them got down to learning songs together at Barry Friedman's house. One they played around with was Young's 'Nowadays Clancy Can't Even Sing', which Furay had learned from the writer in New York the previous autumn.

Meanwhile the search for more musicians went on. Stills tried to contact Young again, calling the number he had in Toronto, but only managed to reach Ken Koblun, then part of a folk group called Three's a Crowd. Come on out, Stills probably told the Canadian, I've got a group and all I need is you. Koblun was keen to play folk rock again, no more immune to hope than Furay, and duly caught the plane. But unlike the American he had an existing group to go back to, and after spending one sunny week waiting for something to happen, he used what money he had left on a cab to the airport, where the Three's a Crowd manager had promised a waiting ticket for Toronto. It was mid-March 1966. Further discouraged, Stills and Furay went back to practising for their non-existent group.

Help was nearer at hand than they knew. Young and Palmer arrived in LA on 1st April and started searching for Stills, the only person they knew in the vast city. From club to coffee-house they trekked, but no one seemed to have heard of him. Cheap lodgings and off-street parking spaces were no easier to find, and their sleeping in the hearse was not popular with the LAPD. Running short of money, they started renting out the hearse to other young people for scene-to-scene transit – a sort of one-vehicle hippie public transport system.

The two men, barely out of their teens, were a long way from home, and although there was probably a better-functioning sense of youth solidarity in 1966 than at any time since, Los Angeles has never been noted as a forgiving place to be when the money runs out. No doubt they could have obtained long-distance support from their parents, but which nineteen-year-olds setting out to discover the outside world want to do that? By the end of their first week in LA, Young and Palmer must have been feeling depressed, anxious, maybe even a little panicky. The promised land seemed in danger of reneging on its promise.

They decided to try San Francisco, but immediately suffered another setback – a huge traffic jam on Sunset Strip. However, it just so happened that stuck in the same jam were ... Stills and Furay. According to Stills, they simply found themselves behind a hearse, noticed its Ontario plates, and realised who must be on board. Furay's account is more satisfyingly circumstantial: 'We were in this white van, stuck in traffic on Sunset Boulevard. I turned to brush a fly off my arm, looked over into the other lane, and saw this black hearse with Ontario licence plates going in the other direction. Then Stephen looked across and said, "I'll bet I know who that is."'

Furay did an illegal U-turn and pulled up behind the hearse, honking his horn. A surprised Young and Palmer suddenly saw in their rear-view mirror the face they'd been looking for. Both vehicles pulled into a supermarket parking lot, and four-fifths of the future Buffalo Springfield got out. Stills must have thought he was dreaming – Young *and* a bass player! A band at last.

Furay claims that they then had to persuade Young and Palmer to come over to Barry Friedman's house and listen to his and Stills's arrangement of 'Clancy'. This sounds about as likely as a snowstorm in Hollywood. Young had been searching for Stills for a week; he was hardly likely to need persuasion, particularly when the invitation included a chance to listen to an arrangement of one of his own songs.

'I was happy to see fucking *anybody* I knew,' was Young's later comment. 'And it seemed very logical to us that we form a band.' They went back to Barry Friedman's house, got stoned, drunk or both, and started playing. Stills, Furay and Young already liked each other's style, and Stills immediately took to Palmer's bass-playing. Somehow, in the most accidental of ways, all the months of wishing and hoping had borne fruit. Fate had smiled on the four of them.

Barry Friedman found them a house on Fountain Street for living and rehearsing in; now all they needed was a drummer. Of those apparently available Stills wanted Billy Mundi, but he took another job, and Young's preference, fellow Canadian Dewey Martin, was chosen instead. He was a few years older than the others, and with much more professional experience, having worked Nashville sessions with heroes of Young's youth such as Patsy Cline, Roy Orbison and Carl Perkins. Sharing, or simply giving in to, the restlessness of the age, he had also headed west, and had formed his own group – the sublimely-named Sir Walter Raleigh and the Coupons – in Seattle. He'd moved on down to LA towards the end of 1965, getting sporadic work drumming for the Dillards, a bluegrass group taking some of their first tentative steps towards the country-rock fusion they would help originate with ex-Byrd Gene Clark. The path to innovation rarely runs smoothly, and in April the Dillards were in temporary retreat, regrouping in the drummerless pastures of pure bluegrass. Dewey Martin was available for alternative employment.

Over the next few days, the five of them – provisionally named the Herd – got to know each other, personally and musically. For Young it was everything he could have hoped for when he left the Canadian winter behind. They had a home, a dollar a day each from Friedman for food, and no demands on their time other than the making of music. And already they all knew they had struck lucky and found something special. 'It didn't take any time before we all knew we had the right combination,' Young said later. 'Time meant nothing; we were ready.'

Not long afterwards, one of them noticed the manufacturer's plate on a steamroller standing in the road outside Barry Friedman's house: 'Buffalo-Springfield Roller Co., Toledo, Ohio'. They had their name, and a few days later they had their first gig.

Watching and listening to the new band, Barry Friedman was suitably impressed. Perhaps he'd despaired of Stills ever finding any musical partners, but he'd always known there was talent in there somewhere, waiting to get out. Now was the time. He contacted a friend who also happened to be the Byrds' road manager, and told him that Buffalo Springfield was exactly the group he needed to open for the Byrds on their upcoming short tour of southern California.

Fate was working overtime on the new group's behalf. Stills, Furay and Young were all musicians who'd independently felt the desire to marry the rhythms of rock'n'roll to the sensibilities of contemporary urban folk, to be both the Beatles and Dylan. And here they were, opening for the group who had made such a musical marriage commercially successful, whose audience could hardly be better chosen for what Buffalo Springfield had to offer.

The first gig was at the Orange County Fair Grounds in San Bernardino on 15th April. The Springfield weren't getting paid much – twenty-five dollars each per concert – but they'd doubtless have played for nothing, and they were having fun. Each day they'd pile their equipment into the hearse, drive to the Byrds' business HQ on Sunset Boulevard and then take a large and impressive-looking Lincoln to the gig location. Afterwards they'd take the hearse home.

Young was still enjoying his relationship with his vehicle: 'Six people could be getting high in the front and back, and nobody would be able to see in because of the curtains. The heater was great. And the tray . . . the tray was dynamite. You open the side door and the tray whips right out onto the sidewalk. What could be cooler than that? What a way to make your entrance.'

Not long after this, though, the hearse went to meet its manufacturer. One day, as the band climbed aboard for the journey home, the drive shaft simply dropped off onto the road. They unloaded their gear and left Mort II where he'd fallen. Eventually noticing the dead hearse, the LAPD checked the licence plate and called up Canada, giving Young's father his first news of Neil's trip to California.

There seems to be unanimous agreement, among both participants and spectators, that from the beginning Buffalo Springfield were good. So good, in fact, that by the end of the seven-date tour, Byrds McGuinn and Hillman were considering offering to manage them. Good sense or idleness prevailed, but Hillman did recommend them to the manager of the Whiskey A Go Go club on Hollywood's Sunset Strip, then one of the prime showcases for LA's booming rock scene. Obviously trusting Hillman's judgement, the man offered the Springfield a six-week residence through the spring and early summer of 1966.

It was at the Whiskey that the band made its name. The music they played there was never recorded, but if the reports of those who played it and those who witnessed it are to be believed, Buffalo Springfield were a more outstanding group than the records they left behind might indicate. On record, the overall sound and energy level suggest a cross between the Byrds and the Beatles, but live they were a funkier, harder band than that, more of a cross between the Byrds and the Rolling Stones.

All three principals seem to have agreed that this was when the band peaked, in the first few weeks of its two-year lifespan. There were several reasons for this. They were doing something new and exciting, living on the adrenalin, and they were doing it together. 'Everybody enjoyed each other,' Furay said later; 'we *depended* on each other. We had these tunes, we had this desire, the shows were magical.' Their diet might consist of hot dogs and peanut-butter sandwiches, but each night they were playing for the hip élite of Hollywood.

They looked good on stage, with each of the five adopting a distinct visual persona. Bruce Palmer, tall and thin, often in a monk's cap, would parade an exaggerated indifference worthy of John Entwhistle. Dewey Martin went in for Carnaby Street flamboyance, all bright colours and cravats. Richie Furay, from the beginning the focal point on stage, wore Beatles-cut paisley jackets, smiled his cute all-American smile, and made the girls scream with his pigeon-toed ballerina variation on Chuck Berry's duckwalk. Either side of him, Stills and Young had begun their long love-hate relationship, adopting enemy personae from the same period of American history. Stills was the manic blond cowboy, sometimes in Confederate guise, while Young had become the brooding Indian. With his first pay cheques he'd bought himself a fringed jacket, and not long afterwards had come across a Comanche war shirt in a shop on Santa Monica Boulevard. He'd bought it and ordered two more.

Of course, they needed to do more than look good. In a city bursting at the seams with groups of youngsters who could play three chords and thought they had something to say, Buffalo Springfield had to be offering something in the way of music. They were all competent on their instruments – Martin, Stills and Palmer probably a lot more than competent – and in Stills and Furay they had two fine, distinctive voices. Both Young and Stills were writing songs that, although fairly nondescript by their own future standards, remained a cut above most of the competition. Above all, having the twin lead guitars, the 'guitar duelling' which Stills and Young made a trademark of their stage shows, was virtually new and very exciting.

At this stage the musical roles within the band appear to have been not only well defined but also generally accepted. Furay was the principal vocalist, Young the primary lead guitarist and Stills the musical arranger, the one who took the individual's songs and made them the group's. Stills's definition of his role was both indicative and ominous. 'I don't dictate exactly what goes down,' he said, 'but I sort of get things going, get the arrangements going.' This was exactly the sort of ill-defined role that would seem so natural in a happy band, yet be so fraught with difficulties in a group of young men increasingly imbued with a paranoid distrust of each other's motives.

This transformation was still in the future, albeit the not too distant future. For the moment, the band exceeded all its members' expectations. The first week at the Whiskey, according to Stills, was 'absolutely incredible'. He wasn't the only one to think so. By the end of that week the word was out. Every record company seemed to want to sign them, every manager wanted to manage them, every dope-dealer wanted to offer them samples, and a bewildering number of girls wanted to go to bed with them. And if this sometimes seemed like a succession of dreams come true, it was hardly the sort of life to foster self-awareness, simple friendship or romantic fulfilment.

Being besieged by sex-hungry women is not an experience this author has shared, but for someone from as conventional a middle-class background as Young it must have been completely disorientating. How could such a lifestyle be accommodated within that search for real love which he was expressing in his songs? How could he feel respect for women when so many of them were throwing themselves at him for no better reason than that he was a rock musician with an appealing image? And how did he feel about himself? No doubt such a lifestyle was often fun, but for someone like Young it must have been an unsettling kind of fun. He was entering a world and a life where it was hard to trust his own feelings and still harder to care about those of others.

The record companies were as hungry as the girls. Dunhill bid $5,000, Warner Brothers doubled that. Group manager Dick Davis, uncertain how to proceed, asked advice from Charlie Greene, ex-manager of Sonny and Cher and now a producer at Atlantic's subsidiary label Atco. He and his partner Brian Stone were impressed by the group's songs and, pausing only to pick up the sheet-music rights, introduced them to Ahmet Ertegun, the much-respected president of Atlantic. He too liked what he heard. 'I loved Buffalo Springfield immediately,' he said later. 'There was something about how Stephen and Neil worked off each other.'

The group signed to Atco for a $22,000 advance. Suddenly there was big money in the air. And somewhere in the shuffle Barry Friedman, who'd made it all possible, got bought out by Stone and Greene.

Almost thirty years on, it's hard to imagine Neil Young or Stephen Stills short of a penny. But back in 1966 – Comanche war shirts notwithstanding – they were hardly living high on the hog. When the Whiskey stint opened, Young was sharing a room in a dilapidated rooming house with a hepatitis case. Their wages for the engagement were $120 a week per man. True, none of the band came from a background that could by any stretch be described as materially deprived, but they were working in an industry where the vast majority of contenders never even smelt a hit, and the successful few were rarely successful for more than a few months. Once their appetites had been whetted by the prospect of serious money, the temptation to elbow each other aside at the trough must have been difficult to ignore.

One probable bone of contention involved the songwriting royalties – who would get his songs on the first album? June Nelson (who worked with Stone and Greene) was present when they signed the first publishing contract. None of them had much of a clue what they were doing. Told that they needed a leader for legality's sake – a somewhat dubious proposition – Stills volunteered and Young acquiesced. Then, according to Nelson, 'the major conflicts began over whose material would be done. Stills knew the more songs he had on the album, the more money he would get. Then everyone realised the significance of the thing in terms of money. So Neil began to say, "Let's get some of my songs done too, Steve."'

There were problems with the management team too. The group had had the impression that Greene and Stone were buying out Friedman, but it soon transpired that they were footing the bill themselves. The new managers were happy to provide cars and accommodation, but getting any actual cash out of them proved less straightforward. 'We always owed,' Young said. 'We never got out of hock. They'd give us an advance and then when an advance came in from somewhere they got it. A lot of things didn't add up right or at least we couldn't follow the addition.'

On top of the pressures of sex and money, there was the more insidious pressure of the times. Fame has always been a heavy burden for some to carry, but in the sixties the problem took on a another twist. The Beatles had bequeathed the age with a collectivist spirit which ran at odds with the romantic loner image of the fifties, while Dylan's contempt for his own and others' celebrity made that unfashionable as well. Whichever way rock's newly famous turned in the late sixties there were feelings of guilt or betrayal lying in wait. Individual fame was no longer something one was supposed to feel comfortable with.

Buffalo Springfield was hardly into the second month of its existence when all these various pressures began to exert their toll, particularly on the less stable trio of Stills, Palmer and Young.

There was an additional pressure on Young. During the first month in LA he had his first *grand mal* epileptic seizure. Bruce Palmer was with him at the time. 'We were standing together in a crowd around somebody demonstrating a Vegematic or some other kind of gadget for chopping vegetables, and when I turned to say something to Neil he wasn't beside me. Then I saw him on the floor having tremors that led to convulsions. I was scared as hell.'

Doubtless Young was too. He was put on daily medication, but disliked the side-effects so much that he often chose not to take it, comforting himself with the belief that keeping himself on an even keel was the best way of preventing further seizures.

Whenever Young has talked subsequently about his epilepsy he has sounded calmly fatalistic about his condition. It was just part of him, he told Cameron Crowe in 1975, 'part of my head, part of what's happening in there . . .'. People watching someone having a seizure saw the physical convulsions, but the sufferer's mind was somewhere else, and that was the scary part, 'realising you're totally comfortable in this . . . *void*. And that shocks you back into reality. It's a very disorienting experience.'

Such acceptance must have been hard earned. Certainly it's difficult to conceive of anyone not being thoroughly scared by their first major seizure, and by the fear that it could happen again at any time and in any place. Even, in Young's case, in mid-performance. Someone already bewildered by a surfeit of drugs, sex and fame hardly needed the sword of epilepsy hanging over his head.

In the summer of 1966 Buffalo Springfield played a series of shows with Johnny Rivers, a Turtles gig at Redondo Beach and, most prestigiously of all, a supporting set for the Rolling Stones at the Hollywood Bowl.

Despite the growing pressures on the five individuals they still, as a group, seem to have had the magic musical touch. And as yet they hadn't yet been through the intense frustration of trying and failing to get that magic down on vinyl, a frustration that, according to Stills, would 'virtually destroy the band'.

The recording of the début album began during the summer, with most of the tracks being laid down in one day, on 18th July. Young had two vocals on the album, and he excitedly took the tape of his first, 'Burned', back to his apartment block that night for the entertainment of the neighbours.

At the end of July the group's first single was released. It was originally intended that Stills's 'Go and Say Goodbye' should be the 'A' side and Young's 'Nowadays Clancy Can't Even Sing' the 'B' side, but at the last moment the record company decided to flip it. This angered Stills, no doubt in part because it felt like a personal demotion, but also because he saw it, quite rightly, as a dumb decision. 'Clancy' was a much better song, but it was not so catchy, it was much too long, and it contained the word 'damn' – three strikes and out as far as most American radio stations were concerned.

Later that summer, while out driving with a friend, Young was stopped by a cop. Lacking a driving permit, he was taken to a police station, where another cop, presumably taking exception to his long hair and clothes, called him an animal. Young gave as good as he got verbally, and was badly beaten for his pains. Brian Stone, arriving with the necessary bail money, was also beaten up and imprisoned.

At this point either Young's condition didn't look too good, or he had another seizure of some kind, because the police decided it might be prudent to take him to a nearby neuropsychiatric hospital for tests. This may well have been the occasion on which a doctor advised Young never to take a psychedelic trip, because there was a good chance he'd never come back.

The whole incident can't have done much for his peace of mind, and overall one gets the impression that the life he was living in southern California was beginning to unravel something in Young's psyche. He wrote to and phoned Pam, his ex-girlfriend in Winnipeg, complaining of pressures from all directions. She found his thoughts 'disjointed', and suspected he was on drugs of some sort. That September he gave a perfect description of her when asked by *Teenset* magazine to describe his dream girl. Young must have sometimes wondered whether coming west to fulfil his musical dreams had meant leaving his romantic dreams behind.

There was still the music. The recording done, the group waited for Greene and Stone's production of the album. When they finally heard it they were appalled. It sounded, in Stills's words, as though 'the guts had been ripped out of the band'. The stereo effects were practically inaudible.

The band pleaded with Atlantic to be allowed to record the album again, but the record company refused. 'Initially refused', according to writer Johnny Rogan, but Atlantic's files show that in fact only one song was re-recorded – 'Do I Have to Come Right Out and Say It?' Since this was done on the same day – 5th December – that the band first recorded 'For What It's Worth', it seems probable that they used an odd hour or so of spare studio time to try and mitigate what they considered the damage.

In the meantime, their live reputation remained high. A three-day stint at the Fillmore in mid-November was a huge success, leaving the group with great hopes for the coming year. So many people seemed to like their music – so many people whose judgement they trusted – that it was hard not to believe that success must be just around the corner.

In one way it was. Stills had witnessed November's major disturbances on Sunset Strip, when the LAPD, ordered to clear the boulevard of 'undesirables', had interpreted the word loosely enough to include anyone under twenty-five (themselves excepted). These events, and the sense of loathing that seeped out of them, came as a great shock to many of the middle-class white kids who found themselves involved.

They also produced two great songs. John Phillips's despairing 'Safe in My Garden', sung with rare beauty by the Mamas and the Papas, announced the effective end of the 'love and peace' movement before most people were aware it had begun. Stephen Stills's 'For What It's Worth' had an equally fine lyric – anger restrained by intelligence, and all the more expressive for it – and a more telling arrangement; the song was driven slowly, relentlessly forward by Palmer's bass, yet full of spaces for the stately lead guitar to echo in.

It sounded different, it sounded catchy, it sounded, to use the jargon of the times, distinctly 'now'. Released, like the first album *Buffalo Springfield*, in February 1967, it then swiftly climbed the chart, peaking at number 7. When the time came to make a second pressing of the album, 'For What It's Worth' was inserted in place of the original lead track 'Baby Don't Scold Me'.

At the time of its release, the newness of the voices, the freshness of its sound, and its few truly original moments largely eclipsed the highly derivative nature of most of *Buffalo Springfield*. The Stills-penned songs on the original album sounded more contemporary than Young's, but only because Stills's writing was more closely aping the new mainstream merger of British beat and Californian folk-rock styles.

Of Young's five songs, 'Nowadays Clancy Can't Even Sing' offers the best of all worlds, with the Stills-Furay arrangement turning a good song into a great track. The three songs that open Side 2 all hark back to the pre-Beatles era, and it's easy to detect the various influences: the Everly Brothers in 'Flying on the Ground Is Wrong', Neil Sedaka in 'Burned', and Ricky Nelson in 'Do I Have to Come Right Out and Say It?' Surprisingly, given the plaintive tone of his voice, Young chose – or was chosen – to sing the most up-tempo of the three. Furay was given the other two, in part because Young lacked confidence in his own voice, but also as a means of compensating Furay for the lack of his compositions on the album.

The lyrics of 'Burned' are quite ordinary, but the other two songs show Young's evolving way with words. The final verse of 'Flying on the Ground Is Wrong' – 'City lights at a country fair/Never shine but always glare/If I'm bright enough to see you/You're just too dark to care' – manages to sound pretty, conjure up nice visual images and hint (albeit in vain) at some deeper meaning. 'Do I Have to Come Right Out and Say It?' captures the fear of commitment to perfection, and is rounded off with as concise an expression of the dilemma as could be hoped for: 'A part of me is scared – the part of me I shared once before.'

It's 'Out of My Mind', though, the least attractive of the five Young songs, that offers the most clues to his future musical development. The guitar line would be echoed ten years later in 'Like a Hurricane', and the subject matter of the lyrics – the threat posed by success and celebrity to one's true self – would be recycled many times over. This is clearly post-Beatles music: Young's guitar solo is flexible and fluid, not tied rigidly to the beat, while the vocal chorus provides an offbeat counterpoint to the melody, like an echo in the singer's disorientated mind.

'Out of My Mind', 'Clancy' and the late addition 'For What's It Worth' carried what originality there was on *Buffalo Springfield*; the other nine songs offered little more than a demonstration of the band's mastery of the new mainstream. It was certainly a good album for its time, but not even a perfect production job could have turned it into a great one.

In early spring, with *Buffalo Springfield* selling steadily but far from spectacularly, the band secured a ten-day residency at Ondine's club in Manhattan, supporting soul star Otis Redding. According to some sources, it was during this visit that they cut Young's 'Mr Soul' in Atlantic's New York studio (others suggest it was recorded on another visit earlier in the year).

The song deserves particular comment: rarely can a rock musician have spelt out his fall from mental grace with such chilling precision. The protagonist of 'Mr Soul' seems to be living in a permanent state of nervous breakdown. Public and peer pressure may have played a part in creating this situation, but he makes no attempt to place the blame on anyone other than himself: 'She said, "You're strange, but don't change," and I let her.' He has connived at his own idolisation, chosen a life that is freezing his face into an image and racing his mind out of control. He's the sick clown, pulling the world down around himself, doing 'the trick of disaster'.

The music, rarely for Young, lets down the lyric. The 'Satisfaction' riff was a plain rip-off, and if any irony was intended it got lost in the mix. Whereas the vocal on 'Out of My Mind' had seemed overdramatic, the whole performance of 'Mr Soul' – vocal and instrumental – is simply inadequate to carry the lyric's strength of feeling.

By this time Young does seem to have been out of his mind as often as not. When the band had a showdown with Greene and Stone in New York, Young was able to supply the distraught Greene with some Valium. It doesn't come as a great surprise to know he had some handy.

Worse was to follow on the same trip. Bruce Palmer was arrested for marijuana possession, and the band, with commitments to fulfil on the West Coast, had no choice but to leave him to the tender mercies of the NYPD. After a brief spell of imprisonment Palmer was tried and deported back to Canada. In one foul swoop the band had lost both its bass player and some intangible factor in the human equation that made it workable.

Back in LA they found temporary bass players. Dick Davis mimed for them on the *Hollywood Palace* TV show, one of Love's bassists stepped in for several LA gigs, and finally Ken Koblun was persuaded to fill the breach. None of these could supply what Palmer had provided musically, which, at its most basic, was the rhythm'n'blues element in the Springfield's potent blend of folk, rock and country styles. Stills called it 'a Bill Wyman kind of Motown feel put under everything'; in essence, Palmer provided a rhythmic counterweight to Furay and Young's tendency towards melodic prettiness.

Just as importantly, Palmer had played a crucial role in the group's internal human dynamic. Stills thought Palmer's relationship with him and Young was the band's 'focal point', and there does seem to have been a sense in which the three of them – all severely freaked out by their experiences over the previous year – needed each other to maintain some sort of functioning balance. Once Palmer was removed, Stills and Young would tend to turn their insanity against each other.

The touring went on. For a couple of months they criss-crossed the States, usually playing second or third on the bill, before largely unenthusiastic audiences. Either Hollywood magic didn't work the same way in the Midwest, or the band really was past its peak.

They came back to LA to start work on their second album, this time with Atlantic boss Ahmet Ertegun handling the production chores in person. The provisional title was *Stampede*; some half-dozen songs were laid down in the early summer. There doesn't seem to be any record of exactly which these were, and the memories of the participants are hazy and contradictory.

Young's contributions included the wonderfully paranoid 'Down to the Wire' – later included on *Decade* – and at least two others: 'There Goes My Babe' and 'One More Sign'. The latter were both acoustic love songs, the first essentially ordinary, the second a particularly lovely example of Young's love-as-one-form-of-vulnerability style.

Three Stills songs are usually mentioned in connection with *Stampede*: 'Uno Mundo', 'Pretty Girl Why' (both of which appeared on the posthumous Springfield album *Last Time Around*) and 'So You Got a Lover', a fine acoustic song. Six other songs – 'My Kind of Love', '(Come On) Here', 'My Angel', 'Neighbour Don't You Worry', 'Nobody's Fool' and 'Down Down Down' may or may not have been scheduled for inclusion. The first three of these were 1966 vintage, and had already been considered of insufficient quality to feature on the first album.

The last-named was conceivably a first run-out for the second section of Young's 'Country Girl', which eventually turned up on *Déjà Vu*.

With the exceptions of 'One More Sign' and 'So You Got a Lover', none of these songs appears to have been particularly strong, and there is no hint of the striking sense of innovation that was to mark *Buffalo Springfield Again*. If anything there seems to have been a move from pop back towards folk. The cover – depicting Stills, Young, Furay and Martin slouching and standing on an Old West sidewalk, with an unidentifiable fifth person sitting head bowed in front of them – was certainly beautiful, but all the musical evidence suggests that *Stampede* was far from being the lost classic of later legend.

The failure to complete the album didn't exactly do wonders for group morale. Ken Koblun suddenly quit, and Jim Fielder became the group's fourth bassist in as many months. Not long into the subsequent Midwest tour, Stills came to the conclusion that Fielder didn't fit the group's sound, and a smouldering dispute began over whether to retain or fire him. Maybe Stills was right, but it is just as likely that Fielder was merely the latest in the line of necessary scapegoats for a group in permanent emotional disarray. The stresses and strains of being out on the road, of trying to retain some sense of reality in a life woefully short on simplicity or honesty, seemed to be taking an ever heavier toll, particularly on Stills and Young.

The musical division of labour that had pre-empted an open struggle for control was also breaking down. Young was no longer willing to have Stills do all the group's arranging, particularly when it came to Young's own songs. As he later told Cameron Crowe, 'I just had too much energy and so much creative flow coming out that when I wanted to get something down, I just felt like, "This is my fucking trip and I don't have to listen to anybody else's." I'd do what they wanted with *their* stuff, but I needed more space with my own. And that was a constant problem in my head.'

As Young invaded his territory, so Stills was busy invading Young's, playing more and more lead guitar. As both would later admit, they were behaving like small boys. In a way this was hardly surprising: the playing of music as part of a group is all but unique in modern Western culture as a non-hierarchical activity; for almost anything else that boys or young men do together, there are pre-set structures and lists of rules, an established way of doing things. There was none for Stills and Young – no way to formalise their relations with each other, no external courts of appeal. They had to accept a shared control over the music, and then reach agreement from day to day, even from note to note, over how to work things through. Considering how difficult most people, in most circumstances, have found such shared control down the ages, it is all too understandable how easy it was, in such unconducive circumstances, for these two young men to come up short.

It had its funny side, of course. One night on stage when Palmer was blissfully playing his bass far too loud, he suddenly found Stills shouting in his face, and slapped him. Stills went purple, and shoved the bassist violently back across Martin's drum kit. Pure adolescent farce. Dewey Martin remembered how another night Stills and Young, after duelling away on stage, came out into the dressing room and 'started swinging at each other with guitars. It was like two old ladies going at it with their purses.'

Young responded to these conflicts in a manner that would soon become characteristic: by removing himself from the battlefield. He and Stills both started turning up late at the studio, preferably after everyone else had gone home. This offered Furay time to record some of his own songs, and at least partial compensation for having to deal with the other two.

On stage their simultaneous presence was still required. Bruce Palmer managed to sneak back into the US in the early summer, but by this time it was too late. The relationship between Young and Stills, which seems to have been used by both as a lightning rod for everything else that felt wrong, was beyond balancing. Young's attendance at gigs was increasingly sporadic, causing cancellation for the whole group on at least one occasion. Things were rapidly coming to a head.

This was unfortunate enough in itself, and made doubly so in the light of the obvious musical strides the group were now making despite their personal conflicts. On 6th June they all went into the studio to record Young's 'Mr Soul' (for the second time) and 'Bluebird', the Stills song that, more than any other, would capture the Springfield's dynamism on record.

Their reputation was growing too. They were due on TV on *The Johnny Carson Show* in New York, and there were hopes of a subsequent spot on *The Ed Sullivan Show*. They had been booked for the Monterey Pop Festival, which, given the quality of all the acts booked – the cream of Californian rock, plus Hendrix and the Who – was obviously going to be a major showcase. The money was beginning to mount; they were even, according to Stills, playing as well as they had ever done.

It was at this point, on the eve of the intended trip to New York, that Young called a meeting of the band and announced that he was quitting. He would later claim that 'something inside of me felt like I wasn't quite on track', that Johnny Carson and Monterey didn't sit easily with his vision of what the band ought to be doing. Stills thought it was 'sheer self-destruct', but was also prepared to admit that by this time they were all acting like madmen. 'That's when Neil had to quit, exactly at the time when it meant the most. He decided that it wasn't worth it, probably he knew the same thing, that Bruce wasn't going to be able to handle it, and he probably thought that I was just as crazy as he was.'

The Springfield went on without Young. Doug Hastings, lead guitarist of the Daily Flash, was enlisted as his replacement. The *Johnny Carson Show* appearance had been aborted, but Monterey could still supply the group with the push it needed. Stills and Byrd David Crosby had become friends over the preceding year, finding common cause in how appalling life in their respective bands was. Their situations were remarkably similar: in losing Bruce Palmer and Gene Clark the two bands had lost their human linchpins, so releasing the potential for conflict between Stills and Young and between Crosby and McGuinn.

Crosby rehearsed and sat in with the Springfield at Monterey, thereby enraging McGuinn and Hillman, who thought such conduct unprofessional. This Stills-Crosby collaboration wasn't just a pointer for the future – the festival was a good one for Buffalo Springfield. Bookings started coming in, including a reasonably lucrative tour supporting the Monkees. And they still had a second album to complete, with or without Young.

He, meanwhile, had spent a couple of months regaining his sense of mental balance, and now felt better able to cope with the strains of life within the group he'd abandoned. The question was, should he go back to them? The calculated answer was yes, and Young has never been less than calculating. For one thing, he knew from bitter experience that putting groups together was easy to do, hard to do well. For another, the devils he knew should be easier to deal with than any number of devils he didn't. Still lacking the necessary clout to secure a solo recording contract, he had no choice but to work as an equal with other musicians. And on the positive side, whatever he thought and felt about Stills, he knew the two of them had a musical bond capable of delivering magic.

But would they take him back? He started angling for re-enlistment, hanging out at the manager's office, and leaving the others with a difficult decision. Their recent successes had been achieved without Young, so why, they must have asked themselves, should they put everything at risk again with someone so unreliable, so prone to put his own interests first and the band's a long way last?

For Stills, the answer was the same as for Young. He knew that they had something special together, that if the new album featured the best songs both could offer it would be better than one featuring just his own. And when all was said and done, everyone knew that Young was an integral part of Buffalo Springfield. A great person to have around when he was together; a great talent, with new songs that sounded astonishingly good. And maybe this time they really could conquer the world . . .

The fuse under the Springfield's career might be spluttering, but there was still time for one classic album to be made before the big bang. Doug Hastings was fired in September 1967, Young taken back on board, and early the following month most of their second album was cut in LA.

Buffalo Springfield Again is more diverse than its predecessor, partly because half the time while it was being made the band members were busy going their separate ways, partly because in the intervening period they'd all been growing so fast, and not necessarily in the same musical direction.

The band's original sound – the earnestly energetic merger of British beat and folk-rock styles – reaches a glorious apotheosis in Stills's 'Bluebird' and 'Rock'n'Roll Woman', leaving the rest of the album open for experimentation. There is the country pop of Furay's 'A Child's Claim to Fame', the hard rock of 'Hung Upside Down', the out-of-place (though strangely impressive) Stax soul-style 'Good Time Boy', the bluesy 'Everydays' and the intimate 'Sad Memory'. On the last two, Young's lead guitar – a sustained whine in one case, a distant echo in the other – may well have been added late in the recording process.

His own three contributions are all memorable. 'Mr Soul' wears its influences – Dylan and the Stones – a little too obviously on its sleeve, but the lyric is a masterpiece of rhyme concoction and economy of expression. 'I was raised by the praise of a fan who said I upset her' really says it all.

'Expecting to Fly' and 'Broken Arrow' are both startlingly original. The former, arranged with Phil Spector's sometime assistant Jack Nitzche, adapts the wall-of-sound ideology to the sort of ethereal ballad that would have been hard to imagine in pre-Beatles times. The lyric is less than special – and often mercifully inaudible – but on this track it's clearly the mood that matters. As the building strings shift from speaker to speaker and the violins unwind, ushering in the massed acoustic guitars and multi-layered vocal, the warm sense of melancholy grabs the listener gently but firmly by the throat.

'Broken Arrow' is something else again, a six-minute journey through several scenes and musical styles. The basic verse/chorus structure is traversed three times, but not simply repeated: there is a steady movement through from the martial beat of the first verse to the almost stately progress of the third, as if the song is passing from youth to age, like a tumbling stream growing into a broad river. And during this progress Young treats the listener to the sound of screaming fans, fairground noises and organ, an emerging drum roll, jazz piano and a fading heartbeat. Rarely for him, there's even an alternation between 4/4 and 3/4 time signatures.

The three verses concern life in a band, a teenager oppressed by parental hypocrisy, and a storybook wedding parade. In each vignette the central characters are trapped in a bubble of isolation: the band behind their limo windows; the boy running down his hall of ignorance; the king and queen marrying for peace, oblivious of the dawn. Each comes, in the chorus, to confront the Indian standing by the river, holding up a broken arrow, 'the Indian sign of peace', according to Young. 'Usually after losing a war . . . a broken arrow usually means that somebody has lost a lot.' Certainly the characters in the song have: they can find peace only at the cost of their souls.

'Broken Arrow' was a fitting climax to an album bursting at the seams with musical ideas – too many, perhaps, for a group already bursting at the seams with personality problems. But emerging from the studio in the autumn of 1967, or listening a few weeks later to the finished product, the five members of Buffalo Springfield must have had a distinct hunch that they'd created one of the most enduring albums of the sixties.

There was no sense, moreover, that musically they'd shot their one and only bolt. Each of them seems to have been full of new ideas. On *Buffalo Springfield Again* Young had gone the furthest in making use of the new multi-tracking possibilities, although in retrospect he would be the most doubtful as to their efficacy. A quarter of a century later he would say that 'even back then I thought the way records were being made in the sixties was wrong. But I didn't know what was wrong with it. It just didn't sound right. I mean, the Springfield records are terrible compared to what the Band sounded like.'

Stills was also fascinated with the possibilities inherent in electronics, but wary of using the new devices and instruments before he fully understood what he was doing. He was suitably sanguine about the ease with which record companies and A'n'R men could be persuaded to sanction such experimentation. As usual, money was the bottom line. It was 'downright infuriating sometimes, but the only way to escape from such limitations is to sell millions and millions of records – then they'll bloody well listen to you'. At the same time he was concerned that 'the old Beatles format isn't gonna make it much longer'. Something else would take its place, but he didn't have any idea what it would be, noting wistfully in passing how expensive light shows were.

Bruce Palmer did know which way he hoped rock was heading: towards 'popular symphonies – a few guitars, flutes and voice, no lyrics . . .'. The Beatles had set them all an example, opening enough musical doors to keep musical explorers busy for years to come. Richie Furay, meanwhile, was headed in the opposite direction, towards the simplicity – some would say regressive simplicity – of country rock.

In an ideal world, the possibilities for fruitful interplay between these musical ideas would have been endless. As 1967 gave way to 1968, the most probable future for Buffalo Springfield remained collective hara-kiri.

The obvious quality of the second album, and the promise of success it seemed to offer, seems also to have precipitated a general grab for larger slices of the growing cake. Richie Furay and, even more dubiously, Dewey Martin, were now demanding space for their compositions. Bruce Palmer was keen to do ragas. Stills and Young, who had enough trouble fighting each other for space, found themselves contemplating only a couple of songs each on the next album. Considering the rate at which both were churning them out this was both pitiful and ridiculous.

The last few months of the group's existence served as a pathetic coda to the underground triumph of the second album. They had enough fame and following to drive them out of their minds, but not enough to reach some indefinable, probably imaginary place where everything would be all right and they wouldn't need to spend so much time at each other's throats.

Business continued as usual. In January 1968 Palmer was again busted and deported, after a brief residency in the San Diego detention centre. Jim Messina was brought in on bass, and presumably proved adequate in Young's estimation, or he wouldn't have enlisted him later that year to help with his first solo album.

The band played musical managers for a while, sacking Dick Davis, employing Elliot Roberts for a couple of weeks, then adopting the Beach Boys' manager Nick Grillo while supporting that band on tour. During this period, at a gig in Florida, Young had a seizure on stage, but fortunately his mother was on hand to take charge. 'No one else knew what to do,' she wrote to his father.

This didn't say much for the rest of the band. Richie Furay, interviewed by *Teenset* magazine around this time, managed to be more revealing than either he or the interviewer presumably intended. Asked about Stills, he admitted that after three years of close proximity he still had no idea what made his partner tick, and then, perhaps realising that this didn't sound too good, asked for some more time to think about it. Later in the interview he suddenly burst out, 'Stephen's bold, Neil's sly, and Bruce is silent but deadly.' Invited to expand on this, he said that Stills would say what he wanted and it was your tough luck if you didn't like it, and that Young was 'tricky about getting things done the way he wants them done'. The interview ended with Furay announcing, 'Boy, being from Yellow Springs, Ohio, I sure don't know how I ended up here!'

On 20th March, Young, Furay, Messina and Eric Clapton were busted in Topanga Canyon for marijuana possession. According to Rogan they were imprisoned for weeks, but given that Clapton was on stage the following night with Cream this seems unlikely. According to Young's father the charges were eventually dropped. Whatever the details, the incident appears to have served as some sort of tacit signal for the dissolution of the group. They fulfilled their remaining commitments – the last of them a Long Beach concert on 5th May – and went their separate ways.

A final album, *Last Time Around*, would be posthumously released that summer, but for Young fans it was something of a disappointment, including only two of his songs (plus one co-written with Furay), one vocal and very little electric-guitar playing.

The collaborative 'It's So Hard to Wait' shows no obvious trace of Young, in person or in spirit, but the other two songs are among his best. 'I Am a Child' features harmonica over countryish acoustic guitars, a wonderfully diffident vocal by Young, and lyrics that evoke the innocence of childhood without slipping into sentimentality. 'On the Way Home' is musically more complex, integrating elements of white rock, Motown and country into its overall sound. Furay does a wonderful job with the vocal, but there's no doubting that it's Young's song, written to the rest of the band, about being in the band. 'I went insane,' he admits, 'like a smoke-ring day when the wind blows.' But he has passed through the madness and out the other side, his adult innocence intact, having learned the ultimate lesson: 'Though we rush ahead to save our time, we are only what we feel.'

With both these songs Young had eschewed the wordiness and metaphorical overload of his earlier work, instead relying on simple imagery and a new directness of expression. Such a honing of his songwriting skills boded well for his new solo career.

One of his first decisions as a solo artist was to ask Elliot Roberts to manage him. They had first met late the previous year, when Young found himself working in the same studio as old friend Joni Mitchell, whom Roberts was already representing. She was making her first album with boyfriend and producer David Crosby, and on discovering that Young was in the same building she suggested they go down the hall and say hello. Crosby demurred – 'That guy is strange' – but Mitchell insisted that Roberts come with her. She thought he would like Young's sense of humour.

He did, and found Young considerably less intimidating than he'd expected. 'I heard all these stories – Neil had left the band twice . . . Everyone was always on eggshells around Neil. Say the wrong word, he's gone. That is all I ever heard. Well, I found it easier to deal with Neil than [with] Stephen. I used to tell people the funny things Neil had said. They'd say, "*Neil?*"'

Roberts's short time with the Springfield had hardly been easy or propitious, but it's hard to believe he would have missed the chance to manage Young even if he'd loathed him. His adoption of Joni Mitchell already showed an eye for talent, and with Young in the same stable Roberts must have felt he'd cornered the market in rock's future.

He immediately got Young a gig guesting with Dave Van Ronk at a Pasadena nightclub. 'We stayed up all night,' Roberts would later remember, 'because we were so thrilled he didn't get booed off.' Young knew some people found his voice appealing, but he doubted whether there were enough of them. He also worried about his songs. It was 1968, and all that hope in the air was conspicuous by its absence in the lyrics he was writing.

Nevertheless, he seems to have had no trouble in securing a solo recording contract. He chose the Warners offshoot Reprise, as much to get away from his former partners as for any other reason. More than a decade later he would repeat, as if it was the most obvious thing in the world, that he 'didn't want to be a member of the Springfield, competing with other members of the Springfield on the same label'. It was as if he was still on stage with them.

The advance from Reprise was used as a down payment on a beautiful wooden house high in Topanga Canyon. While he was waiting for the deal to go through, he met and befriended a man of around his own age who was to play an important part in his life and career.

David Briggs had left home in Wyoming when he was fifteen, done all sorts of jobs in the next few years, and finally found his way into the music business as a record producer. Driving up Topanga Canyon one day he stopped to offer a longhair a lift, not knowing that it was Neil Young. The latter was equally surprised to discover that Briggs's house was one that had been used by the Springfield in days gone by.

The two men immediately hit it off, and a lasting friendship began. Both could be prickly characters, and perhaps a mutual recognition of this fact made it easier for each of them to accept the other for who he was. They certainly enjoyed sharing ideas about music, and Briggs was soon heavily involved in the planning and preparation of Young's first solo album, visiting studios with him to test their different sounds, and bringing in friends to help out with the actual music-making.

During this period Young seems to have stayed away from professional gigs. He played lead guitar on one Monkees song ('You and I') and shared the credits on another ('As We Go Along') with Ry Cooder and Danny Kortchmar, but otherwise steered clear of session work. He seems to have relished the chance to escape the limelight, and to seek out the solid emotional ties he needed after the battering of the last couple of years. He found one in Topanga Canyon itself, another in the four-storey redwood house which he devoted much of the year to fixing up. And last but far from least, he met Susan Acevedo at the nearby restaurant she managed, the Canyon Kitchen. She had a seven-year-old daughter, Tia, and soon Young was living the sort of family life he hadn't known since his parents' separation. He and Susan married in December of that year.

'I just started really digging on being home,' Young told *Fusion* magazine. 'I have another life that doesn't have anything to do with rock and roll, you know . . . that, I think, is a reason why I think I might be a little different from most of the people who live rock'n'roll twenty-four hours a day.'

The domestic atmosphere was well captured in an article for the *Toronto Star* written by Marci McDonald. Young's 'incredible house on stilts high on the side of the canyon' was 'filled with the things that make him happy'. She listed them: Spanish-American antiques, skin rugs, home-made art, a recording studio, pedigree cats and a dog, 'a sunny blonde named Susan with hair that flows down to her waist' and her 'equally sunny seven-year-old daughter, Tia'.

Even by the standards of 1968–9 this sounds decidedly dubious, as if Susan and Tia were merely items on a list of *objets d'art*. At least McDonald noticed that Susan was a functioning *objet*, piling food on the table, lighting more candles, then curling up at Neil's feet, 'her hair shining in the candlelight'.

Outside there were goats on hand to keep down the vegetation, and a garage to house the first of Young's collection of historic automobiles – a 1940 Lincoln. It all sounds like a male hippie heaven, caught in that short moment between sexual liberation and women's liberation. A few more years and men with Young's intelligence and sensitivity would find it harder to have their sweet potatoes and eat them. When McDonald ended her article by writing that 'even in the shelter of Topanga Canyon there are the coyotes', her words were truer than she knew.

Neil Young, according to its author, 'was very much a first album. I wanted to prove to myself that I could do it. And I did, thanks to the wonder of modern machinery.' It was also a highly accomplished piece of music-making, one that has stood the test of time a lot better than most of its contemporaries.

Intrinsic quality apart, the most obvious reason for this longevity lies in the simple strength of the melodies, and the almost jewel-like settings in which Young placed them. The only piece of musical extroversion on *Neil Young* was the acoustic epic 'Last Trip to Tulsa', which, perched at the end of the album, seemed almost to stand outside it. For the bulk of the album, Young took a collection of melodic ballads somewhat similar in style to those on the first Buffalo Springfield album, and treated them to the benefit of all the studio expertise he had gathered in the intervening period. The result was a series of songs and moods that seemed to flow into each other, like varying shades of rich dark hues on a canvas.

Despite the optimistic feel of the opening instrumental 'Emperor of Wyoming', the overall mood is far from upbeat. The only aggressive song, 'The Loner', looks into the mind of someone – perhaps Stephen Stills, perhaps Young himself – who has trouble relating openly to anyone, while 'The Old Laughing Lady', which comes complete with ghostly piano, strings and gospel chorus, drags the river of alcoholism. 'Here We Are in the Years' casts a wider net, as it quietly, forcefully builds into one of the more musically effective condemnations of ecological vandalism.

Between the songs that keep this wary eye on the world, Young serves up four cameos of romantic angst. 'What Did You Do to My Life?' is not much more than a throwaway, but the Byrds-like 'If I Could Have Her Tonight', the dark, cascading 'I've Been Waiting for You' and the aching 'I've Loved Her Song' remain three of the loveliest tracks he has ever recorded. 'But if she came to me, would she be kind?' he asks in the first, before pinning his hopes on 'a woman with the feeling of losing once or twice' in the second. Here was a voice for the times, for 'relationships' rather than love affairs, for all the doubts of a generation confronting a mismatch of old desires and new expectations.

The concluding 'Last Trip to Tulsa', though sitting uneasily alongside the rest of the album, does conjure up a raw power of its own, both in the apocalyptic menace of the acoustic-guitar work and in the bizarre imagery of the lyrics. There may well be a story in there somewhere – even several stories – but the overriding impression is of rampant paranoia. In one verse Young tells of pulling into a gas station but being afraid to ask for the gas – 'The servicemen were yellow, the gasoline was green/Although I knew I couldn't, I thought that I was gonna scream' – while in another he wakes up to find an Indian trying on his clothes.

Young himself, a year or so later, would say that he considered 'Last Trip to Tulsa' 'a mistake', but in retrospect one can see that it offered, in all its awkward rawness, a clearer signpost to his future than the rest of *Neil Young*. In the same interview, he described the making of 'I've Been Waiting for You' – how the track had been spliced together from recordings made in different cities – and how time-consuming it was to make an album that way. Doing it once seems to have deterred him from ever doing it again; from this point on, live spontaneity would always be his primary objective in making records. Overdubbing was one thing, playing another, and never the twain should meet again.

Any artist putting out their first solo effort is conscious of the need for a good reception. So to Young, who'd put a great deal of effort into his, and who was feeling basically satisfied with what he'd achieved, it must have come as cruel blow to discover how far the mix on the final mastered version had been miscalculated.

It was partly his own fault for having adopted an untried new process for giving stereo records the concentration of mono on radio. As with many such technological breakthroughs, the initial advance was more than cancelled out by the accompanying side-effects, which in this case turned out to be a flattening-out of the sound on the turntable. Young's lead vocals were so far back in the murk that they lacked all clarity.

The following year, after the album's release, Young would persuade Warners to issue a remixed version in the US, but whether or not he made the effort to have it remixed before release is not known. It seems likely that he was unsure, both of whether he should and of whether he could, given his freshman status at Warners. An interviewer from a local LA paper found him 'nervous about the album, as nervous as if it were the first time he'd been in a studio. During the interview he worries about a single, about the sequence of songs on the album, and about the mix – the relationship of instruments and vocals. He plays it and is alternately proud and fretful, wanting it to be the best he could possibly do, thinking first that it is, then that it isn't, then that it is, and so on.'

For the moment he lacked either the clout or the clarity of mind to remix it, and in January 1969 *Neil Young* was duly released. That same month he undertook a brief solo acoustic tour to promote the album, taking in, among others, New York's Bitter End, Toronto's Riverboat and Ottawa's Le Hibou. It was not a particularly happy experience. Audiences were thin and generally lukewarm, and Young was subjected to the indignity of a strip search on entering Canada. Roberts and Young joked that the poster at the Bitter End was bigger than the crowd, but the public's lack of enthusiasm can hardly have been a confidence-builder.

The only reason Young had the bookings in the first place was that Roberts had promised the clubs his other act, the more saleable Joni Mitchell.

With the first solo album selling slowly, and no apparent hunger among the public for his live presence, Young must have returned to LA wondering what he should do next. Fortunately he didn't have to look far.

A few years earlier two exiles from the East Coast, Billy Talbot and Danny Whitten, had met in an LA club called the Peppermint West. At a party a couple of weeks later they started singing together, along with a friend of Billy's named Lou Molina. They sounded good, took it seriously, and even managed to swing a record deal with Liberty. Lou's cousin Ralph, who'd been hanging out in Florida, was called out to join them. Under the name Danny and the Memories they cut one single – which hardly set the West Coast on fire.

Psychedelia was becoming all the rage and they changed the group's name to the Psyrcle. At first the intentions were vocal/acoustic, but seeing an early Byrds gig changed their minds. It was time, they decided, that they learned to play some electric instruments. Whitten already played a little guitar, Ralph took drums and Billy Talbot opted for the bass. Lou had disappeared by this time, and Ben Rocco, the designated lead guitarist, decided he would rather get married. Two brothers from San Francisco, George and Leon Whitsell, were drafted in as replacements. A final addition was Bobby Notkoff, an electric-violin player whom Talbot had met through a woman friend.

The name changed again, this time to the Rockets, and they started playing gigs around southern California. They didn't get as many bookings as they'd have liked, but they attracted enough attention to secure another record deal. The resulting album, *The Rockets*, was produced by Barry Goldberg and released on White Whale in March 1968. One particular friend of the band's both loved it and found himself inspired by it. As Billy Talbot noted years later, 'Listen to "Let Me Go" on the Rockets' album and you can hear the birth of "Down by the River".'

A girl called Autumn had brought Young to meet the future Rockets during the recording of the first Springfield album, and he'd been dropping in at Talbot and Whitten's house in Laurel Canyon ever since. He liked them, liked playing with them, and doubtless found them a shelter from the often raging storm that was life in Buffalo Springfield. He seems to have been particularly drawn to Danny Whitten, whose almost painful sensitivity perhaps mirrored his own. Years later, Elliot Roberts would say of Whitten, 'Whatever very soulful is, he had it. Very strong guy, but you could see that you say the wrong word and you'd slap him in the face. We all liked Danny. He was obviously very talented and Neil was drawn to him instantly.'

During early 1968, as the Springfield disintegrated, the Rockets saw more of Young, often in the company of Robin Lane, a woman folk singer and mutual friend. They would play acoustic guitars and sing up at Whitten and Talbot's house, with Whitten giving Young constant encouragement as regards his singing. Early in 1969 the Rockets (reduced to a foursome by the Whitsells' return to San Francisco the previous year) got an extended gig as the house band at the club where the Springfield had made its name – the Whiskey A Go Go on Sunset Strip. Young, back from his promotional tour, saw them here and, on at least one occasion, sat in with them.

It was during these weeks that some major shift occurred, either in Young's musical development or in his awareness of it. It wasn't so much a road-to-Damascus-style shaft of light as an accumulation of circumstances: his dissatisfaction with the first solo album and with the seemingly endless recording process that had produced it; the long history of the Springfield's failure to capture their live sound on record; and a narrowing of the gap between the music he loved to listen to and the music he loved to play.

Young decided once and for all that he didn't want to be the Beatles. If he was going to play in a band – and he seems never to have seriously considered spending the rest of his career alone with an acoustic guitar – then that band would play and record like a live band, make mistakes, sound raw, sound *human*. They would be, in Young's mind at least, much more akin to the Rolling Stones than to the Beatles, with one crucial difference: in his band there would be only one writer, only one leader.

On all the relevant counts the Rockets scored highly. They were not the sort of musicians who were likely to take the world by storm on their own, and one suspects they were not the sort of people who would particularly want to. There would be no equality of talent or commercial viability – Young would be in control. It would be *his* band.

But were they good enough? There was only one way to find out. Laid up with flu in his Topanga Canyon house, Young wrote a couple of 'strange songs' – 'Down by the River' and 'Cowgirl in the Sand'. Once recovered he asked Whitten, Talbot and Ralph Molina up to his studio for a recording session. Before long, these three would be known as Crazy Horse.

Of all Young's albums, *Everybody Knows This Is Nowhere* probably holds the securest place in the hearts of his most die-hard fans. There are several possible reasons for this, not least the most obvious – that it is simply one of the greatest albums in the history of rock music.

Easier said than justified. Unlike his first solo album, *Everybody Knows This Is Nowhere* would prove strongly indicative of the paths Young's career was to follow, introducing all three of the major styles he would return to again and again: guitar-dominated hard rock featuring extended instrumental work-outs, country rock and confessional acoustic folk. But despite its apparent heterogeneity this album possessed a unity – or perhaps a whole greater than the sum of its diverse parts – that few others could match.

There's certainly an emotional unity that transcends the various styles, a sense of yearning which, although almost comfortably melancholic, finds its own salvation in the honesty and simple directness of its expression. This is further mirrored in the music, which is also simple, also direct, no matter whether the guitars being played are acoustic or electric. On all the songs the changes are simple folk changes, a fact that led one critic to categorise Young's electric music under the highly appropriate name of 'garage folk'. With this music Young achieves what is considered the most difficult task in any artistic medium – a simplicity that doesn't deny complexity.

The title track is particularly revealing, in that there exists a recording of the same song made for the first album. The *Neil Young* version, with its wistful vocal, beautifully layered guitars, strings and flute solo, sounds pretty but passive. The *Everybody Knows* version is stripped-down, foot-stomping rock, but not an iota of the song's meaning has been sacrificed. Young has realised that emotional honesty doesn't necessarily entail speaking in a whisper.

He said he wrote the opening 'Cinnamon Girl' for a girl he saw in the street, but the words, though poetic enough – 'A dreamer of pictures, I run in the night/You see us together chasing the moonlight' – can't compete with the descending bass line, the Byrds-like ringing guitar behind the bridge, and the flashing burst of lead guitar following the joyful realisation that 'your baby loves to dance'. This is simply great rock'n'roll, late-sixties style.

'The Losing End' is just as straightforward, only the mood is morose rather than joyful, the rhythm a resigned country plod. There's even an 'All right, cousin, hit!' introduction to the guitar solo.

The two long ballads are quite different. 'Round and Round' is almost hypnotic, perhaps in part because of the way it was recorded, with Young, Whitten and singer Robin Lane rocking back and forth in front of the mikes. The lyric is not profound, but it hardly needs to be when the experience it's describing – the vain attempt to keep a doomed relationship alive – is such a common one. It's the directness that tells, with the intimacy of the subject more than matched by the intimacy of the performance. 'Running Dry' is not quite so successful – next to 'Round and Round' both words and performance seem slightly overblown – but there is the added compensation of Bobby Notkoff's almost traumatic violin solo.

Each side of the album ends with what, by the standards of the time, was an extremely long song. In the ten-minute 'Down by the River' he shoots his baby, but only metaphorically. 'There's no real murder in it,' Young claimed; the song was mainly about blowing a relationship. The lyrics do, however, admit of other possibilities. The lines 'This much madness is too much sorrow/It's impossible to make it today' make sense in relationship terms, but in 1969 they also seemed every bit as relevant to the political situation. And the same was true of the song's opening line: 'Be on my side, I'll be on your side.'

The eleven-minute 'Cowgirl in the Sand', according to its tongue-in-cheek author, was an impression of beaches in Spain he'd never visited. Its three heroines – 'cowgirl in the sand', 'Ruby in the dust' and 'woman of my dreams' – all seem to share the same promiscuous lifestyle. 'When so many love you, is it the same?' Young asks in the chorus, echoing an increasingly widespread feeling that greater sexual liberation was equal parts blessing and curse. Unfortunately, the succeeding line – 'It's the woman in you makes you want to play this game' – left a lot to be desired, even in 1969.

But although both these songs have interesting lyrics, their main purpose is to serve as overarching structures for the extended instrumental passages Young wanted to play on his electric guitar, and it is these, more than anything else, that account for the album's enduring popularity. In 1969, jamming in rock music was the preserve of guitarists like Clapton, Hendrix and Allman, all technically gifted, all with their music grounded primarily in the blues. Young, though a lead guitarist of long standing, didn't fall into either category. Nor did he want to play the sort of lead guitar that normally marked the traditional guitar hero – fast and flashy. On the contrary, he wanted to play it slow and full of passion, and to hell with good technique.

All of this made him somewhat special. Young's guitar-playing on songs like 'Down by the River' is perhaps as close as many rock fans get to classical music or jazz, in that he is using his instrument not so much to explore its musical possibilities as to serve as a direct line to his emotions. Young paints aural landscapes on these extended pieces, and mostly in primary colours, inviting his listeners to stretch their own sensibilities, to hear their own stories. The beat laid down by Crazy Horse never varies – at least not on purpose – giving the listener the same solid ground to stand on as the lead guitar has to play across. At one level this is easy music, but, like the simplest computer game, it can accommodate its listener at any level of complexity.

Everybody Knows This Is Nowhere was like a starter kit for Young's career. He would hone its parts in future years, but he would never improve on its raw spirit. Whether such music would make him a star was, of course, a different matter.

3

FUR COATS AND PERSIAN RUGS

In the summer of 1968, while Young was settling into Topanga Canyon, his erstwhile partner Stephen Stills was finding what seemed like musical heaven in nearby Laurel Canyon. After the Springfield's demise he had begun hanging out with David Crosby, who was also unemployed, having been fired from the Byrds in the middle of making *The Notorious Byrd Brothers* the previous autumn. And one evening in LA the two of them ran into the Hollies' Graham Nash and they found that together their three voices came close to magic. A long six months later Nash left the Hollies, and the threesome spent December getting an act together in a rented flat on Moscow Road in London's Bayswater district. Apple turned them down, but Atlantic proved loyal to Stills. Back in the US, they recorded *Crosby, Stills and Nash* in February 1969.

It seems to have been a happy time for all three of them. Nash was revelling in the creative freedom he felt the Hollies had denied him, Crosby was at last working with musicians who appeared to be as interested in music as in money and fame, and Stills was relishing the musical control he'd been increasingly denied as a member of Buffalo Springfield. 'They let me run with it,' he said later. 'There were no egos. Everyone was surprisingly co-operative,' he added wistfully.

The album was released in June to generally good reviews. Twenty years and many imitations later, it's hard to credit how fresh it sounded, how new. The blend of voices, of course, was and is a matter of taste. This author would rather hear Crosby's voice sandwiched between McGuinn's and Gene Clark's, Stills's voice on its own, and Nash's, if at all, in its lower registers. But for the purposes of this book it's important to understand what made the threesome special and, in particular, just how special they themselves thought they were.

Art Garfunkel, whose voice has a similar tendency to sweetness, offered an illuminating analysis of the three men's voices, and particularly of Crosby's: 'You have the brilliant Graham, who's so adaptable in that upper range and has such a perfect cutting edge and is ideally suited to combination from his Hollies experience. You have Stephen, who has a real personality of a voice, and you have David, the velvety sort of cement in their sound . . . the middle man does the stuff that makes the chord work, but you never notice it . . . There's a Zen-smooth kind of exhale in David's delivery. He has great come-from-the-heart feel in his singing and he loves rock'n'roll. You can hear it.'

Friend John Sebastian found the blend 'magical, otherworldly harmony, like nothing I'd ever heard before'. Engineer Bill Halverson couldn't believe how tight they were; Ahmet Ertegun and Phil Spector, invited to an early hearing of 'Suite: Judy Blue Eyes', were 'blown away'.

It was not just their technical ability as singers. Joni Mitchell noted the 'tremendous amount of affection and enthusiasm running back and forth among them'. It was almost as if they were in love with each other, and the warmth of feeling spilled out into their music and washed over their private audiences.

Nor was it simply the vocals. Both Stills and Crosby were fine guitarists, and Stills in particular was making great efforts in the studio to come up with new sounds. Acoustic guitars on record had rarely sounded as vibrant as on *Crosby, Stills and Nash*, while the album's full bass sound was something Stills had spent time developing in his work with Judy Collins.

The three of them had a new sound, and they were well aware of it. Crosby thought they'd 'lucked onto something so special, man. You could hear it plain as day.' Nash went further over the top: 'Those first album sessions got to levels of unbelievable connection. When you find someone that you're psychically linked with, it's a fortunate thing. When you find *two* people like that and you're in the same room with them, it's *scary*.' 'We worked together and still gave each other room,' Stills said. 'I've never felt such support since.'

With all that going for them, one wonders why they even considered inviting Young to join them.

There were good musical reasons for adding *someone*. First and foremost they needed some help to take their music out on the road. Stills had no intention of their becoming the new Simon and Garfunkel – always assuming that any of them could have written lyrics half as good as Simon's – but for an electric band they would need either another guitarist or a keyboard player, preferably someone who was both.

The first choice was Stevie Winwood, at that time between legs of Blind Faith's one, immensely lucrative tour of the US. Stills and CS&N drummer Dallas Taylor went to see him in England, trudging through knee-deep mud to Winwood's country cottage, only to find that this particular member of rock's first supergroup had already had enough of such aggregations. They then tried the Paul Butterfield Blues Band's Mark Naftalin. He didn't say no, but he wouldn't say yes either.

Meanwhile, back in the US, Ahmet Ertegun's brain had been turning over. He had always been an admirer of the Stills-Young combination, and he hadn't become one of America's most successful music entrepreneurs – and president of Atlantic – by being the kind of man who would overlook the potential of a grouping like Crosby, Stills, Nash and Young. Four writers and four voices, sensitivity and politics, acoustic and electric – could this really be the long-awaited American Beatles, a real band of real individuals?

Whether Ertegun ever did reach such a conclusion, and work towards its realisation, will probably never be known. Once the initial idea had been floated, everyone involved – the four musicians, their managers, their friends – must have had an inkling of how powerful such a line-up would be – in commercial terms, in artistic terms, even in political terms.

Crosby, Stills and Nash would need a little help in taking the big leap. They had to overcome a natural conservatism, a delight in what they already had, and the fear that Young – or at least the Stills-Young combination – would prove once again a disruptive force. But gradually they were persuaded, or persuaded themselves, that the game was worth the candle. They could handle it. They could handle Young, they could handle themselves. There was no shortage of confidence in their talent, in the strength of their 'vibes', in the spirit of the times. Love was coming to us all, and who were they to let a little personal difficulty stand in the way of such a new and sweet-smelling manifest destiny?

The actual process of getting Young to join seems to have been conducted along the lines of a ritual courtship. According to Ahmet Ertegun, he asked David Geffen and Elliot Roberts – who had somehow divided up the CS&N managerial chores between them – to dinner one evening in June 1969. 'After dinner I started to play these Neil Young records and I told them that as happy as I was to see Stephen Stills with Graham and with David, I was very sad that Neil Young was no longer with Stephen. There was a certain magic between them when they were with Buffalo Springfield, and that evening they said, "You know, we ought to talk to Neil."'

The next step, though, was to convince Stills. Another dinner was given, this time for Stills and Geffen, and Young was back on the turntable, singing, among other songs, 'I Am a Child', whereupon Ertegun began to wonder aloud whether Young should be added to Crosby, Stills and Nash. 'There's something about Neil Young that goes with this,' he said – presumably not referring to the grown man's continuing ability to be a child.

Stills allegedly disagreed, but nevertheless passed the suggestion on to his two partners. Maybe Crosby was the next one to get dinner, because Nash remained most vociferously opposed: 'I was against Neil joining at first. I felt a little threatened, because the three of us had made this *thing* of CS&N, this album, this image, this *sound*, and I felt afraid that it was going to change.' But by this time he seems to have been in a minority. Stills was given the task of approaching Young, and found a warm welcome from his old partner. Young told Stills that the vocals on *Crosby, Stills and Nash* had knocked him out. According to Stills they 'talked about being *brothers*, about being a little older and about how we should be able to play in a band together'.

It's hard to believe that Young hadn't been prepared for this visit by either Elliot Roberts or Ertegun himself. He was certainly not knocked off his stride by Stills's suggestion that he join the group as a sort of glorified back-up, someone who would fulfil all the musical functions Stills thought they needed but who would otherwise stay in the background doing what he was told. Young not only wanted his name on the marquee – henceforth the group would have to be called Crosby, Stills, Nash *and Young* – but also intended to do his share of the writing and arranging. If Stills wanted him then Stills would have to surrender his musical domination of the group. Stills's objection – 'Aw, c'mon, everybody'll know who you are, man' – was somewhat disingenuous, to say the least.

Soon afterwards, Crosby, Stills and Nash went up to Young's house together. He played them 'Helpless' and, according to Crosby, 'by the time he finished, we were asking him if we could join *his* band'.

Why did Young agree to join? Did he see CSN&Y as a way of getting his name in lights, of making stacks of money? Or, to put the same expectations another way, did he envisage the new band offering him an audience for his music that he would find harder to reach, so quickly, either on his own or with Crazy Horse? Certainly the dispute over whether his name got tagged onto the end of the group's – which according to Young took about a month to resolve – seems significant in this respect: there was not much point in playing to wider audiences if they didn't know who the hell you were.

There is also no doubt that he often derived great creative satisfaction from playing with Stills, had a lot of respect for Crosby, and did indeed find their three-part harmonies a joy to listen to. The sort of music CSN&Y would play was far from inimical to Young; it wasn't the only type of music he liked to play, but it was certainly one type. And there would always be his own solo spots. And Crazy Horse.

The downside to all this must have been equally apparent. He'd be back in a band, competing with three other egos in the madhouse environment of touring. And one of them would be Stills, whom he *knew* to be about as stable in such situations as a neurotic jack-in-the-box. And he'd be back in the studio with the same three egos, arguing about arrangements and anything else that could be argued about.

But this time, Young must have hoped, it would be different, and for one simple reason: he *wanted* to play with these guys but he didn't really *need* to. He had his own back-up band in Crazy Horse, and he had no intention of giving it up. Total control in that department could go hand in hand with a lack of too much responsibility as regards the other. In CSN&Y 'I didn't have to be out front', he said later. 'I could lay back. It didn't have to be me all the time.' He was being selfish, but which of them could claim to be playing with the others out of the kindness of his heart? Young, at least, made no secret of how he saw the arrangement. Before joining Crosby, Stills and Nash, he made it 'clear to both sides' – to them and to Crazy Horse – 'that I belong to myself'.

He had been given the chance to have the best of both worlds and he grabbed it. He admitted that there was a side to his music that was 'too technically advanced for Crazy Horse', and that in this respect CSN&Y offered him an outlet, but there was no doubting which band he preferred to play with, and which he considered more important. He compared CSN&Y to the Beatles and Crazy Horse to the Rolling Stones, adding that the latter were his favourite group. With Crazy Horse he could 'make records that are not necessarily hits, but which people will listen to for a long time'. But since, for the moment at least, there seemed little hope of the Crazy Horse music paying for itself, there was no choice but to subsidise it from his earnings elsewhere, to accept that 'the CSN&Y thing supports Crazy Horse'.

Young could hardly have been clearer. For its other three principals CSN&Y was something altogether special, the focus of their music and their lives. For him it was an opportunity, a way to reach an audience, to express one part – not even the most important part – of his musical persona.

The flaw was built into the mechanism from the beginning.

With Young on board, they set about finding a bass player. Stills's first choice was Kenny Passarelli, but the others thought he was too young. Stills then suggested Bruce Palmer – partly, according to Crosby, because he liked his playing, partly because he wanted to help him out. No doubt Young concurred with the choice of his old friend.

Palmer lasted only a couple of weeks, through rehearsals at Peter Tork's house and the recording of four songs, which included 'Horses through a Rainstorm' (written by Graham Nash and English rocker Terry Reid) and a new version of 'Helplessly Hoping', both of which would turn up more than twenty years later on the *CSN* CD boxed set. He doesn't seem to have impressed either Crosby or Nash. The former found him 'unstable', and the latter 'stormed out' when the bassist missed a chord. Palmer himself, while admitting he was 'rusty', found nothing to admire and 'not a lot of joy in the way they made music; it was aloof and distant. They were cold, calculated and sometimes abusive.'

His replacement was Greg Reeves, a nineteen-year-old Motown session player recommended by Ricky Matthews. He was good, and probably more in awe of the band's principals than Palmer had been. Four giant egos was enough for any group.

CSN&Y played their first live gig at the Chicago Auditorium on 16th August 1969, the second at Woodstock a few days later. Crosby, Stills and Nash took the stage at three a.m. on the second night of the festival and, following what would become the regular pattern of the CSN&Y stage show, performed 'Suite: Judy Blue Eyes' as a trio before bringing on 'a friend of ours – Neil Young'.

To say that Young's feelings about Woodstock were ambivalent would be to overstate his enthusiasm. In the words of the later 'Hitch-hiker', he had no desire 'to see or be seen'. A 1979 comment – 'I saw the movie and I wasn't in it, so maybe I wasn't too good there, I don't know' – was more than a little hollow: CSN&Y's electric set opened only after Young had made clear his refusal to be filmed. Nash was surprised: 'I never understood why Neil didn't want to be part of that,' he said, adding, with a naïvety that's hard to credit, 'It was like he didn't want to be *connected*.'

Certainly Young had his doubts about festivals. The sound quality was usually deplorable, reducing the music to not much more than an excuse for the parading of what he suspected was a largely artificial collectivist ethos. His favourite memory from Woodstock would be a personal one. On their arrival the band discovered that the helicopter pad was several miles from the stage area and no lift had been arranged. Young chanced upon an empty pick-up, climbed aboard and drove it across, with fellow guitarist Jimi Hendrix perched on the bonnet like a psychedelic hood ornament. In later years Young would regard 'stealing a pick-up truck with Hendrix' as 'one of the high points of my life'.

Woodstock certainly did the band as a whole no harm. In *Rolling Stone* Greil Marcus wrote a rave review, calling them 'visually one of the most exciting bands I have ever seen . . . Crosby finally looks exactly like Buffalo Bill . . . Stills with his pageboy haircut and Mexican serape . . . Nash one of those undernourished-in-childhood English kids . . . Neil Young, as usual, looked like a photo from Agee's *Let Us Now Praise Famous Men*, dustbowl gothic, huge bones hung with very little flesh, all shaped by those odd piercing eyes that have warmth even as they show fear . . .' There were many bands at Woodstock, but according to Marcus, that particular night belonged to CSN&Y. Their performance was 'a scary brilliant proof of the magnificence of music'.

Immediately after the festival they played five sell-out nights at the Greek Theater in LA, hitherto not a venue associated with radicalism of any kind. A short trip to England to play a free concert in London's Hyde Park was first planned and then abruptly cancelled, before a series of gigs at New York's Fillmore East was announced for the end of the month.

These concerts, and the events surrounding them, offer a rounded picture of the band in their dubious prime. Fillmore chief Bill Graham called his staff together and told them that CSN&Y were the American Beatles, and that he wanted it to be 'very special'.

So did the band, who were not above being demanding. According to Jonathan Kaplan, 'Each one of them had to have a different cuisine catered in their dressing room every night from a different land. So Stephen had Jewish and Graham had Italian and David had Chinese and Neil had Japanese. Then the next night, it all switched around. They never ate the food anyway. But one only wanted Coors in his cooler and another only wanted Bud. If the right one wasn't in the cooler, they would be out the door.'

And then there was the matter of a Persian carpet, required on stage according to the terms of the band's contract. One was found easily enough, and vacuumed to everyone's satisfaction, but for some reason it wouldn't stay still. 'They kept making me recentre the rug,' a Fillmore employee later recalled. 'I remember them saying, "This is *not* centre stage." And they would make me move the rug two inches this way. And then I would have to move it two inches *that* way.'

During this period any problems on stage were rarely group-threatening, with one notable exception. On the night Bob Dylan turned up to see them, Stills asked the others if he could do an extra song in the bard's honour, and they agreed. He then did three extra songs. Since Stills's solo set was the last of the four, none of the others could retaliate. This probably added fuel to Nash's fury, and when the intermission came he let Stills have it. 'I remember him standing in front of me with a can of Budweiser. And while we were talking, Stephen was getting so pissed he was *crushing* the can in his hand and beer was foaming all down his arm.'

It looked as if the band was going to break up then and there, but Elliot Roberts persuaded them at least to finish the show. And having spent forty-five minutes doing a better-than-passable imitation of schoolboys in a playground, the four of them went back on stage and played what was reputedly one of their best ever electric sets.

In fact, throughout this time they hardly seemed capable of putting a foot wrong, musically. At the end of the last show the audience refused to leave, and Bill Graham was reduced to putting hundred-dollar bills under the dressing-room door to coax them back. Young kept demanding more, until he thought he had a big enough wad to throw at the audience. Nash told him to forget the idea: this was New York, and he'd start a riot.

Then tragedy struck. On 30th September, Crosby's partner in love, Christine Hinton, was killed in a car accident. The band went their separate ways for a fortnight, with Nash accompanying the stricken

Crosby out onto the empty ocean, and Young renewing his acquaintance with Crazy Horse for a show at the Santa Monica Civic Auditorium.

Crosby returned, determined to bury his grief in his music. The band did an extended gig at San Francisco's Winterland, then set off on the Carry On tour across the US. They did a set at Altamont, but didn't hang around. Unlike some of their fellow performers, CSN&Y had picked up a shrewd idea of the violence in the air the moment they'd stepped off their helicopter. They played and ran, literally.

What was so important about this band? Why was it possible to mention them in the same breath as the Beatles? Partly, no doubt, it was wishful thinking. America needed its own Beatles, needed a band that could reflect an American-dominated world and an American-dominated youth culture. Two Americans, one Englishman and a Canadian was just about the perfect mix. There was even an Afro-American on bass.

And in one other crucial sense CSN&Y really did reflect something wider than music. The disintegration of the Beatles had mirrored the disintegration of the counter-culture community and its hopes, but for a brief year CSN&Y managed to recreate its appearance, to reflect hopes that were no less real for being doomed. No matter that the vision was flawed, simplistic, downright naïve. It was still one of the least irrational responses on offer to a vicious war waged by a vicious system, a society riven by racism and greed.

CSN&Y had enough musical substance to be Beatles-substitutes – a then unique fluency in both acoustic and electric styles. They combined the excitement of being a new group with the continuity that came from the best of rock's history: Californian folk rock and the English beat boom. They had distinct visual personalities on stage. Even their love lives seemed like quality soap opera – although sometimes the plot appeared to involve little more than a question of who was sleeping with Joni Mitchell.

And they had a vision, albeit one that walked a thin line between the simple and the simplistic. Essentially it was just a matter of honesty, in politics as in personal relationships. In the latter case it was simply a matter of recognising your own feelings, and learning to express them in whatever ways seemed appropriate. In the former, of telling it like it was. Railing against the war, against racism, against the ignorance and the greed that made such behaviour not only possible but necessary. The powers that be did not constitute the only targets. Each individual had to search his or her own soul as well: if all the banners had to offer was 'hooray for our side' then it was time for a rethink.

Young was an integral part of the group because, more than any of the others, he reflected the doubts. Without the ballast he provided, the band would have teetered on the edge of ideological flatulence. Young rounded it out – 'Helpless' made 'Carry On' acceptable. He enabled them to reflect, however imperfectly, the community as it then was, still full of righteous anger and hope, but now bearing the added burden of doubts and resignation.

On stage they were certainly magic. I saw them at the Albert Hall in London early in 1970 and thought them the best band I'd ever seen. The music in itself – particularly the electric set – was probably not that wonderful: after all, the live album *Four Way Street* was presumably compiled from their best performances, and that often verges on the sloppy. It didn't seem to matter. Crosby and Nash encompassed everyone with their stoned smiles; Stills's manic energy and Young's brooding intensity added the counterpoint. It was more than music. It was an oft-repeated cliché that this band created mini-Woodstocks wherever they went, but that notion, paradoxically, did them less than justice. Wherever they went they recreated a sense of community in a world that was rapidly becoming more individualised, a sense of sharing in a world where self-interest was increasingly the measure of morality, and a sense of not being alone in a world that seemed to be heading for hell by the quickest route – all of which was worth a great deal.

Creators of community, purveyors of honesty; they gave themselves a lot to live up to. Far too much, in fact, for any group of four men not long out of adolescence, let alone *this* foursome. And there was always the in-built contradiction: people who get rich and famous evoking community are pretty soon far removed from the community they think they're speaking for. The link becomes dishonest.

In mid-September the band were faced with the choice between a lucrative, sales-boosting appearance on the *Hollywood Palace* TV show and a free concert in front of a relatively small, live audience at the Big Sur Folk Festival. In deference to the spirit of the times, and to the important place it occupied in their own sense of how they should behave, they chose the latter.

So far, so politically correct.

For costume, Crosby, Stills and Nash chose the huge fox-fur coats they had worn for the centrefold of their album cover. They were warm, they looked beautiful, they looked expensive. It was the latter that enraged one spectator, and he had imbibed enough alcohol to say so. How could they flaunt such conspicuous wealth – those coats and those beautiful guitars – and still have the nerve to think they could speak for ordinary people?

It was a good question, and Stills's answer from the stage says a lot more about the late sixties than the movie *Woodstock* ever could. 'Like the guy was saying,' he began sympathetically, 'we look at these fur coats, fancy guitars, fancy cars and say, "Wow, man, what am I doing?", you know, so when somebody gets up and freaks out like that, it kind of strikes a nerve and you end up right back in that old trap, and where that guy is at is in that same trap and that's getting *mad* about something. And that ain't nothing, you know, and I had some guys to love me out of it and I was lucky. We just gotta let it all be. Because it all will be however it's gonna.'

Don't get angry? This from the man who used to end his solo spot in CSN&Y concerts with a musical 'poem' full of righteous indignation called 'America's Children', who wrote the enraged 'Word Game' about South Africa, who would be a more than willing participant in 'Almost Cut My Hair' and 'Ohio', two of the angriest songs of the era? Why was it okay to be angry about those things, but not about a few rock stars flaunting their wealth?

This is harsh on Stills, of course. How else could he have replied to the accusation? By taking a vow never to display any of his wealth in public? Or to give it all away? None of these guys was a saint, and in some ways they seem to have tried harder than most. In their arguments with each other they used to bring up each other's lyrics, and tell each other they weren't living up to what they preached. But the contradictions at the heart of their position as stars could never be resolved.

Sex was no easier a subject than money. Each of the four had well-publicised – not least by themselves in the lyrics they wrote – love relationships. How could any or all of them square that with Jonathan Kaplan's memories of a CSN&Y visit to the Fillmore: 'I'm not going to name names, but at a time when I and most people were certainly aware of the position in which women had been placed in a male-dominated society, rock and roll was maybe a step down from football in the way that women were treated.'

Who knew there was a step down from football?

* * *

Recording for the band's first album, *Déjà Vu*, began in October, continued sporadically into November, and was then resumed in January 1970. In all, a staggering eight hundred hours of studio time were consumed in its making.

The first sessions in particular were unhappy affairs. Crosby was grief-stricken by the loss of Christine, Nash was about to split with Joni Mitchell, Stills was still lamenting his break-up with Judy Collins, and Young's marriage to Susan was on the downslope. Nor did the four of them appear to be getting on very well with each other. Engineer Bill Halverson noted that they were rarely all in the studio at once, and that, 'unlike the first CSN album, the feeling was not comfortable'.

Young was the least co-operative and, in Halverson's opinion, 'never even seemed a part of the group'. Of the seven songs he had no hand in writing, he played on only two – 'Almost Cut My Hair' and 'Woodstock'. Not surprisingly, he argued that the recording process should be as spontaneous as possible, and on 'Almost Cut My Hair' this view prevailed, with the result that Crosby's sublimely excessive song became easily the most exciting piece of music on the album.

As for 'Woodstock', Young claims that Stills's original live studio vocal was wonderfully expressive, but that the others insisted on replacing it with a more 'perfect', more sterile version. 'That pretty well typifies the whole deal there,' he said years later. 'Most of the things, they were so concerned with making them perfect that they were better before they started messing round with them.' In retrospect even Stills admitted that Young 'might have been right'.

'Everybody I Love You', the song Young co-wrote with Stills – it was actually two songs placed end to end rather than a genuine collaboration – sounds as if it was recorded in layers, but on the songs for which he was solely responsible – 'Helpless' and 'Country Girl' – Young was able to insist on virtually live recordings, with little more than the backing vocals added at another time.

These two were not the only Young songs considered for inclusion on *Déjà Vu*. The nondescript 'Sea of Madness', which turned up on the Woodstock album, was attempted again in the studio, as were the more promising ballads 'Everybody's Alone', 'Birds' and, probably, 'Wonderin''. A CSN&Y version of the last-named would have been delightful, but maybe Young was still planning to include the song on his next solo album.

*　　*　　*

Rolling Stone gave *Déjà Vu* the accolade of two reviews, one in traditional style, the other an allegorical tale by J.R. Young. In the latter, a bunch of hip and happy counter-culturists are feeling the strain of waiting for the long-promised album. Their stoned reveries are interrupted by the arrival of a visiting stranger. He is made of tougher, more revolutionary stuff, and pours scorn on their radical pretensions. Music and dope are no way to overthrow the system, he says: *Déjà Vu* is not the answer – it's the problem. The happy bunch think about it, are convinced, and decide to blow up the local record store. Returning from their successful mission they find the stranger stoned out of his skull, blissfully listening to the newly-released *Déjà Vu*. 'But, but, but . . .' they splutter. 'I know, I know,' the stranger drools, 'but it sounds so *good*.'

Which just about sums up the album. Halfway through the opening 'Carry On', as Crosby, Stills and Nash take off, in perfect harmony, into 'love is coming, love is coming to us all', it sounds so good you can almost believe them.

The content is another matter. Four of the ten songs – 'Carry On', 'Teach Your Children', 'Déjà Vu' and 'Our House' – are basically CS&N affairs, and on none of them do the lyrics move beyond the hippie kindergarten. Their idealistic smugness sets Stills's acoustic solo '4+20' in almost too great a relief: a beautifully understated sigh of despair, it is even good enough to survive a place in the running order behind the appalling 'Our House'.

The other five songs are real group efforts. 'Woodstock' might have been improved by the rawer Stills vocal, but it's doubtful: even the existing one seems in constant danger of overpowering Joni Mitchell's less than interesting melody. Perhaps it's the overblown hope of the lyrics – bombers turning into butterflies! – but this song seems to feature Crosby, Stills and Nash at their most sterile. It's done to perfection, with the accent on the done.

'Everybody I Love You' is more of the same, without even the saving grace of a real lyric. 'Almost Cut My Hair', by contrast, shows the band at its best. Many thought the lyric facile, but letting your 'freak flag fly' was some kind of statement at the time, and a risky one at that in some places. Like 'Long Time Gone' this song was supposedly inspired by Robert Kennedy's assassination, and the hook line – 'I feel like I owe it to someone' – encapsulated the counter-culture's sense of embattlement as the sixties ended in a welter of killings and betrayals. But it's the music that makes the song, in particular the instrumental section, where Stills and Young climb a mountain with traded lead-guitar runs, and Crosby's exultant whoop tops it all off. These thirty seconds capture the band's harder live sound better than anything on the later *Four Way Street*.

Young's two songs are very different. During the recording of 'Country Girl' he was overheard telling Greg Reeves that 'what we've got to do is listen with an eye to simplicity. Think how we can make it bigger by simplifying it.' Unfortunately, he succeeded only in making it bigger, and the finished product falls between the two stools, cluttered as a Phil Spector record but lacking – apart from the one moment in which Nash's voice soars out past Mars – the accompanying grandeur. Young's solo performances of the song around this time had a simple strength the recorded version lacks.

'Helpless', though, can rarely have been done better than here. One of Young's most important songs, it benefits enormously from the Crosby-inspired 'ooooh's and Stills's bluesy piano. Lyrically it looks back to Omemee and childhood, to a past that can never be relived, to that intertwining of landscape and innocence that seems to lie at the heart of Young's view of himself and the world. 'All my changes were there', but now 'the chains are tied across the door', and there can be no going back to his own making, no disentangling of who he is and always will be.

Such fatalism was almost like a slap in the face of everything Crosby, Stills and Nash stood for, and it's no surprise that many saw Stills's later song 'We Are Not Helpless' as a reply. The world of 'Helpless' is a world that changes slowly, if at all, a world in which humans are at the mercy of forces greater than themselves. Like a beggar in a rich man's church, the song exposed the pretensions of those around it. In its light the political pretensions of the album appeared shallow and transient.

It may have been greeted as a musical manifesto for the new age, but *Déjà Vu*'s only two moments of stark emotion are Stills's '4+20' and Young's 'Helpless', both of them deeply personal songs, more concerned with the prisons within than with those without.

Once the album was in the can, sometime towards the end of January 1970, the band went their separate ways: Stills back to England, Crosby and Nash out onto the ocean again, and Young back on the road, this time with Crazy Horse. This was a successful tour, no doubt in part because Young's profile had been heightened by his membership of CSN&Y. At this stage, a month before its release, *Déjà Vu* already had pre-sales in excess of two million.

Young and Crazy Horse played mostly material from *Everybody Knows This Is Nowhere*, spicing it with a few new songs such as 'Wonderin'' and 'Winterlong'. The Fillmore East show on 6th March, which has figured on a large number of bootlegs, found Young and Whitten in sparkling form. When these electric performances are compared with those on CSN&Y's *Four Way Street*, recorded only three months later, the difference is striking. Young and Crazy Horse seem to be working on the edge, generating tension and drama as a band, whereas it is as if CSN&Y, for all their talent and commitment, have already settled for giving the people what they expect.

Young was interviewed several times during this period, and the picture that emerges of his state of mind is – by Young's standards – reasonably clear. By the beginning of the March, when he talked to *Rolling Stone*'s Elliot Blinder, he was already contemplating the limits on his time and energy. With most of two tours behind him and another looming ahead, he was beginning to wonder how much longer he could keep it up. The same went for making records. There was one in the works, but after that, who knew when there would be another, 'of any kind, with anyone'? He thought he might just 'stop for a while . . .'.

Playing in two bands might have solved his musical problems, but it hadn't done much to preserve his sanity. It was 'like living two different lives', he said. 'People who see me and come over and want to talk to me because of Crosby, Stills and Nash are weird compared to the people I know through Crazy Horse, and then there's the people I know who don't have anything to do with either one of them, who are a whole other trip, and by the time the day's over I'm just completely screwed up.'

The level of success he'd found with CSN&Y hadn't helped. Everything seemed so extreme – the applause, the level of reaction, the sums of money involved. It was 'hard to relate to after what I was doing before'.

There was not much privacy on the road, and not much more at home, where fame had turned his house into a minor tourist attraction. During the latter part of 1969, he and Susan had found a hobby – making home movies with a newly-purchased Beaulieux Super-8 camera. If this new interest served as an escape from the pressures of the music, and gave the two of them something they could do together, it also expressed real artistic ambition on Young's part. For now, they were showing their work at the Topanga Community House, but later ...

Young's intellectual interests around this time are hard to ascertain. He had grown up in houses full of books – his father a writer, his mother a quiz-show panellist – but for the last five years he'd been living in Californian music circles, and he seems to have adopted their jackdaw approach to culture. When interviewed by Robert Greenfield in New York, he read out headlines from the *National Enquirer*: 'DRUG ADDICTION WILL SURROUND YOUR CHILDREN THIS SUMMER' ... 'POISON PLANET – EARTH'S TEN YEARS ALL THAT IS LEFT' ... 'VISITORS FROM OTHER PLANETS WERE HERE IN PREHISTORIC TIMES'. It was more exciting than the *Village Voice*, he said – 'not to put down the *Voice*'. Young was aware that his fans would expect him to find the hip *Voice* more interesting, but he didn't. The mysteries of Stonehenge, statues in Peru, a mural of a rocket ship inside an Egyptian pyramid – all of these were much more fascinating. 'You can't think about that ... you can't ...' he said, smiling in wonder.

The report of his conversation with a guy from RAW (Right-A-Wrong) is even more revealing. The activist had turned up during a dressing-room interview to enlist the rock star's support for a campaign to legalise marijuana, but the conversation quickly turned to pollution and the environment, with Young optimistically offering the opinion that five more years of popular pressure would force a change in business and government behaviour. This assessment looked pessimistic to the guy from RAW, but Young told him, 'You won't get these big plants to shut down and change things, so ...'

'Within four or five years,' the activist interrupted enthusiastically, 'there might be a very violent revolution, man, that will stop every wheel turning!'

'I can dig it,' Young said. 'I hope not, though, cos if it is I'll be in Big Sur [laughing] ... I'll be in Big Sur with my guns.'

It would be nice to have seen the expression on his face as he said this. A mixture of seriousness, irritation and mischief-making amusement perhaps. Doubtless noticing the raised eyebrows of both activist and interviewer – he was a star, so they'd be polite – Young went on, 'Yeah, I'll get a big cannon if they're gonna have a revolution. I'll sit up on top of my studio there, with my material gains after the game, and uh, contemplate my future ...'

At this point the interviewer left a pregnant pause, before bringing the interview back to music.

It was an enlightening exchange. Young was not half joking, half serious, he was simply dressing up seriousness in a joky manner. The use of the word 'they' in 'if they're gonna have a revolution' was no accident. Young was a star in his dressing room; no matter how absurdly the world was being run – and he knew full well it was being run by knaves and fools – there was no way he was going to pretend that he was a revolutionary.

In the gaps between tours, the hours between gigs, Young worked on the writing and mental arranging of a new solo album. In claiming that the albums he made with Crazy Horse were meant to last, that they were the art that CSN&Y's more entertainment-inclined music paid for, he had raised expectations in others, and probably in himself as well. Now, after three months of CSN&Y's New Age love and politics, he decided to make an album that would be musically positioned somewhere out on the country edge of pop.

Songs apparently available for selection included Young's own 'All the Things I Gotta Do Girl', 'I Believe in You', 'Winterlong' and a traditional favourite he'd learned in high school, 'It Might Have Been'. The latter two had been featured in the electric set during the winter tour with Crazy Horse.

And then there were a further nine songs whose titles would later be listed, for no apparent reason, on the *After the Goldrush* lyric sheet. 'Birds' and Don Gibson's morose classic 'Oh Lonesome Me' would appear on *Goldrush*, while 'Sea of Madness' had already appeared on *Woodstock*. 'Sugar Mountain' would surface on any number of single 'B' sides, and become difficult to avoid at some stages of Young's career. 'Wonderin'' would turn up more than a decade later on *Everybody's Rockin'*, shorn of most of its wistful beauty.

'Dance, Dance, Dance' and 'Everybody's Alone' would both become bootleg staples. The former was a reworked traditional number, much along the lines of the later 'Love Is a Rose', while the latter was a melancholy ballad with an attractive melody that demanded freedom, yearned for commitment and announced a despairing awareness of singularity. According to Rogan, both 'Big Waves' and 'I Need Your Love to Get By' were performed on the 1970 (presumably Crazy Horse) tour, but if so, no one seems to have been around with a tape recorder.

It's possible that the subsequent listing of these nine songs on the *Goldrush* lyric sheet was intended by Young as an indication of how the album was originally conceived. If this was the case, it's a good thing he changed his mind, because most of the songs he introduced later were significantly stronger.

Choosing the songs was only a beginning: there was also the style of their presentation, and in this matter Young was apparently burdened with either confusion or conflicting desires. On one hand he was aiming, he said, 'to make records of the quality of the records that were made in the late fifties and the sixties, like Everly Brothers records and Roy Orbison records and things like that ... They were done at once.' They'd mostly been made in Nashville, but the location was unimportant: it was the spontaneity that made them sound the way they did, the fact that everyone was playing at once.

It's easy to see what he was getting at. There was a simplicity, a clarity, a straightforwardness about the records of those he mentioned, and of others like Ricky Nelson or the young Elvis. There was even an emotional directness, despite the fact that the artists in question were often performing lyrics written by others. If he could add that simplicity and directness to more personalised, more subtle lyrics, Young must have thought, he would really be onto something.

But he was also pulled in a different direction. Jack Nitzche had helped Young arrange 'Expecting to Fly' back in 1967, and 'The Old Laughing Lady' in 1968. He was, like the Everlys or Orbison, a master of pop, but any similarities between them ended with an emphasis on simple melody. The Everlys' ''Til I Kissed You' was to the Crystals' Nitzche-arranged 'Da Doo Ron Ron' what water was to mud. One was full of space and light, and sounded as if it had been done in a single live take, while the other boasted grand pianos queuing up behind each other, and sounded more produced than performed.

Young was drawn mostly to the space and the light, but not exclusively so. In the spring of 1970 he and Crazy Horse made a recording of 'Winterlong' which Nitzche had arranged. 'If you listen,' Young told one interviewer, 'you can really hear the Crystals.'

On 4th May 1970 about five hundred students at Kent State University in Ohio mounted a protest against the ongoing involvement of US forces in Vietnam and Cambodia. The National Guard were called in, stones were thrown, and they opened fire, killing four and wounding many more.

Young and Crosby were staying in Pescadero, a small California coastal town not far from Young's ranch, when it happened. According to Crosby, he saw Young staring at the famous newspaper photograph of one student kneeling bewildered by the body of another, handed him his guitar, and watched him write the song. He called the rest of the band and told them to book studio time that night. 'I got Neil to the airport,' Crosby goes on, making it sound as if the effort of writing the song had turned Young into an invalid, 'and we got a plane and flew down.'

They recorded 'Ohio' along with 'Find the Cost of Freedom', a slight piece Stills had unsuccessfully submitted for the movie *Easy Rider*, and gave the tapes to Ahmet Ertegun, who flew them to Atlantic Records' New York HQ that night. All but uniquely in rock, a protest record was out within ten days of the event it was protesting against. And according to Crosby, it was released 'with the finger firmly pointed right where the guilt lay: Nixon and the warmongers. At that point we were powerful. We affected the world, right then.'

Did they? Did 'Ohio' have any lasting impact? Many radio stations did refuse to play it, and Vice-President Agnew was moved by it to denounce rock music as anti-American, but you could still buy the record at the local store – and who cared what Spiro Agnew thought about anything anyway.

In some ways 'Ohio' expressed the impotence of rock better than any other record before or since. It did indeed point the finger in the right direction, naming an American President as a murderer. In three brilliantly concise, telling lines – 'What if you knew her/And found her dead on the ground/How can you run when you know?' – Young asked *the* question, not just of the events at Kent State or of the wider Indo-Chinese situation, but of politics in the Western world in general. It's the question that has haunted, and still haunts, anyone of his generation with both a conscience and some inkling of how this world is really run.

The music and the performance more than matched the lyric. The bass rumbled with anger, the vocals and guitars cried with passion; it was worth the price for its fade-out alone, with Crosby screaming 'How many? How many more?' as Young's lead soared like a sun over the battlefield.

It was CSN&Y's best record. It said everything there was to say, said it powerfully, beautifully.

And maybe a few Americans had second thoughts about life, liberty and the pursuit of happiness at other peoples' expense. But the murderer Nixon remained in office, and would in fact be re-elected two years later. In the meantime, active opposition to the war would dwindle as American ground troops were withdrawn.

CSN&Y went back on the road, starting in Boston on 29th May. The cracks were already widening, as witnessed by the presence of a new bassist. Greg Reeves had been fired in April for having ideas above his station – demanding a place in the playlist for his own material – and Calvin 'Fuzzy' Samuels had been brought in to replace him.

This time around, apparently, there would be no holds barred. The camaraderie that had bound together the original threesome had evaporated in the heat of success, leaving everyone involved with both the chance and the inclination to 'grandstand'. Whether Stills sought to hold things together by assuming control, or simply created resentment by being too domineering, is hard to tell. Like the chicken and the egg, Stills and resentment seem to have gone hand in hand around this time. While he thought he was 'just trying to act like a pro', Nash was regarding him as a 'monster dominating force'.

Stills was by no means the only one to blame. The beatific grins Crosby and Nash bestowed on their audiences were not simply the result of sunny dispositions: at times the twosome seemed to be carrying the global dope industry on their shoulders.

On this tour, unlike the first, the four of them were often taking the band's problems out onto the stage with them. As usual the electric set was the more problematic, presumably in part because there were more chances to strike macho poses and blow each other off with the volume-control knob.

Stills blamed Young: '"Southern Man" was the best of the conversation pieces, but it really was the only one that was dependable. It was slow, there was room to fuck up ... but the unfortunate reality was that it was Neil's song, therefore he paid more attention. We never got that kind of commitment and interaction going in some of my pieces or some of David's or Graham's.'

Many of the people around the band – managers, roadies, friends – behaved in just as adolescent a fashion as the principals. Like baseball coaches they screamed from the dugouts, goading on their respective champions, and like spectators at a motor-racing meet they waited for the crashes. It worked. Stills and Young increasingly took to cutting up each other's vocals with their electric-guitar playing. And after fighting each other musically on stage, according to Ron Stone, 'they'd go into the dressing room and try and kill each other'.

Stills wasn't Young's only adversary. In Denver, angered by Dallas Taylor's drumming, Young simply stalked off stage. According to Taylor, 'Neil thought I was fucking up his songs on purpose.' He gave a reasoned denial of the charge, but no one seemed surprised by the *idea* of fucking up someone's songs on purpose. As for Taylor, he had to go. 'I was outside the dressing-room door when I heard Neil say, "Either Dallas goes or I go."'

Dallas went, but the band was already in the throes of disintegration. Not long after, in Chicago, the tie was broken. 'We couldn't relate to each other on a rational level,' was how Nash explained it, 'and when we can't do that, we can't play.' Stills had a different view: 'At one amazing meeting I watched Neil, David, Graham, Elliot and God knows who else smoke an ounce of weed and blow off a $7 million year, purportedly because I was being a showboat . . . We all lost right there, that day, to indulgence. We lost it all.'

Shortly afterwards he was further mortified when Nash moved in on the woman he'd just fallen in love with, Rita Coolidge. Crosby immortalised the whole sordid business in the song 'Cowboy Movie', and the band – much richer but not noticeably wiser – called it a quarrelsome day.

For Young, broken bands were becoming a way of life. In May, in the weeks before he was due to go out with CSN&Y, he'd been rushing to complete his solo album when Danny Whitten, almost overnight, became addicted to heroin. 'There was no reason,' Billy Talbot said later. 'In those days, people just started shooting right up. Didn't snort nothing. He just shot some speed, the next day some smack, and from then on he was a junkie.'

And totally unreliable. Young, doubtless experiencing a mixture of shock and anger, fired Crazy Horse on the 24th, the album half-completed. He then sent out urgent requests for help from Stills and Greg Reeves. His father thought there was 'some possibility that he fired the whole band in an attempt to shock Whitten off his road to disaster'. If so, it didn't work. Young rehired Ralph Molina to play drums and did what work he could before taking off on the CSN&Y tour.

After that tour was over, or perhaps along the way, it seems he remembered a young man who had invaded the Crazy Horse dressing room in Washington the previous year and played them a virtual audition. Nils Lofgren had, in his own words, 'freaked them out. I just started talking about my songs and music – for like half an hour. The energy I was putting across was so intense – nothing like how it must have been for them in LA. Then Neil handed me a guitar, and they just sat there listening . . .'

Young asked him to come and play on the rest of the album sessions. 'Sure, but why not Whitten?' Lofgren asked. He wanted Nils to play piano, not guitar, Young said, neatly sidestepping the question. Lofgren protested that he didn't play the piano. Young knew better, and after practising for a couple of days and nights at a friend's house Lofgren agreed with his new mentor. 'He knew I played accordion and the right-hand work is the same, so all I had to do was get my left hand together. He wanted a plain, simple style – and it worked.'

Once gathered, the musicians began recording in a professional studio. But either the hours weren't flexible enough, or something else wasn't right. Young hired a mixing board and they all went back to his basement studio.

Eventually, Talbot and the disgraced Whitten were invited back to add vocal support and to play on a couple of cuts. Jack Nitzche came with them, but only played on 'When You Dance I Can Really Love'. He doesn't appear to have been, at least in this period, the sort of man anyone would want as a character witness. According to Lofgren, 'Jack would get drunk a lot and talk a lot. One second he'd be sitting there drivelling away about how much he loved Neil's music, then the next thing you knew he'd be yelling and screaming at him, calling him names and refusing to play.'

Exactly *which* songs Young was putting on record *when* is hard to tell. The original 'countryish pop' album either got ditched at some definite point or, as seems more likely, slowly evolved over several months into something else. Young has always claimed – as does the album sleeve – that *After the Goldrush* was based on an idea for a screenplay by his actor friend Dean Stockwell. The plot followed three people – one of them a moody musician – through the day on which a tidal wave swallows Topanga Canyon.

Listening to *Goldrush* one is hard pushed to find anything that bears much relation to this notion. 'Don't Let It Bring You Down' (which

Young said he wrote about a visit to London) and the title track are both apocalyptic enough, but that's about all. More plausible perhaps is that several of the songs survived the abandoning of the original context, and that *After the Goldrush* represents several themes or none at all.

Lofgren noted a surge in Young's productivity, remarking that songs 'started flowing out of him'. David Briggs recounted how Young 'would sit upstairs in the living room working on a song and then we'd all go downstairs to the basement and turn on the tapes and away we'd go'. The whole album seems to have taken only a few days, in fact almost too few. Though he was pleased with it, Young initially worried that anything done that quickly couldn't be that good. 'He wasn't sure there was enough in it,' Lofgren said.

Time would prove him wrong, at least as far as the record-buying public was concerned.

There's no doubt that *After the Goldrush* was Young's ticket to the big league, but the nature of its immense appeal remains open to question. Was the album so popular because it offered such an emotionally satisfying reflection of its times? And if so, how well has it worn?

The answer to the first question has to be yes. *Goldrush* offered an emotional snapshot of a generation (or at least its affluent agenda-setters) beginning to come to terms with recognising that the sixties had raised more expectations than could be fulfilled. A greater awareness of how the world worked hadn't made it work any differently; more liberated attitudes towards sex and love co-existed uneasily with the old hankering for something that lasted. There was a dawning realisation that the hunger for change, while both understandable and laudable, might also reflect a failure to live in the world as it was. Limiting yourself to one partner in love might seem restrictive, but after five or six, wasn't there a sense that something had been lost? Things that had seemed so simple and straightforward were beginning to look like hard work.

After the Goldrush was a testament to the struggle, full of determination and understanding and more than a trace of self-pity. Read through from beginning to end the lyrics didn't suggest a feast of melancholy, but Young's voice tended to colour them that way, and since this struggle for honesty and a deeper-than-Hollywood love was such a righteous one, the melancholy could at least partly be enjoyed. It was this fusing of the two sensations, of both a reaching upwards and a sumptuous wallowing, that gave the album its topical power. The times they were a-changin', but not that fast and not that much. *After the Goldrush* affirmed the need to keep on trying as it offered comfort and an empathetic hand to those who caught themselves not living up to the new ideals.

All of this might have given the album a rather limited shelf-life, had it not been for other factors in its make-up. The most obvious of these is the basic strength of the songs. As on the first album, simple, beautiful, hummable riffs and melodies seem to trip over each other. Unlike those on the first album they are not half-buried in the production; the sound is basic and clear, each instrument audible. The acoustic guitar is dominant, but rarely alone; the album might sound folkish, but this is folk with a pronounced beat, in some ways the definitive *acoustic* folk-rock album. Piano, variously played by Nils Lofgren, Jack Nitzche and Young himself, is also more in evidence than on most Young albums of the sixties or seventies, providing variety without clutter. Overall, the combination of Young's voice and sparse instrumentation brings out the pained honesty, the 'realness', that lies at the heart of the songs.

A second source of the album's vitality – paradoxically so, considering its melancholic reputation – is the range of emotions given rein in the different songs. There is despair, anger and sadness, but there is also hope, acceptance and flashes of joy to light the gloom. 'Till the Morning Comes', despite its fragmentary lyric suggesting anger and threats, reaches musically for the sunlight in a manner that lifts the heart, and the singer's realisation, in 'When You Dance I Can Really Love', that 'I can love, I can love, I can really love' perfectly captures the moment's joyful surprise of realising we were more than we thought we were.

At the other extreme, 'Don't Let It Bring You Down' is a harrowing journey through any city's night, and the title song 'After the Goldrush' an equally apocalyptic trip, this one through time. The single couplet 'I was thinking about what a friend had said/I was hoping it was a lie', with its storybook representation of the gap between how we see ourselves and how others see us, offers a clue to Young's popularity: such an ability to hone and give dramatic expression to common concerns is not widely shared.

The spirit of the times may be omnipresent – with lines like 'Finding that what you once thought was real is gone and changing' just as applicable to the culture as to a relationship – but beyond a vague sense of rampant alienation there is only one passing nod to politics: the musically corrosive, ideologically simplistic 'Southern Man'. Interestingly for his own future, Young, a resident of multicultural LA, seemed in the song to be identifying racism only with the distant South and, moreover, in a manner that suggested the past rather than the present. For the moment the music was good enough to bury such doubts, with Lofgren's piano rattling chains and Young's guitar howling wildly at the moon. In one passage he keeps playing the same crazed note over and over, like an assassin sending redundant bullets into a corpse.

There are two great love songs on the album: 'Birds' and 'I Believe in You'. Both have gorgeous melodies, both were thematically unusual at the time of the album's release – and still are, if to a lesser extent. In 'Birds' the protagonist offers comfort to someone he has rejected – 'Tomorrow, see the things that never come today' – while in 'I Believe in You' he urges a lover to let faith in the depth of his feelings carry her through their mutual doubts. On both these songs Young demonstrates another rare ability: that of writing about love, from the heart, in such a way so as not to insult either his own or the listener's intelligence.

Of the other songs, mention should be made of the Don Gibson-written 'Oh Lonesome Me'. Young cited this as something he couldn't have done with Crosby, Stills and Nash, but it's hard to see any reason why: the chorus, like that of 'Helpless', seems tailor-made for their harmonies. The real reason, which Young probably intuited rather than thought through, was that they wouldn't have *wanted* to do the song. It was somebody else's, it was country, it was old. Or, as they might have said, it wasn't self-expressive, wasn't radical, wasn't 'now'.

Crosby, Stills and Nash were still trying to merge Dylan and the Beatles: their musical roots seemed to go back no further than 1964. Young's clearly went deeper, and herein lay the greatest source of the album's strength. Though happy to acknowledge the influence of Dylan and the Beatles, not to mention the Rolling Stones, Young also felt no qualms about paying homage to Roy Orbison, Hank Williams, the Crystals. 'When You Dance I Can Really Love' was stripped-down Spector, 'Oh Lonesome Me' a hard-edged Everly Brothers, and 'Birds' echoed Orbison's emotionalism while recycling his words. On top of everything else, *After the Goldrush* was a great pop album.

When CSN&Y had played in San Francisco that June, one of the road managers told Young about a 140-acre ranch for sale some forty miles south of the city in the foothills of the Santa Cruz Mountains. Young went to have a look, fell in love with the land, and after a couple more visits with Susan decided to buy.

The price was $340,000. Young paid cash, which made more emotional than financial sense. Feeling insecure about his future – after all, who could predict how long rock stardom would last? – he preferred to sink most of what he had in the place. That way, it could never be taken away from him.

He probably needed something to hold on to. Susan and he had found it impossible to reconcile their marriage with his career. He was often on the road without her, and she, a strong person in her own right, filled her life, and their house, with friends. When Young came home seeking refuge he found a group of people he hardly knew, and no doubt expressed his dislike of the situation. Given the circumstances, one is drawn to the conclusion that he was right from his side, and she from hers.

She had accompanied him on the Crazy Horse tour, but by then there seems to have been too much dividing them to be outweighed by what still held them together. They reached a final parting that summer, and Young moved into a hotel while he waited for his purchase of the ranch to be completed. The Topanga Canyon house was later sold – Young had grown tired of endless drop-in visitors and gawping fans.

All in all it must have been a difficult time for him, with professional success finding few echoes in his personal life. The marriage break-up, according to his brother Bob, 'hurt him deeply'. He even spent some time in Omemee that summer – perhaps returning to the place of his roots in search of something he feared had been lost.

Success was clearly a two-sided coin. On one side a ranch in the hills, on the other a failed marriage.

After the Goldrush was released in September. *Rolling Stone* managed an elegant put-down by Langdon Winner, in whose judgement 'none of the songs here rises above the uniformly dull surface . . .'. He wasn't alone: many critics apparently felt obliged to sharpen their knives on Young, as part of the then current fashion of decrying anyone who dared to sound even vaguely serious. Ken Emerson called several of the songs pathetic, and thought Young's ability 'to mouth such clichés with such compelling conviction . . . less a gift than an indication of lack of character'. He went on, 'If these songs are to be enjoyed, it must be as camp parodies.'

This must have surprised those who went out and bought the record –

which people did, in droves. That autumn *After the Goldrush*, along with James Taylor's *Sweet Baby James*, seemed to be floating out of every nook and cranny in the Anglo-American world.

Young had clearly arrived, and it was his own talent that had brought him such success. CSN&Y had given him a platform, but *Goldrush* was as strong an album as *Déjà Vu*, if not stronger. And for all those who had discovered Young through CSN&Y, there were many others – this author included – who had loved his work with Buffalo Springfield, loved his first two solo albums, and been to see CSN&Y primarily because of Young's involvement.

It should have been a great time for him. Everything he'd worked for over the last ten years had borne fruit. He had yearned to be a successful musician, and here he was paying a third of a million dollars for a ranch, all of it earned through his music. The sense of vindication must have been awesome.

Young must also, at some periods of his life, have felt 'Why me?' with rather more justification than most of us. As *Goldrush* sent his star into orbit that autumn, he put his back into spasm lifting a slab of polished walnut, and for most of the next two years would be at least partly incapacitated.

It wasn't the first time he'd had trouble with his back, but this time he felt worried enough to contact a specialist. A few days before keeping the appointment he saw the movie *Diary of a Mad Housewife*, loved Carrie Snodgress in the title role, and managed to get her phone number from a friend. She agreed to meet him, and they made a date for after his hospital visit.

The medical prognosis was worse than he'd expected. The specialist told Young he had a crumbling spinal disc, shouldn't be on his feet, and should be in traction. Neil called Carrie to cancel their date, but she came to see him anyway in the hospital. It was the beginning of a beautiful friendship.

Young was in and out of hospital for a couple of months, and spent at least some of his time planning the next album, a live double. He was also determined to get out on tour again as soon as possible, even if the state of his back restricted him to a seated, solo acoustic set. In any case it's doubtful if he would have wanted it any other way at this point. Another CSN&Y tour was out of the question, and his relationship with Crazy Horse wasn't exactly in very good shape. For the moment he was musically alone, and probably happy to be so.

Elliot Roberts fixed up the tour Young wanted, mostly small clubs and halls. It began in Washington on 30th November with three nights at the Cellar Door club, then moved on to Carnegie Hall in New York for two concerts on 4th and 5th December.

These last two dates were like a dream come true for Young, and not just because of the demand for tickets – the first concert sold out in twenty-five minutes – which must have been eminently satisfying in itself. No, it was the prestige associated with the venue: Carnegie Hall was a place where *artists* played. 'You have to be good at Carnegie Hall,' he told his brother. 'The money you make there isn't important. I'd do it for nothing – it's playing Carnegie Hall, that's the important thing.' The whole family was there to see him, though not together: Rassy and Scott came on different nights.

He did one night at the Fillmore East, then went back home for Christmas. The tour restarted in January, circling North America – with particularly gratifying sell-outs in Winnipeg and Toronto – to end in LA's Royce Hall on 1st February 1971. Three weeks later Young flew to London to record a live TV special and play the Royal Festival Hall.

He had enjoyed the tour immensely: it was 'real personal . . . very much a one-on-one thing with the crowd'. One interesting feature of his performances was his transforming of electric numbers into acoustic, a habit that he'd acquired with CSN&Y and which would continue throughout his career. 'Down by the River', 'The Loner', 'Ohio' and 'Southern Man' all received the treatment.

He also introduced more than a few new songs, including seven of the ten that would make up his next album, *Harvest*. (Although its completion and release were still more than a year away, only 'Are You Ready for the Country?', 'Alabama' and 'Words' were as yet unwritten or unperformed.) He even gave the début performances of the three ballads later to appear on the live *Time Fades Away*.

There were only a few sour notes. At the Boston Music Hall in January he lost his temper, warning the audience that he wasn't 'together enough tonight to put up with any shit', and that if they made too much noise he'd simply leave. At Carnegie Hall the previous month he'd been annoyed by shouted requests, firmly informing the guilty parties that he didn't 'take playing here lightly at all and I think that you should have enough faith in me to know that I would plan ahead and include all of the songs that I thought you'd want to hear'.

More seriously, at the same concert he told the audience that his next song was one he'd be doing with Johnny Cash on a TV special in a few weeks' time. This caused one heckler to shout out, 'Why? Why with Cash, man?'

Young didn't bother to answer, but the question was indicative of something that would come to haunt him over the next few years – a growing sense of confinement within the prison of his audience's expectations.

4

HARVEST OF SOULS

Imagine the scene: Young's limo pulls up outside the luxury flat in London's Grosvenor Square that has been rented for him, and the uniformed doorman grandly informs the singer that his new neighbours are King Hussein, Raquel Welch and Michael Caine. Young asks to be driven somewhere else.

This story appeared in one of the British music weeklies, and may even have been true. The reader was not, of course, told what happened next. Was Young perhaps persuaded that finding another flat at such short notice might prove difficult? It seems unlikely that he slept under a newspaper on the Embankment.

The picture this incident paints of him, as someone either embarrassed or bored by celebrity, was probably true as far as it went. But it was far from the whole story, as an almost childlike pride in his reception by the London Symphony Orchestra made clear. He had hired them to provide orchestral backing for two songs on his next album and, as he told his father, 'they were really into it. They treated me like *somebody*.' Success was still a new enough experience to elicit wonder, not to mention the usual bouts of rock-star self-indulgence. Whoever his neighbours were that time in London, they can't have got much sleep – Young was asked to leave his place of residence for making too much noise after hours.

He returned to America in time for his record company's announcement of the live album's imminent release. The track listing issued to the music press showed six previously unreleased songs: 'Old Man', 'Dance Dance Dance', 'See the Sky about to Rain', 'The Needle and the Damage Done', 'Bad Fog of Loneliness' and 'Wonderin''. Two of Young's compositions for Buffalo Springfield – 'Nowadays Clancy Can't Even Sing' and 'Flying on the Ground Is Wrong' – would also make their first appearance on record with the author on vocals.

The weeks went by. No album appeared, and no explanation was offered as to why. Finally the release of a completely different album, *Harvest*, was said to be in prospect. But this too failed to appear, and Young's fans were forced to make do with *Four Way Street*, a live double album culled from CSN&Y's shows in New York, LA and Chicago in the early summer of 1970.

Four Way Street was a major disappointment. Like Buffalo Springfield, CSN&Y had failed to capture the quality of their live performance on record, although by this time – towards the end of the second tour – there was undoubtedly less quality to capture anyway. The electric set in particular seems to have suffered from the deterioration of the relationships between the principals. 'Pre-Road Downs' was uninspired enough to begin with, and nothing had been added to the studio version of 'Ohio'. Deep within the lengthy jams framed by 'Carry On' and 'Southern Man' there are hints of how exciting Stills and Young's guitar interplay could be, but they soon pass. Only Crosby's 'Long Time Gone' transcends its studio version, thanks largely to the unrestrained passion of the vocal.

The acoustic album is better, but not much. The performance of Young's 'On the Way Home' is disastrous, transforming a beautiful song into a flat-footed dirge. He does provide the album's other highlight, though: a version of 'Don't Let It Bring You Down' that could send a shiver down a statue's spine. Young's joky spoken intro – 'Here's a new song that's guaranteed to bring you right down . . . it's called "Don't Let It Bring You Down" . . . sort of starts off real slow and then it fizzles out altogether' – sets a new standard in false senses of security. The performance is gut-wrenching, welding the song's glimpses of a civilisation cracking at the seams into a vision of almost total hopelessness. Beside this, the acoustic version of 'Cowgirl in the Sand' can offer little more than pleasant light relief.

Four Way Street was released in the spring of 1971, around the time that Young and Carrie Snodgress started living together at the Broken Arrow ranch. Within the constraints imposed by a back that allowed him only four hours on his feet each day, he seems to have been as happy as anyone could hope to be.

The back went out three times more before his operation in August 1971, and the period of convalescence lasted right through the following winter and into the spring. Advised that swimming and uphill walking would aid in the regeneration of his back muscles, Young had a hilltop swimming pool built on the ranch. Like the Topanga Canyon house, it was a testament to his taste and to the style of the times: dark interior walls, stone paths and weathered wooden pool-house. As his father proudly noted, it wasn't a typically Californian pool.

During this period, which accounted for most of 1971 and a large chunk of 1972, he found it difficult to hold up a guitar, even when wearing a specially-designed brace. Standing on a stage was next to impossible for any length of time, so touring with a band was out of the question. According to Young he couldn't even 'physically play an electric guitar'.

He had a lot of time – too much, probably – in which to think about all the things that had gone right for him, and all the things that had gone wrong. In later years he would claim that his state of health had not only affected the musical options open to him, but also reduced the imaginative energy he brought to the whole creative process. As he told Cameron Crowe, 'My whole spirit was prone.'

Musically, he had already explored more avenues than most of his contemporaries. He had been an integral part of roughly egalitarian bands, the undisputed leader and creative controller of others, and a solo performer in his own right. He had already developed three clear styles for himself. The first, which made its début on *Buffalo Springfield Again*, had been heavily influenced by the Beatles, the Beach Boys and, through Jack Nitzche, Phil Spector. This style was studio-centred, dramatic and – despite *sounding* both lyrically and musically complex – essentially a late-sixties development of early-sixties pop. Young simplified things a little for his first solo album, but the philosophy of his music-making remained much the same: he was producing a performance rather than merely performing. This first style had since been abandoned, apparently for good. CS&N's studio perfectionism, which might have rekindled Young's enthusiasm for such an approach, seems to have had the opposite effect, and confirmed his disapprobation.

The second style, developed with Crazy Horse on *Everybody Knows This Is Nowhere*, was rawer, more basic. It was characterised by two electric guitarists – one usually playing lead and rhythm, the other playing rhythm and lead – conducting a musical dialogue over a simple, heavy, rhythmic base. The song structures were just as basic, allowing extended improvisation between the verses and/or choruses.

The third style, which featured on *Goldrush* along with variations on the second ('Southern Man' was garage folk plus the piano, 'When You

Dance I Can Really Love' garage folk à la Spector), was a predominantly acoustic, lyrically confessional music. By combining pop's emphasis on melody with folk's emphasis on sincerity, Young had created a very potent brew: the listener could hum along without risk to personal integrity.

Most critics expected – and most of the punters who had loved *After the Goldrush* no doubt wanted – Young to rehash the third successful style on his upcoming fourth album. After all, if solo albums one and two hadn't made it, and solo album three had, then you'd repeat solo album three, right? That was the way the pop industry had always worked.

In Young's case it appeared even more self-evident, given his current circumstances. He'd abandoned his first style, and it was hard, if not impossible, to imagine pursuing the second with his back in a brace and without Danny Whitten. The former would doubtless heal in time, but there were more doubts about Whitten, who showed no sign of coming back from where the junk had taken him. If Young still wanted to be the leader of an American Rolling Stones he would probably need to search out new partners.

For the moment, it seemed, he had no option but to pursue his third style, and it's doubtful whether he had anything else in mind when he arrived in Nashville early in February 1971 to record the TV show with Johnny Cash. The new songs he was carrying with him – 'Heart of Gold', 'Old Man' and 'Bad Fog of Loneliness' – would all have fitted, melodically and lyrically, on *After the Goldrush*, and when Young decided to hire a few hours of studio time in Nashville he may well have had such a sound in mind. As it was, one thing led to another, and he found himself with a new, fourth style, not to mention two new musical collaborators – both of whom would still be with him twenty-three years later.

Country music had, of course, been a major element in the musical synthesis that was rock'n'roll. Elvis Presley's early singles were almost religiously split between countrified rhythm'n'blues and rhythm'n'blues-ified country, while later white performers like the Everly Brothers owed a much greater debt to country than to rhythm'n'blues.

Country music was white music, the folk music of the white South, and as such it was – and to a large extent still is – deeply imbued with conservatism, particularly in matters of sexuality, politics and religion. Not to put too fine a point on it, country music's audience and practitioners both sprang from and reflected a deeply racist culture.

At this time, though, there was another aspect to consider. Rock musicians, confronting the dissolution of those hopes for a new society that so many had trumpeted in their music, had little choice but to seek out new grounds for optimism, and a new spiritual home that was untainted by political failure. Since most of them were urban animals, and identified social problems with the city, the country seemed to offer both real distance from the problems and a place to begin afresh.

Adding a country lick or two to rock rhythms was one – somewhat ridiculous – way to signal this shift in cultural priorities, but country music had rather more of substance to offer than that. As hopes of change for the better turned, slowly but inexorably through the 1970s, into fears of change for the worse, country music was well equipped to offer solace and not a little understanding. It might spring from a conservative and racist culture, but it had also traditionally championed old verities and moralities against the dislocations, physical and emotional, of 'progress'.

For anyone with liberal intent, country music was a two-edged sword, offering an ideal medium for the exploration of themes of moral uncertainty and corrupted innocence, but carrying with it the baggage of a culture only a century beyond slavery, and a mind-set still in thrall to psychopaths in hoods.

All of this could doubtless not have been further from Young's mind when he arrived in Nashville. James Taylor and Linda Ronstadt were there for the same show, and he figured 'since we've got all these people around, perhaps we should cut some things'. Quadraphonic Studios were hired, and the word went out for musicians.

One of those who heard it was Tim Drummond. Five years or so older than Young, Drummond had played with Conway Twitty in the early sixties before becoming the only white man in James Brown's band. Touring had taken its toll, and he had settled in Nashville as a session player. One day in February 1971 he was walking down the snow-covered street when a friend told him that Neil Young was over at Quadraphonic looking for a bass player.

Drummond went across and got the gig. They were probably working on 'Heart of Gold' when Young decided that the formula of simple acoustic guitar, drums and bass wasn't enough. It was all a bit one-dimensional, 'all bottom'. He 'wanted to hear some colour', and asked Drummond if he knew any pedal-steel players. Luckily – it was still snowing hard outside – Drummond knew a guy named Ben Keith who lived only two blocks away.

Keith answered the call and duly arrived. 'I didn't know who anybody was. I thought, the guitar player in the corner plays a hell of a guitar. Who is that? They said, James Taylor. I said, who's that guy over there? That's Neil Young.' He set up his steel guitar, plugged in and started tuning it with the aid of a harmonica, playing 'big wide long notes'. Young told him to do the same on the pedal steel, just playing those keening notes under each chord, and a cascade of shorter notes under the changes at the end of the choruses.

They did much the same with 'Old Man' and, eventually, most of the rest of the album. The result was a new, lighter sound, countrified rather than country, more in keeping with life on a ranch than with life in the city, more in tune with a part-mythical American past and present than with any residual dreams of a better urban future.

The band were dubbed the Stray Gators and the album, like the previous two, would be named after its second song, in this case 'Harvest'. The dark, paranoid figure seen scurrying through the city on the sleeve of *After the Goldrush* would be transformed, on the new album's cover, into a check-shirted man wreathed in sunlight, albeit visible only at one remove, in the reflective surface of a shiny brass doorknob.

Although *Harvest* would go on to become the bestselling of all Young's albums, it would never receive much in the way of critical acclaim, and even Young himself would damn it with faint praise in later years, in one breath calling the album his 'finest', in the next noting how restrictive an adjective 'fine' was. No doubt the album's poor critical reputation arose partly as a direct consequence of its commercial success, but by no means entirely: on its release John Mendelsohn claimed, in a mostly well-argued review, that *Harvest* found 'Young invoking most of the LA variety of superstardom's weariest clichés in an attempt to obscure his inability to do a good imitation of his earlier self'.

More than twenty years later the album seems neither as good as its sales suggest nor as poor as its critical reputation. It does boast Young's first real clinker of a song (the indescribably inept 'There's a World'), but it also includes several that are still justifiably popular today, and one or two touches of sheer genius. Overall, the album sustains both a mood and a sense of its time with consistently listenable music.

The first two tracks set the tone. A wonderfully long intro drags the listener into 'Out on the Weekend'; the drums are mixed forward and amazingly clear, the pedal steel has a blue-sky purity, the harmonica sounds down-home enough to bottle. Young's wistful voice comes in: he's on the road but looking back, full of joy he can't relate to, floating in a dreamy sort of sadness. 'Harvest' has a different melody, a different rhythmic pace, even more incomprehensible words, and the same relaxed angst. Both songs invite identification with lines, not stories; like dreams they seem so full of recognition, yet so short on sense.

Young has rarely revived these two songs, which is not the case with 'Heart of Gold', 'Old Man' and 'The Needle and the Damage Done', all of which have featured in his live performances at regular intervals over the last two decades. 'Heart of Gold', with its potent mixture of instantly recognisable melody, yearning arrangement and a lyric that takes a universal theme to the edge of daftness, went to number 1 on the singles chart, probably much to Young's surprise. If puppies could be made into music they would sound like this.

'Old Man' offers slightly more in the way of lyrics, and an equally memorable melody. Though neither this song nor 'Heart of Gold' has the depth of Young's best work, both demonstrate the power of simplicity in his songwriting, and they are good for what they are. 'The Needle and the Damage Done' is even better. A simple folk acoustic tune only two minutes long, it tells its tale of addiction with chilling directness. There's no blame, no shame, only regret and sadness. Considering that the track was recorded live at UCLA's Royce Hall, Young's expressive vocal is beautifully controlled.

At the song's end, the first chord of the closing track, 'Words', cuts across the applause like a door slamming shut. It's just another concert, just another song. 'The king started laughing and talking in rhyme, singing words, words . . .' The guitar takes up the story, a slow procession of staccato notes, angry but resigned. 'Words' is nothing if not a coherent statement of how Young was feeling about being a rock star.

'A Man Needs a Maid' bore much the same relationship to his private life. The title gives rather a false impression: far from being an endorsement of male chauvinism, it is actually an admission of male inadequacy. He wants a maid because then he'll know the rules; in real relationships it's never that simple. As he says, in an obvious reference to Carrie that retains its universal implications, 'I fell in love with the actress/She was playing a part that I could understand.' A man needs a maid, but that says more about the man than he'd like to admit.

Buffalo Springfield. Left to right: Richie Furay, Dewey Martin, Bruce Palmer, Stephen Stills, Neil Young.

A band by any other name: Young, Crosby, Stills, Taylor and Nash.

Looking out into the darkness. CSN&Y at Woodstock, August 1969.

Tonight's the Night, 1973.

On tour with CSN&Y, 1974.

On Zuma Beach, 1975. Left to right: Ralph Molina, Billy Talbot, Frank Sampedro, Young.

The Last Waltz, 1976, with Joni Mitchell.

With Rick Danko and Robbie Robertson of the Band.

Like a hurricane . . . On tour with Crazy Horse, 1976.

Young and 'road-eyes' during the Rust Never Sleeps tour, 1978.

With Nils Lofgren on the Trans tour, 1982.

Transformer Man's dad.

Meanwhile, a man still aspires to a real relationship of equals. 'To live a love, you gotta be "part of" . . . when will I see you again?'

The song asked questions that were relevant in 1972, and remain so today. Young's stage performances of the song around this time, alone at the piano, had a power that was unique in his acoustic repertoire. In his realisation that such rawness would seem out of place on *Harvest*, and would need to be shrouded in orchestration, he himself provided one of the more telling comments on the album's limitations.

1972 was definitely a year for taking stock. The release of *Harvest* in March found Young still mostly confined to the ranch, and if the need to rest his mending back was sufficient reason for this reclusiveness, one suspects that in any case he harboured little desire to re-embrace the world.

Talking to Cameron Crowe in 1975, he said that at this time he had felt something was dying – without specifying what. In another conversation four years later he hinted that it was his sense of connection with the outside world that had withered. He'd achieved what he'd set out to achieve in career terms – had the 'world on a string' to quote a song from the following year – but as that song said, it 'doesn't mean a thing . . . it's only real in the way that I feel from day to day'. The more the outer world gave him what he'd thought he wanted, the more the inner world raised doubts about the worth of it all.

'Heart of Gold' might be number 1 on the singles chart, but, as he said years later, 'I realised I had a long way to go and this wasn't going to be the most satisfying thing, just sitting around basking in the glory of having a hit record. It's really a very shallow experience. It's actually a very empty experience. It's nothing concrete except ego-gratification, which is an extremely unnerving kind of feeling.' It felt like a wall building up around him, hemming him and his music in. Slowly but surely through 1972–3, in an increasingly conscious manner, he would seek to reverse the process, to take the wall down.

This is not to imply that Young spent the next eighteen months perched on a fence agonising about the state of his psyche, only to say that in any consideration of his future life in music he was acutely aware of looming traps and the need to avoid them. In the meantime ordinary life went on, and a comfortable life it was by most standards. He and Carrie had each other, and for the first eight months of 1972 they were expecting their first child. A son, Zeke, was born on 8th September.

With *Harvest* outselling any of his previous albums, money was obviously not going to be a problem in the foreseeable future. If Young wanted to go trekking in Nepal, buy an ocean-going yacht or create a stereo system several hundred yards wide, then he could. And in the latter case, did. Graham Nash recalled being invited out onto Young's small lake in a rowing boat, thinking his host wanted a private chat. But no. In mid-lake Young raised his arm, and seconds later one of his songs came booming across the lake from two directions. He had set up the barn and the house as reverberation points for two powerful speakers. When friend Elliot Mazer appeared on the shore to ask how it sounded, Young shouted back, 'More barn!'

His interest in movies was also taking up a significant amount of time and, presumably, money. He'd been working on one specific project – which would reach the screen as *Journey through the Past* – since at least 1971. It's hard to judge how clear an idea Young had of his own cinematic intentions, in part at least because the final product would be so much easier to describe in terms of what it wasn't than in terms of what it was. The film laid no claims to story-telling, of either the fictional or the autobiographical variety. Nor was it intended as a music film, despite the inclusion of performance footage and an extensive soundtrack. These were included solely as part of the deal with Warners, who had agreed to put up money for the film only on condition that they had a record to sell.

Young put the finishing touches to the movie sometime around the summer of 1972. Whatever they were expecting, Warners didn't like what they got, and decided to postpone distribution until the following year (when they would pull out altogether). In the meantime they remained eager to release the soundtrack double album, even though it contained only one new song and now lacked its cinematic justification. This was gross stupidity on someone's part, because the album could only hurt both Young's reputation and Warners' future profits. Why he went along with it is even harder to fathom. One can only assume he either found he was legally trapped or had his mind on other things.

Music was not likely to be one of them that year. He played what would prove his only live gig of the year at the Mariposa Folk Festival in Ontario on 16th July, and sang only four, well-worn songs: 'Helpless', 'Heart of Gold', 'Harvest' and 'Sugar Mountain'.

It's impossible to know with any real certainty, but 1972 also seems to have been a thin year as far as his writing was concerned. Only one song is known to have originated in the ten months prior to November's tour rehearsals, and that's 'War Song', written around the specific issue of America's continued involvement in Vietnam, and in response to a particular situation – McGovern's candidacy in the 1972 Presidential race. 'There's a man says he can put an end to war' runs the chorus, and there's no doubt that the song has its heart in the right place. Unfortunately there's not much else to recommend it: the lyrics are at best banal, at worst inept. 'They shot George Wallace down/He'll never walk around' would have had trouble qualifying for 'Eve of Destruction'.

Musically the song was even less inspired – a sort of determined plod – but its arrangement did offer an interesting precursor of the sound Young would bring to the Time Fades Away tour and album, a cross between his Crazy Horse and countrified styles, with the dialogue he'd once conducted with Whitten now taken up by his angry electric guitar and Ben Keith's sad/tragic pedal steel.

In the autumn of 1972, his back apparently recovered, Young decided to tour again. With the exception of his brief appearance at Mariposa that summer, he had now been out of the public eye for over eighteen months. It was time to reap the harvest, in more ways than one.

A huge tour was scheduled, as if Young wanted to make up for lost time. He would be on the road for three months, visiting sixty-five cities, the last seven of them in Britain. The band he chose to accompany him was a peculiar mixture of the Stray Gators and Crazy Horse, and would later even include members of CSN&Y. A Nashville rhythm section of Kenny Buttrey and Tim Drummond was supported by Ben Keith on pedal steel and Jack Nitzche on piano. The decision to saddle himself with the latter's erratic behaviour may not have been one of Young's wisest, but it seems almost inspired when compared with his choice of second guitarist and vocal support. Danny Whitten had been a junkie for two years now, rendering his own band Crazy Horse unable to tour in support of their excellent first album.

In the autumn of 1972, as Young was gathering everyone to the ranch for rehearsals, the word was that Whitten was trying hard to kick his habit, and the decision to invite him aboard may well have been taken partly by way of encouraging the process. It wasn't mere charity, though: Young had probably got as much out of working with Whitten as he had with anyone, Stills included, and, as the upcoming tour would amply demonstrate, he badly needed the kind of guitar and vocal support that the pre-junkie Whitten would have provided.

The rumours of his friend's recovery, however, turned out to have been somewhat exaggerated. Whitten was off heroin, but ingesting large quantities of other drugs by way of compensation, all of which rendered him just as unworkable. When rehearsals began in mid-November he could neither play what was required nor appreciate the extent of his failure. Moving from one song to another without realising he had done so hardly constituted an acceptable level of musicianship. A sad Young did the only thing he could – he fired him. Whitten was given a plane ticket and fifty dollars, and driven to the airport. Back in LA he spent the money on a dose of pure heroin; he died the same night.

Young was of course stunned. And perhaps something more. He had loved Whitten as a person, and the man's death no doubt ushered in a time of grieving. But it's as if Young also experienced Whitten's death as symptomatic of a wider loss, one for which the sense of grief, though less personal and less intense, would prove harder to dispel. He told Adam Sweeting in 1985 that it had seemed as if Whitten's death had 'stood for a lot of what was going on. It was like the freedom of the sixties and free love and drugs and everything . . . it was the price tag. This is your bill . . .' When Sweeting asked him if he'd felt any guilt for encouraging such self-destructive behaviour in others, Young said yes: 'I didn't feel very guilty, but I felt a little guilty.'

In this frame of mind Young went on with preparations for the tour, deciding, for reasons that are more understandable than apparently sensible, not to replace Whitten. Only a couple of weeks later the soundtrack album *Journey through the Past* was released, and the reviews did nothing to cheer him up. The film itself was still unseen, the album not much more than a collection of Young out-takes with a few oddities – bits of Handel's *Messiah* and the Beach Boys' 'Let's Go Away for Awhile' – thrown in for good measure. The only new song, 'Soldier', was one of Young's worst, a nothing melody married to a lyric only one step up from 'There's a World'.

Coming after *Harvest*, which for all its much-criticised blandness had been another fresh departure, *Journey through the Past* seemed like a blatant rip-off – the same old songs, often done worse than before, at a double-album price. The whole package left a sour taste in the mouth, and made it all the more crucial that the upcoming tour be successful.

At first there was no reason to doubt that it would be. All the huge arenas sold out almost immediately, as if the demand for Young had been simply building and building during his extended leave of absence. The early audiences went away more than satisfied, having enjoyed an acoustic set reprising many of the songs that had made *Goldrush* and *Harvest* so popular, and an electric set which one reviewer described as 'unbelievable, brutally loud, soaring rock'n'roll'.

It didn't last. Young's throat was in bad condition from the outset, and with no vocal back-up to ease his load it could only grow worse. By the concluding third of the tour the usual level of vocal control was gone, with the result that his singing was often little more than a succession of hoarse shouts.

The early success of the tour also took a toll on solidarity within the touring party. With so much money in the air, people started grabbing for more: both the roadies and the band. Young, accustomed to considering these people his friends, doesn't seem to have known how to react. With Danny Whitten's death hanging over the tour – centre stage whenever 'The Needle and the Damage Done' or 'Don't Be Denied' was played – and a year of warily pondering the cost of his own success behind him, Young found himself watching people he'd thought he knew turn resentful for the want of a few dollars more.

'It turned him against everything,' Elliot Roberts said. The state of his throat was reason enough not to talk; the sense of betrayal made him even more reclusive and paranoid. Even the music had deteriorated; by some perverse twist of fate the band always appeared to be capable of producing what Young wanted at sound checks, but never in actual performance.

He met the financial demands and the tour went on, although without Kenny Buttrey – for whom the whole experience had proved too stressful – and now devoid of most of what camaraderie it had begun with. Young started drinking heavily, and his performances became both more ragged and, at times, more rivetingly real. He found the audiences too loud during his acoustic set, too quiet in the electric portion of the show. He started screaming at them to wake up.

The tour needed an injection of *bonhomie* just to stay alive, and as it headed west Young called up some old friends. Linda Ronstadt joined as the opening act in March; Crosby and Nash – whom Young had briefly joined on stage the previous October – came on board for the last three weeks. They played rhythm guitar and offered much-needed vocal and moral support.

The two men had their own problems to share: Crosby's mother was dying and Nash's girlfriend had just been murdered by her brother. It was an opportunity for the threesome to remember why they liked and needed each other, and since there were no doubts as to who was in charge, there was no reason for them to rediscover why they had so often found each other impossible to work with. Stills, wondering out loud why he never received a call, was being disingenuous in the extreme: he had never been one of nature's back-up men.

Crosby quickly picked out Jack Nitzche as one of the villains of the piece, but selecting one culprit for the woes of the Time Fades Away tour was like blaming one American general for the war in Vietnam. No one was blameless. Greed, arrogance and lack of self-awareness all seem to have played a part in making the tour an unsatisfying experience for everyone involved.

It ended abruptly, and in a manner in keeping with what had gone before. 'It was at the Oakland Coliseum,' Young told an audience at New York's Bottom Line a year later; 'I was singing away – "Southern man, better keep your head, don't forget what the good book said" – and this guy in the front row, he was about as far away as you are from me, he jumped up and yelled, "Right on, right on, I love it!" He felt really good, I could tell. And all of a sudden, you know, this black cop just walked up to him, you know, and it just was the scene the way he looked at him, and he just crunched him. I just took my guitar out and put it on the ground and got in the car and went home . . .' He later told Ray Coleman that 'it was like I was watching myself on TV and someone had pulled out the plug I was playing on, but I couldn't believe what I'd just seen. I was disconnected. Then I got out of that place and I said to myself, "Who needs it?"'

In the same interview he looked back on the whole tour with a jaundiced eye. His ego had been satisfied by the huge audiences, but it was hard to communicate meaningfully with 20,000 people. He wanted to be able to see the people he was playing for. In future he would settle for smaller numbers having a deeper experience. As for the strains of success, and how to overcome them, he told Coleman that he was still 'passing through, feeling my way. I haven't come out at the other end yet, and I'm not dead. I've got to go on living, being myself, really.'

It's doubtful whether the ranch any longer offered Young a carefree refuge from the problems associated with his musical career. The relationship with Carrie, which had apparently flourished during the

seclusion occasioned by his back problems, seems to have started showing signs of strain soon after his re-entry into the professional world.

Nor was there any solace to be found in a cinematic triumph. After
Warners' defection Young had eventually found a new distributor, spent
an irritating amount of time on gaining clearance for the use of certain
music and visuals, and then waited nervously for the première, which
finally took place on 18th April 1973 as part of the Dallas Film
Festival.

Journey through the Past was eighty minutes long, and had cost
$350,000 to make. It featured a central character, referred to throughout
as 'the graduate', who wanders through the movie and its creator's
version of America. In the process he gets beaten up, is dropped off
in the desert, witnesses a junkie fixing up, and cheerily lectures the
audience on environmentalism in a junkyard under a freeway: 'Well,
man, you know, rebuilding cars instead of making new ones.' The
mostly invisible villains are sixties staples: big business, the military and
the Church – though it does seem Young was more incensed by the
latter than most of his contemporaries. The hooded men on horseback
surging down a beach towards the camera were already familiar from the
soundtrack album cover; in the film they function as a recurring dream
or nightmare, visually striking but lacking any meaningful context.

The same could be said of the movie as a whole. It is full of bright
ideas and interesting visuals, it is occasionally – and surprisingly, for
those who'd come to see Young as a brooding whinger – very funny,
but it has no real thread save Young's internal musings. This was not
an accident; it was exactly what he'd intended. It was the way he liked to
make music, and it was the way he wanted to make films – spontaneously,
on the run, without the prison of a script. If the strengths of such an
approach do to some extent show through in *Journey through the Past*,
it has to be said that the weaknesses are more obviously apparent.

Young himself said, 'I just made a feeling. It's hard to say what the
movie means.' But the maker of a film should have at least some idea
of what he's made. Movies are not songs, and the kind of creativity
that works over three minutes doesn't necessarily, or even often, work
over eighty.

Some critics were kind, preferring to see the movie as evidence of
Young's potential rather than as anything significant in its own right. It
was, they thought, a good first try. Others were less obliging, but Young
did himself no favours if he really believed, as he maintained, that the

negative reaction was the film community's way of keeping him at bay. He made more sense when he said, 'It wasn't made for entertainment. I'll admit, I made it for myself.'

By some huge stroke of luck and talent he had found that the music he wanted to make was also, most of the time, the music others wanted to hear. The same was not apparently true of his movies.

His other creative product that year was a live album recorded mostly on the recent tour. Young would later claim that the 'only redeeming factor' of *Time Fades Away* 'was that it truly reflected where I was at', but though far from a great album, it had rather more going for it than that.

The opening title track tells a third of the story. Over a loping piano Young's rough and weary voice offers a disjointed newsreel of junkies, Presidents and 'riding subways through a haze'. In the chorus a father earnestly exhorts his son to be in by eight – which seems a less than adequate response to the perils of the world depicted in the verses. If Young is perhaps trying to equate too much discipline early in life with too little self-discipline later on, then he's a making a ham-fisted job of it.

There are two other songs in this angry, accusative vein: 'Yonder Stands the Sinner' and 'The Last Dance'. The former, which somehow manages to be both mocking and self-mocking, self-deprecating and self-righteous, features an even more off-the-wall vocal and one of the album's few guitar solos. The latter, clocking in at almost ten minutes, has a ludicrous, almost offensive lyric, wherein Young urges his listeners Peter Fonda-style to abandon their tedious nine-to-five existences and do their own thing in their own time. The song is saved by its music, with Ben Keith's pedal steel and Young's guitar combining to great effect. It's the counterpointing of these two instruments – the active anger of the guitar and the passive sadness of the steel – that gives the whole album its colouring and individuality.

There are three ballads, two of which – 'Journey through the Past' and 'The Bridge' – are fairly rudimentary affairs. The former, which at least has a good melody, examines the loss of his Canadian roots and friends in the context of his new home. 'The Bridge', inspired by Hart Crane's poem of the same name, is another of Young's 'long-haul' songs for those who wanted the world and wanted it now. Both are pleasant, but neither is particularly memorable.

The core of the album lies, appropriately enough, in the three songs at its centre. 'LA', written five years earlier, expresses Young's love-hate relationship with the city in unique style: by offering a guarded welcome to an expected earthquake. His lead guitar simmers angrily, and Ben Keith's pedal steel draws graceful wails, across the predicted landscape of 'an ocean full of trees'.

'Love in Mind' is a mere hundred seconds long, but unlike some of the other songs on the album seems fully realised. 'I used to call this girl up from the road,' he told a Royal Festival Hall audience in London. He was in love with her, even though they'd never actually met. 'I used to talk to her all the time on the phone, usually late at night because of the time difference. And I'd wake up in the morning feeling so good.'

The song defiantly captures that sense of peace, flicking past religious hypocrisy and civilisation's repression of natural feelings to that place within where his 'love still shines'. 'I've got nothing to lose I can't get back again,' he sings, ostensibly about the risks of giving himself in love, though the point of view is just as applicable to the damage inflicted by fame.

The autobiographical 'Don't Be Denied', though musically repetitive, is the album's one great song. Written in the shadow of Danny Whitten's death, it builds in intensity through four verses, the heavy guitar riff banging each one shut, like the chained door to the past in 'Helpless'. Young's voice strains at the story with an out-of-tune urgency that is often harrowing, reiterating the single chorus line – 'Don't be denied' – like a hard-won mantra. Don't be denied, either by broken family or school bullies, or by impossible dreams or agents. Don't even be denied by riches and fame, by the fact of being 'a millionaire in a businessman's eyes'. In the last resort, all that matters is to be true to yourself. Like 'Love in Mind', 'Don't Be Denied' is about cutting through the crap to find out who you really are and what really matters.

In the words of another current song, Young could see clearly now all the obstacles in his way. Eighteen months after *Harvest* the grace and the flow have vanished, and with them any lingering self-satisfaction. The doubts expressed in 'A Man Needs a Maid' and 'Words' have multiplied; the country, far from supplying any answer, has just shifted the problems to a prettier place. 'Alabama' is within as well as without. If there was ever any hope that the world could be smoothed away, it has gone.

Time Fades Away offered a necessary break with his past, akin to a clearing of the musical palate. It may be largely a lacklustre affair, with a sometimes distressingly petulant and resentful tone, but few albums have explored self-doubt, guilt and regret with such teeth-gritted determination. Young himself, years later, told of people telling him how much they loved the album. All he could do, he said, was 'look at them', adding with a laugh that 'not many have said that to me'.

After the Time Fades Away tour Young presumably had no immediate desire to spend a prolonged period of time in company with the Stray Gators, and with Crazy Horse reduced to a rhythm section by Whitten's death there was little likelihood of his renewing any partnership with them in the near future. There were rumours of a Buffalo Springfield reunion that spring: the others were willing, but accepted, in Furay's words, that 'Neil doesn't need it'. Nor apparently did he want it.

A reunion with Crosby, Stills and Nash was more conceivable. Young was doubtless grateful to Crosby and Nash for their recent support, and he and Stills were, as ever, moths to each other's musical flames. And, lo and behold, it turned out that all four of them were taking holidays in Hawaii during the first half of June. 'So,' as Nash put it, 'the timing seemed right and we all had good songs we'd been kind of saving for CSN&Y.'

Once in the islands they rehearsed on Crosby's boat and at the house Nash had rented on Maui. Young had written a new song with a catchy, even jaunty melody masking lyrical themes of loss and betrayal. It also had a name that seemed made for an album, and 'Human Highway' was adopted as the putative title song of the latest offering in CSN&Y's bittersweet history.

Other songs intended for consideration included Crosby's 'Time after Time' and 'Homeward through the Haze'; Nash's 'Wind on the Water', 'Prison Song', 'And So It Goes' and 'Another Sleep Song'; Stills's 'You'll Never Be the Same', 'My Angel', 'See the Changes' and 'As I Come of Age'; and Young's 'Hawaiian Sunrise', 'Sailboat Song' (later known as 'Through My Sails'), 'New Mama' and 'Mellow My Mind'.

They even had a photo for the cover, taken by Nash, with the four of them posed in holiday togs between palm trees, sea and sky. The executives at Atlantic could probably hear the distant ring of a million cash registers.

It was only an echo. Tim Drummond and Johnny Barbata were summoned to Young's ranch, but by the time the four principals had reconvened the mood had changed. Like a tetchy posse chasing an elusive fugitive they managed to record versions of 'See the Changes',

'Human Highway', 'And So It Goes' and 'Prison Song'. And then the arguments really started. Should they tour first, get tight, and then finish the album? Or should they get the album done and then go out? Needless to say they ended up doing neither. Everyone somehow got angry with everyone else, constructive criticism became impossible and, in Nash's pungent summary, it 'turned to a piece of shit'.

Since all this was happening at Young's ranch the Second Law of Rock Dynamics – 'In Any State of Potential Anarchy, Stills Will Seek Control and Young Will Disappear' – was difficult to enforce. But not impossible. According to his father, Young was on the way to a session – presumably somewhere else on his ranch – when David Briggs, who had been a sorely-missed exile in Canada for the last couple of years, suddenly turned up. Let's go to LA and play rock'n'roll, Young suggested, and the pair of them did. What Crosby, Stills and Nash made of this can only be guessed at.

It would have been a great scene to end a docudrama with. Perhaps Young should have focused his cinematic endeavours along the lines stressed by creative-writing teachers and stuck to what he knew. If he'd had the cameras rolling through this latest CSN&Y imbroglio he might have come away with a great film.

Though Young was probably as upset as anyone by CSN&Y's latest failure to behave like adults, he had other, more depressing things to think about. There was the cool reception given to his movie, and the growing problems at home with Carrie. The aftertaste of the Time Fades Away tour was no doubt still lingering on his tongue. And somewhere at the back of Young's mind the manner of Danny Whitten's death continued to cast a shadow over his music and his life.

He arrived in LA to find that Bruce Berry, CSN&Y roadie and friend, had followed Whitten to a premature grave. Whether Young felt in any way responsible for this death no one but he could say, but some of his on-stage theatrics during the Tonight's the Night tour would suggest he felt at least some sort of existential connection. In any case the fact of Berry's death can't have helped but reawaken the hurt of Whitten's.

Young's immediate reaction was to find some means of expressing his feelings in the way he knew best. Like a blind man grabbing for the familiar he gathered in Nils Lofgren, Ben Keith and the remnants of Crazy Horse and tried to tell it like it was. Styling themselves the Santa Monica Flyers, Young and the band did two gigs at the Corral Club in Topanga Canyon on 11th and 12th August with Joni Mitchell and the Eagles, then kept on playing together in the rehearsal hall at Studio Instrument Rentals, which was owned by Bruce's brother Ken. When he felt they were ready, Young hired a mobile recording truck.

With the rump of Crazy Horse together for the first time since Whitten's death, and Berry's brother looking on, they held an Irish wake for the two victims – played them, in Young's phrase, on their way. They drank a lot – in Young's case, mostly tequila – and smoked a lot. The aim was to 'get right out on the edge', and by the middle of the night that's usually where they were. It might mean they had trouble functioning as musicians (in fact, as the album would show, it often meant exactly that) but they'd be 'just wide open', which mattered more. There was emotion and spirit to spare. 'We knew it was different when we were doing it,' Young said later. It was all live, with 'everybody playing and singing at the same time. There was no overdubbing on those nine songs that were done at SIR. That's the way the old blues people used to do it. It was really real.' By all accounts a calculating man, for once Young seems to have been content just to let things happen.

On one night they did five songs – 'Tonight's the Night', 'World on a String', 'Mellow My Mind', 'Speakin' Out' and 'Tired Eyes' – back to back, talking drunkenly between songs as the tape rolled. 'Roll Another Number for the Road', 'Albuquerque', 'New Mama' and a second version of 'Tonight's the Night' were recorded on other nights.

Nine songs about drugs and music, love and death. For the participants there was some sort of exorcism – which, after all, is what wakes are supposed to achieve. Whether such an out-of-tune outpouring of emotion could be turned into something any record company would want to put out was another matter.

Young worked on it. In the first place he didn't really have enough for an album, not much more than thirty minutes' worth. Other songs were needed from somewhere, and they would serve the added purpose of breaking the relentless anguish of the original nine, which Young thought essential if the album was to be rendered halfway listenable for record-company executives and his fellow human beings. He 'had to get the colour right, so it was not so down that it would make people restless'.

The songs chosen to lighten the load were 'Look Out Joe', a saga of war and drugs which Whitten had helped work on shortly before being fired the previous November; 'C'mon Baby Let's Go Downtown', a song about drug-dealing which had been recorded live on the 1970 Crazy Horse tour with Whitten on lead vocals; and 'Borrowed Tune', a song about being wasted by fame and fortune. If this was sugaring the pill, then Vietnam was an exercise.

The SIR recordings needed remixing, since half the time the vocalists had been swaying too hard to hit the microphones. And then there was all the stoned and drunken chatter to cut out. In retrospect Young would regret even this level of editing, but in the circumstances – *Journey through the Past* had flopped, and *Time Fades Away* was not about to fare much better – he probably had no choice.

The story of Bruce Berry's life and death, as recounted in the two versions of the title track, begins and ends *Tonight's the Night*. One minute the roadie had been singing songs and playing along on Young's guitar, 'real as the day was long', the next he was dead as Danny Whitten, 'out on the mainline'. In the ten songs in between, Young tries to make sense of his own and others' relationship to a business, a lifestyle and a wider culture that offer such encouragement to self-destruction. The music throughout is ragged and starkly drawn, and often almost sagging with weariness.

'Speakin' Out' opens with a burst of energy on piano and guitar, but seems tired out before the first verse is half sung. Young is hoping that love will carry him through, but mention of the 'notebook' behind his partner's eyes doesn't suggest any great faith in his own optimism. Fame and fortune are obviously no help, as the cracked vocal and its lucid message on the next track make abundantly clear. The 'world on a string doesn't mean a thing' – it's as simple as that.

And as isolating. 'Borrowed Tune', sung with an aching intensity to solo piano accompaniment, finds him alone, enclosed, far from others, commenting on the struggle. 'I'm climbing this ladder,' he sings, and 'hoping it matters'. The voice, and the song's central image of a frozen lake, suggest it won't. It's a land at peace, but the 'shaking hands' still 'grab at the sky'. There's no peace like madness, the song seems to say, and madness is no peace at all.

The album climbs out of despair and into the drug euphoria of 'C'mon Baby Let's Go Downtown'. It's great rock'n'roll, with an added resonance: that's the late Danny Whitten singing that 'sure enough, they'll be selling stuff when the moon begins to rise'. In this context his performance feels like a twist of the knife, and it leaves Young with only one place to go: into the hangover of 'Mellow My Mind' – and the most painfully out-of-tune vocal on the album.

The second side shuffles the same themes. 'Roll Another Number for the Road' has Young contrasting Woodstock's hopes with the reality, and admitting that he's 'been standing on the sound of some open-hearted people going down'. Everyone involved in the game bears some responsibility for the way it's played, even for the fact that it's played at all. In 'Albuquerque' he's 'starving to be alone, independent of the scene that I've known', but he knows it's not possible, that his desire to be somewhere where 'they don't know who I am' is not one that can be satisfied within the rules of this game.

'New Mama', with its celebration of his son's birth, almost manages to dispel the clouds, but in the context of the album a line like 'I'm living in a dreamland' can only seem double-edged. 'Look Out Joe' and 'Tired Eyes', in which Young turns his gaze outwards, offer some relief from the self-laceration, but it's only temporary. 'He tried to do his best, but he could not,' the narrator of the second song laments, and the line stands as a requiem for Danny, for Bruce, for friends and colleagues, for all who let them die, for the whole goddam circus. And we're back where we started: 'Tonight's the night . . .'

T.S. Eliot thought that mankind could not stand too much reality, but seventy years on from *The Waste Land* chance would be a fine thing. *Tonight's the Night* works as catharsis because it does manage to scrape the bare bones of reality, not through either a blind raging of emotions or the power of reason, but through its appeal to that place within where thought and feeling become indistinguishable. The music is as full of human failings as the lives it celebrates and laments. And on a good day a sense of what's real can be its own therapy.

The record company hated what they heard, and refused to consider releasing the album, but there was no way anyone could stop Young taking it out on the road. Elliot Roberts can't have been too keen on unleashing this particular tour, and according to Young's father he began searching out the smallest and most obscure halls he could find, but if this is true someone sadly misinformed him about London's Royal Festival Hall.

The night of 20th September marked the opening of both the tour and its first venue, the Roxy Theater in LA. The owners, rock tycoons Lou Adler and David Geffen, had probably rubbed their hands with glee when they secured Young to open the Roxy for them; if so, they can't have savoured their triumph for long. The barely-lit stage set consisted of a moth-eaten palm tree, a wooden Indian and a grand piano from which hung a selection of boots. Hubcaps littered the floor.

The band performed nine new songs from the SIR sessions and generously threw in 'Cowgirl in the Sand' as an encore. No 'Heart of Gold', no 'Helpless', no graceful sadness to shroud the pain. In fact Young seemed more interested in drowning it. His own liquid intake was becoming prodigious, and one night he decided to share his pleasure by offering the entire audience a round of drinks. Adler and Geffen were not amused.

With every song from the heart there comes a time when the emotion that originally inspired it has faded, and the re-creation of that emotion becomes a matter of performance, not simple self-expression.

The same was necessarily true of the entire Tonight's the Night concept. Originally an outpouring of grief, anger and who knew what other emotional responses to both specific events and an entire way of life, it slowly turned into a form of theatre. Young would later claim that he stepped outside himself to make the album. 'Every song was performed,' he told Bud Scoppa. 'I wrote the songs describing the situations and then I became an extension of those situations and I performed them. It's like being an actor and writing the script for myself as opposed to a personal expression. There's obviously a lot of personal expression there, but it comes in a different form, which makes it seem much more explicit and direct.'

This sounds self-contradictory, but it does at least point out the thin line between self-expression and performance in this context. When the tour restarted towards the end of October, and as it continued on its way, Young was clearly often straddling that line, both telling *a* story and telling *his* story.

Canada was the next stop, with three university gigs in Ontario. The mangy palm tree, fake moon, glitter boots and hubcaps were all along for the ride. Young, sporting black shades, very long hair, whiskers and beard, would proudly tell the audience that it was all cheaper than it looked.

The band crossed the Atlantic. In Bristol they played three versions of 'Tonight's the Night', and with each one they tore away another layer of pretence. In Glasgow one fan endured 'a God-awful noise for ninety minutes'; then in Newcastle he noted that Young seemed to have the world on his shoulders, and that reaching the high notes no longer appeared to be something that unduly concerned him. At London's Royal Festival Hall he sang eight new songs to a dumbstruck audience, then announced he was going to do one they'd heard before. It turned out to be 'Tonight's the Night', which the band had opened with forty-five minutes earlier.

One of the best accounts of the tour was issued by Young himself, in Dutch, as an accompaniment to the *Tonight's the Night* album when it was finally released eighteen months later. It was written by Constant Meijers, who had hit on the idea of offering to bring Young some bottles of his favourite tequila – José Cuervo Gold Brand – from Holland in exchange for a concert ticket. The offer was accepted, and Meijers was met at the airport, where he received his ticket and the promise of a meeting with Young after the show.

The concert would leave Meijers wondering, 'What on earth was happening to Neil? Where was the magic gone?' The sound quality, the band's co-ordination, Young's piano-playing and singing – they were all appalling. Young downed wineglasses of tequila in one gulp and 'mumbled for minutes on end about anything and more'.

Or so it seemed. In fact there was quite a lot being expressed in Young's apparent ramblings. 'There is one member of the band for whom I feel a special affection. One day he came and knocked at my cellar door in Washington DC where the President of the US lives ... Impeach the President, and ... eh ... What a situation. WHAT A SITUATION ladies and gentlemen. Where's my cigar? I won't be seeing you again for a few years so I can do what I like! Ha ha ha.'

So much for audience expectations. Several of the songs were dedicated to Danny Whitten, the man who'd come knocking at Young's 'cellar door' in 'The Needle and the Damage Done'. But a death like Whitten's was not an isolated incident, not an aberration. Not in this culture, anyway.

'You buy a newspaper on the street in the morning,' Young mumbles, 'and you open it at page two straight away because you can't read page one ... photos of all the people ... now I'm in the desert ... the Americans are there. Let's think about the desert this evening. In the desert there's a lion; some people are standing on one side of the lion and some on the other. Everybody knows what I'm talking about, so everybody can draw their own conclusions. We're going to play a song, ladies and gentlemen, to try to cheer ourselves up. It wasn't very good in the desert, was it? I didn't like it much there, anyway.'

A couple of songs later he admits, 'Nixon loves me, I'm good for the economy. Do you understand what I'm trying to say? What more can I say? Four dead in Ohio?'

The audience applaud. 'I don't want applause for something like that even though I think I know what you mean. It's strange. Look at it from my point of view. You don't have to, but you can try. Take Miami Beach. There are all sorts of people there. And they get up real early, ladies and gentlemen.' He walks away from the microphone, out to the very edge of the stage, and shouts at the audience, 'I can assure you that the people get up at six in the morning. Really, ladies and gentlemen!'

There's a sense here of violent dislocation, that Young is both enjoying himself intensely and in the throes of enormous anguish. It's a show and it's not a show. Everything he's ever done is on the line here, and it's not really important in the grand scheme of things.

Meijers went back to meet him in his dressing room as arranged, and found him 'looking like a beaten dog, abandoned on a chair, his head hanging between his shoulders', with Nils Lofgren and David Briggs trying to reassure him that it had been a good show. 'I was shocked that they didn't ask for more,' Young said. And he obviously meant it. Having, by the simple expedient of not giving people what they either wanted or expected, slapped the audience in its collective face, he was surprised and shocked that they hadn't asked for more.

In Boston, on the final, short American leg of the tour, he had a run-in with an erratic microphone. After complaining at length about a buzzing noise, he smashed it across the stage and stormed off, before returning to apologise – 'I know it was childish of me to storm off that way.' At several gigs his mumbled ramblings turned into an obviously scripted, imaginary dialogue between Young and Bruce Berry, in which the latter, apparently sacked from CSN&Y for 'losing' Crosby's guitar – the suspicion being that he'd sold it to finance his drug habit – has his appeal for re-employment rejected.

It was a show and it was real. It had to be real, or it couldn't have functioned in the cathartic way it did. Young thought he had 'slipped out' of himself, and appeared in later years to be almost claiming that the whole thing had been a premeditated exercise. It seems more likely that the need to confront what had happened to him over the preceding few years, to come to terms with the negative aspects of his success –

including, perhaps, things he had found out about himself of which he wasn't too proud – had led him, mostly by accident, into some sort of controlled release. As a musician he had naturally turned to music as the instrument of this release, and the *Tonight's the Night* enterprise – from the writing of the original songs through their performance in a theatrical context – had doubled as both artistic product and a long therapy session.

In the process, as he said quite rightly, both his audiences and he himself had been stimulated. Those who had come to see the shows 'had their minds totally turned around and that's more than you can say for most concerts'. Future luminaries of the British punk explosion would later cite the British concerts as a major influence. As for Young himself, 'It was really healthy for me. I was the same person for too long.' At last he had found the opportunity to 'obliterate everything' that he was – to 'wipe the slate clean'.

One sign that something had been exorcised was Young's reaction to the record company's rejection of *Tonight's the Night*. 'I would describe that as a rocky day,' he told Adam Sweeting a decade later. 'They couldn't believe how sloppy and rough it was, they couldn't believe that I really wanted to put it out.' But rather than get angry or upset he simply started work on a new album. As usual being on the road had inspired him to write, and for the first time since late 1970 he was overflowing with ideas for new songs. In another indication that a break had been made with the past, the musicians he chose to record with did not – with the exception of Ben Keith – include any of the Santa Monica Flyers.

Many of the new songs, like those on *Tonight's the Night*, were about his relationship to fame, music, his past, the world, rather than his relationship with Carrie. He was also writing songs about the latter, but most of these would not surface until the following summer, and the album after next.

The two of them were certainly not getting enough out of their relationship. Young was manifestly reluctant to go home that summer or autumn, as attested to by both the reports of his half-sister Astrid and his own comments from the stage the following May. 'I hadn't been home for two months . . . trying to get my act together,' he told the Bottom Line audience, in a long spoken introduction to 'Motion Pictures'.

The discovery that winter that their son Zeke had a mild form of cerebral palsy may have brought the couple temporarily back together, but the writing seems to have been on the wall. Carrie's original decision to sacrifice her career for love might have made sense when she and Young were together on the ranch, but with him rarely around she started recreating an independent life of her own. In the words of Young's unreleased song 'Homefires', they had become 'young lovers who live separate lives'.

The appearance of David Crosby as a guest musician at Young's latest recording sessions was one more sign that the previous summer's fiasco had not irrevocably damaged the relationships between the CSN&Y principals. There had already been one mini-reunion in the midst of Young's Tonight's the Night carnival, when he joined a Crosby-Nash-augmented incarnation of Stills's band Manassas on stage at San Francisco's Winterland. Two months later, in the same city, he again sat in with Crosby and Nash. And 1974 had not long been under way when rumours started flying of a major reunion tour in the coming summer.

The necessary moves and counter-moves involved in bringing everyone together around an agreed plan occupied most of the first three months of the year, but there was little doubt that everyone was committed in principle. Crosby, Stills and Nash had not been unsuccessful over the last few years – all three had produced reasonable solo albums, without setting the world on fire – but there was a definite sense in which their careers had become shorn of focus. Elliot Roberts was apparently much in favour of the tour, probably because he saw it as an ideal opportunity for Young to re-establish his credibility with the mainstream audience. Young must have recognised it as the same, and also as something that would give him the chance to make another break with the past.

No group seems to have had shorter memories than CSN&Y – their career could almost be used in a study of marijuana's effects on memory loss. Nash told one interviewer that since all their previous problems had been in the studio they would tour first, then make a record.

The decision was also taken to play only venues holding 30,000 or more. Young's feelings about big arenas, so cogently argued after the Time Fades Away tour, were conveniently put to one side. After the event it would be Crosby and Nash – particularly the former – who echoed Young's earlier sentiments, but the fact remains that all four of them must have signed up for the summer of 1974 knowing full well where they were going to play.

One of the selected venues – the Ontario Speedway in southern California – held 200,000. This was going to be the first ever stadium tour, and the eventual gross proceeds from admissions, T-shirts, programmes and merchandising were expected to be in the region of $10 million.

In the spring of 1974, before descending once more into the CSN&Y bear pit, Young made one interesting purchase and did two interesting gigs. The purchase was a bus, which he had customised as a mobile home for touring. The window-roof sections of two old Studebakers were welded into the roof of the bus to provide observation turrets, while the interior was divided into bedroom, lounge and kitchen areas, each complete with hand-carved wooden fittings. The legend 'Buffalo Springfield' was emblazoned on the rear.

The first of the gigs, on 26th March, was a two-part benefit concert with the Eagles at Cuesta College in San Luis Obispo. A total of $11,500 was raised to help with the building of a Native American work-cultural centre. In addition, Young donated two buffaloes to the organisation concerned, the Friends of Red Wind.

The second gig was a one-night stand at the Bottom Line in New York on 16th May. This much-bootlegged performance featured eleven songs, of which only 'Helpless' had previously appeared on record. A further six of the songs offered a mixed bag: the familiar 'Dance Dance Dance', the sixteenth-century folk song 'Greensleeves', 'Roll Another Number for the Road' from the shelved *Tonight's the Night*, an acoustic 'Long May You Run' (which both Young and the audience seem to have found hilarious) and two revealing songs about Young's love life.

The first of these two was announced as 'Citizen Kane Junior Blues', but it would be known thereafter as 'Pushed It over the End'. It essentially takes the feminist to one side and asks her (or him), don't you think you're going a bit too far? Don't you think you're letting ideological conviction run away with you? Don't you see what you're doing to us men?

In the early seventies, as now, there were indeed people who put ideas above people, and who, in the words of the song, took a good idea and 'pushed it over the end'. It's also true that women's liberation – to use the shorthand term – created problems for all those who had grown up with a certain set of gender expectations. Young was pointing this out in his song, and in a not altogether unkindly way. The song's heroine Millie may keep 'ten men in her garage', but 'she works hard'. And the male protagonist does keep coming back to her.

Against this, 'Pushed It over the End' is undoubtedly sexist at heart. The opening lines – 'Good-looking Millie's got a gun in her hand/But she don't know how to use it' – state the male claim to a monopoly of power as clearly as it could be stated. Millie doesn't know to wield her new power, because she's a woman. And because she's such a loose cannon all these 'poor men' are 'falling down'. Young makes no attempt to suggest a way forward: as usual he is content just to say what he's feeling.

It's hard, particularly twenty years later, to condone such an oppressively male song, but it's also hard to think of anyone else artistically courageous enough to take on such a difficult subject for no other reason than that it concerned him.

The second song, 'Pardon My Heart', was one of a series that Young said at one time he considered too revealing to release. Unlike the others (many of which would be performed on the CSN&Y tour) this one would, none the less, eventually see the official light of day, on 1975's *Zuma*.

The remaining four songs were from the forthcoming *On the Beach*: 'Revolution Blues', 'On the Beach', 'Motion Pictures' and 'Ambulance Blues'. On stage at the Bottom Line, Young continually made jokes between songs about how depressing they all were, and he seemed to have a point.

When it appeared later that summer, *On the Beach* was welcomed as something of a return to form after the disappointment of his previous release, *Time Fades Away*. Reviewers saw it primarily as a despairing reflection on both Young's psyche and Nixon's America. Ian MacDonald of the *NME*, however, made even greater claims – subsequently endorsed by Rogan in his biography. *On the Beach*, according to MacDonald, was Young's equivalent of Lennon's first 'primal-scream' solo album, a cathartic rejection of the performer's personal and artistic past, the storm before the calm.

MacDonald, of course, hadn't heard the unreleased *Tonight's the Night*, or he might have reconsidered. Later critics, who had the benefit of such hindsight, should have known better. *Tonight's the Night* was the agonising, ecstatic breakthrough, *On the Beach* more akin to a bout of post-coital sadness. The one thing conspicuous by its absence on this album is passion.

On the Beach is a good candidate for Young's most cerebral album, at times witty, at others infuriatingly enigmatic, more often interesting than compelling. 'See the Sky about to Rain', the oldest song on the album, has a grace most of the rest lack, but shares the generally fatalistic feel. 'Vampire Blues' is a throwaway disguised as an ecological rant. 'Motion Pictures', which Young wrote in a motel after staying away from home for several months, is the closest the album comes to a love song. More of a stoned reverie than a song, it seems in constant danger of fading out all together.

Throughout *On the Beach* the music sounds subdued to the point of weariness, as if Young has had the musicians playing for days on end. Nowhere is this more noticeable than on the relatively up-tempo 'Revolution Blues', his fantasy of armed gangs descending Manson-like on LA's star-packed canyons to slaughter the likes of him. The musical ingredients all appear to be present, but something intangible has been left out: there's no drive to the song, no real fury. It's possible that Young was trying for a repressed-violence feel to the music, but if so he succeeded only with the repression. It's not the fault of the song: future live acoustic versions of 'Revolution Blues' would carry the punch that the *On the Beach* version so palpably lacks.

Lyrically, it is one of Young's harder-edged efforts. He had met Charles Manson socially on a couple of occasions, and found his personality mysteriously compelling. In later years he remembered how Manson 'would sing a song and just make it up as he went along, for three or four minutes, and he would never repeat one word, and it all made perfect sense and it shook you up to listen to it'.

By the time Young wrote his 'tribute' Manson was in prison, but the mixture of genius and evil that Young felt he represented was not only still out there in the world, it was in everyone. Dylan once told a shocked group of American liberals that he had seen something of himself in Kennedy's alleged assassin Lee Harvey Oswald, and Young seems to have had the same sort of feeling about Charles Manson. A simple division of the world into good guys and bad guys was no longer possible, if it had ever been. In this life he might be a star living in LA, but it wasn't that much of a stretch to imagine himself as one of a gang coming down from the mountains to kill people like him.

The other four songs – 'Walk On', 'For the Turnstiles', 'On the Beach' and 'Ambulance Blues' – are meditations on the costs of success and related themes. The opening 'Walk On', whose forced sprightliness sets the tone for the whole album, is beautifully succinct – 'Some get stoned/Some get strange/Sooner or later it all gets real/Walk on' – in its refusal to get sidetracked. 'For the Turnstiles' offers a more oblique dissection of celebrity's attraction and impermanence, but in the end the message is the same: the realisation that explorers end up as stone statues for the big parade, while no doubt humbling, is no reason to give up exploring.

'On the Beach', like the album, shares its title with Nevil Shute's novel of global nuclear suicide. This, although perhaps coincidental, remains hard to ignore on an album so packed with apocalyptic references. The song itself is more heartfelt and less contrived than most on the album. A slow blues propelled by rippling rhythm guitar, it's also more musically interesting, with prominent bass and more inventive percussion than Young usually uses. Lyrically the verses are a catalogue of doubts about his progress to date. Success, far from fulfilling his original expectations – 'I'm living here out on the beach/But those seagulls are still out of reach' – has provided new problems, like 'needing a crowd of people' he can't face 'day to day', like ending up 'alone at the microphone'. The only escape is to get out of town, but he doesn't come across as being too convinced that will work any better. By this time the repetitiveness of the music has made his life sound like a luxurious treadmill.

'Ambulance Blues', which MacDonald thought Young's finest achievement to date, is straightforward folk, with a guitar part unconsciously stolen, as Young would admit years later, from Bert Jansch's 'Needle of Death'. The lyrics offer an extended journey through the writer's past, with several references to the Toronto period: the street Isabella, the folk club the Riverboat, even Toronto itself in its abbreviated form 'TO'. Despite this, there's no attempt to write straightforward autobiography: the listener is offered Young's history as a context, then left to interpret particular lines and verses as he or she sees fit. At the time of the album's release most people identified the perennial liar of the last verse, who 'had a different story for every set of eyes', as Richard Nixon, but there's no evidence that that was Young's intention. The same could be said of the 'kidnapping' verse, which many people assumed referred to the then current case of Patty Hearst's abduction by the Symbionese Liberation Front.

It doesn't really matter. I've always seen the couplet 'All along the Navajo trail/Burn-outs stub their toes on garbage pails' as a comment on the damage 'civilisation' has wreaked on what was once another people's homeland, but who knows what Young had in mind? The phrase 'you're just pissing in the wind' was allegedly directed at CSN&Y by Elliot Roberts, but what he meant by it has never been made clear. Was he telling them to stop allowing their egos to get in the way of their talent? Or was it some sort of political statement, a suggestion that all this talk of love coming to us all was not only daft, but also counterproductive? Again, who knows?

'I guess I'll call it sickness gone', by contrast, seems a crystal-clear reference to Young's sense that he was re-emerging from a depressed period. 'An ambulance can only go so fast' is simply one of the great lines in the history of rock, a platitude worthy of any Zen master, equally applicable to Young's career, the new age or a medical vehicle.

Finally, the cover more than anything on the record was indicative of Young's renewed light-heartedness. It may or may not have been intended as a satire on Joni Mitchell's *For the Roses* centrefold, but it certainly worked as one. She on her cover stands blonde and naked on a rock, looking out over the shining water, the brave new future incarnate, while Young on his stands fully dressed, staring into grey skies, a buried Cadillac and newspapers full of Nixon's disgrace littering the beach around him.

He still had a better idea than most of what was going down, but he hadn't lost his sense of humour.

He would need it. Rehearsals for the CSN&Y Tour to End All Tours – dubbed the Doom Tour by Crosby – began towards the end of May at the Broken Arrow ranch. Young had ordered the building of a forty-foot stage in a redwood grove close to his studio. Russ Kunkel (drums), Tim Drummond (bass) and Joe Lala (percussion) were also on board, and the seven of them set out, in Stills's words, to achieve 'some form, from which we could ' fly and on which we could land'. In this regard they succeeded. Criticisms would be levelled against many aspects of the tour, but the quality of the music created by the band would not often be one of them.

At first everything was apparently hunky-dory. The opening gig, in Seattle on 9th July, was a triumphant return. Forgetting themselves in the excitement they played for four hours, in the process putting such a strain on Crosby's voice that he couldn't sing the following night. Nash admitted he'd been apprehensive, but said he wasn't any longer. Stills and Young were leaving room for each other to play, more aware 'of the "us" than the "I"'.

Drummond confirmed the general feeling about Young. He was 'a changed man ... really one of the boys now ... more open than he used to be'. He even looked different. The long hair, beard and general appearance of a deranged professor had vanished, giving way to long sideburns, reflector shades and the old patched jeans. Drummond thought that Young wasn't 'feeling the pressure any more'; if this was the case, part of the reason might have been that he'd learned, from bitter experience, to keep his distance from all the craziness. While Crosby and the managers travelled on one Learjet, Nash and Stills on another, Young, son and friends motored blithely down American highways in the bus.

His choice of what to perform on stage was also significant, with songs from both *Tonight's the Night* and *On the Beach* (which would be released during the first month of the tour) conspicuous by their absence. Instead, a few old favourites – particularly those associated with CSN&Y, such as 'Helpless' and 'Ohio' – were mixed in with primarily new love songs like 'Traces', 'Love-Art Blues', 'Pushed It over the End' and 'Homefires'.

The other three principals, by contrast, offered little in the way of new material, which evidently both annoyed and saddened Young. He would later call it the 'kiss of death' as far as he and the band were concerned, which may seem somewhat extreme, but there's no doubt that the other three were less than willing to risk their refound success by breaking new ground. Young's 'Revolution Blues', one of the few *On the Beach* songs they did perform on the tour, was a case in point. Crosby really didn't like doing it, because, in Young's words, 'it was so much the darker side. They all wanted to put out the light, you know, make people feel good and happy and everything, and that song was like a wart or something on the perfect beast.'

There were other, bigger warts to worry about. From the beginning the band were accused of doing the tour for money and money alone. For other bands this might have been a compliment, but for one with CSN&Y's record of earnest radicalism it was not an accusation to be swallowed without a suitable amount of hand-wringing. Both Crosby and Nash blamed everyone else for the fact that no one could hear or see them in the venues they were playing, conveniently forgetting that they had agreed to the whole deal in the first place. Young mused philosophical about it being 'a huge money trip', which in turn was 'the exact antithesis of what all those people are idealistically trying to see in their heads when they come to see us play'. He told one journalist what a 'high' it was to 'get really personal with 60,000 people', having said the previous year how impossible it was to communicate properly with 20,000.

Stills at least sounded as though he was being honest when he told Cameron Crowe, 'We did one for the art and the music, one for the chicks. This one's for the cash.' But was he? According to Crosby, Stills's real motivation was ego-gratification: getting off on playing enormous places, having people like Joni and the Beach Boys and the Band to open for them, being the biggest group in the world.

All the old contradictions were still there. They were a people's band whom the people could hardly hear from their distant vantage points, a people's band who were not only raking in millions of dollars for their performances, but living like royalty in between gigs at which they sang about four students who'd died four years earlier in Ohio. In each hotel room there would be the custom-made pillowcases, each with its Joni Mitchell-designed tour logo silkscreened in five colours, in the dining rooms the teak dinner plates with the same logo burned in wood. There were hookers on the payroll – presumably not bearing Joni Mitchell logos – for anyone in need of sexual snacks, and a suite would be open round the clock for the dispensing of the other necessities of life on the road: champagne, iced shrimp and capsules of cocaine.

Most of these goodies may, as some claimed, have been used by those surrounding the band rather than by the band themselves, but the responsibility for this gratuitous consumption had to rest with those who were ultimately in charge. This corruption – no other word fits such a level of dissonance between stated ideals and actual behaviour – was bound to affect relations between the principals, and also the musical performances. Bill Graham, the promoter who organised the tour, called them 'these four *nudniks* . . . All I heard from them was "*I* don't talk to him. He don't talk to me. In the second half, *I* do the piano solo first. But he does *two* solos! I only do *one* solo. I'm not going to follow that with my acoustic guitar."'

As for the musical problems, fortunately most people were too far away to hear. Crosby tells how Young and Stills would 'start competing on guitar simply by turning up. We clocked them once and they got up to 135 decibels. So Nash and I were unable to sing harmonies. It was a drag.' Stills once more blamed others for goading him and Young on, but didn't bother to explain who was to blame for the two of them letting it happen. He also added that 'Crosby's Alembic twelve-string was the loudest motherfucker you ever *heard*. Half the time Neil and I would have to turn up to hear past the bastard, who was between us.'

And so ended another chapter in the glorious history of CSN&Y.

There was a footnote, however – the projected album. Young later articulated that it didn't get made because it didn't get made, and that anyone who thought otherwise just couldn't understand why the four of them would turn down such an opportunity to print money.

There may be some truth in this, but it has to be said that it's a lot easier to turn down a fortune when you've just made one. The tour had grossed millions and *So Far*, a 'best of' album culled from just two albums and a single, had recently reached number 1 on the US chart. It is perhaps fair to assume that, for the moment at least, the edge had indeed been taken off CSN&Y's collective financial appetite.

But the sad, deeper truth of the matter was that yet again they had found it impossible to tolerate each other for long enough to produce something *shared*. The desire had been there, but not the will to see it through. In December they had managed to record Crosby's 'Homeward through the Haze' and Nash's 'Wind on the Water' at Sausalito's Record Plant, but that proved to be all. One day in January, according to Elliot Robert's assistant Leslie Morris, 'they were sitting on the floor arguing like kids, wasting costly studio time'. The argument was allegedly between Stills and Nash, and concerned a single harmony note. Someone suggested they adjourn to Nash's house, whereupon everyone went outside. Crosby later said he 'could feel the pendulum swing right then. And Neil goes, "Well, see you guys tomorrow." And he never came back.'

Who could blame him? Nash later claimed that Young had used the 1974 tour, like the rest of his association with Crosby, Stills and Nash, as a springboard for his own career – but so what if he did? By the time the foursome reached Sausalito early in 1975, Young was well out of what he called his 'dark period': he might enjoy playing with Crosby, Stills and Nash, but he had no need of them. In some ways, it might be argued, he needed to put them behind him.

His personal life had also undergone a revolution in the months following the tour. After the Wembley Stadium gig in September he'd visited Holland with Mazzeo and David Cline – the two friends from

San Mateo County who had shared the driving chores in the bus – and talked enthusiastically about his future plans, which then included a 'water album' to be titled *Mediterranean*.

Someone suggested driving down through Africa, and Young seemed keen on the idea. But he also realised, with a little help from his friends, that he needed to find out if there was any life left in his relationship with Carrie. He flew back to America and the ranch for one last, vain try. By the end of the year Carrie had moved out with Zeke.

And Young too had left the ranch, having discovered, with Cline's assistance, that he was being ripped off by many of those around him. 'I just had too many fucking people hanging around who don't really know me. They were parasites, whether they intended to be or not. They lived off me, used my money to buy things, used my telephone to make their calls. General leeching. It hurt my feelings a lot when I reached that realisation. I didn't want to believe I was being taken advantage of. I didn't like having to be boss . . .'

The whole place was a financial disaster area. Young hired Cline to turn things round and went to live in a new house he'd bought in LA's Zuma Beach. Once owned by Scott Fitzgerald, this beautiful house became Young's base for the next few years of his mostly bachelor existence. He had no regrets about his music over the last few years; on the contrary, it was 'radical work' and he was justly proud of it.

For now, the clouds had lifted. He was free of the recent troubled past, free of the ranch, free of the responsibility of a partner in love and life. He had money and talent to burn.

The next few years would be astonishingly productive.

5

THE UNSEEN HOMELAND

In the months immediately before and after the latest CSN&Y fiasco Young was busy putting together another album of his own. *On the Beach* had been released only the previous summer, but already, with its downbeat, defensive tone and societal focus, it seemed a relic of days gone by. The new album, provisionally titled *Homegrown*, was no more upbeat, but it was much more melodic, and probably his most accessible album since *Harvest*. The lyrics ranged from the breathtakingly direct to the obscurely allegorical, but the subject matter was fairly consistent: *Homegrown* was basically a requiem for his relationship with Carrie.

The available songs included 'Pardon My Heart' and 'Pushed It over the End' from the May 1974 Bottom Line gig, and all the songs that had had their début performances on the road with CSN&Y: 'Homefires', 'Love-Art Blues', 'Traces', 'Hawaiian Sunrise', 'Star of Bethlehem' and 'The Old Homestead'. Three other little-known songs – 'Try', 'Separate Ways' and 'Vacancy' – were contenders for inclusion, along with five that would eventually be released: 'Love Is a Rose', 'Little Wing', 'Deep Forbidden Lake', 'Human Highway' and 'White Line'.

Of those songs that have never been officially released, 'Homefires', 'Traces' and 'Love-Art Blues' were lyrically the most interesting. 'Homefires' had the singer still wanting a life centred round home and family, but admitting that his current partner was no longer the one he wanted to share it with. 'Traces' was more cryptic, on the one hand noting how easy it was to find true love, on the other stressing the impermanence of everything. 'Love-Art Blues' had Young accepting at least some of the blame, lamenting the need to choose between music and love, but realising he had lost the latter through choosing the former. All three songs had typical Young melodies, apparently effortless, vaguely reminiscent, graceful to a fault.

He said later that the whole album scared him, that it was 'a little too personal'. The songs were '*too* real'; he'd be 'too embarrassed to put them

117

out'. Why putting them on an album was more embarrassing than singing them in concert – with the inevitable bootleggers taping away – is hard to understand. And in any case he apparently *was* intending to put at least some of them out, until a strange accident changed his mind.

The tape containing the resequenced *Tonight's the Night* songs had not spent the last year gathering dust in a vault. On the contrary, it had been just lying around the house. 'It was like a joke', Young said. 'My kid was playing with the master tapes when he was two and a half. He'd get up every morning and go turn it on, start rewinding, going back and forth.'

Somehow a copy of this tape made his way onto the back of the tape containing *Homegrown*, which Young played to an assembled party of friends at his Zuma house one evening in the spring of 1975. The gathering was depressed by *Homegrown*, and the sudden, unheralded assault of *Tonight's the Night* worked like a proverbial cold shower, thoroughly invigorating its listeners.

Hearing the two albums back to back, and watching the reactions of his guests, Young 'started to see the weaknesses in *Homegrown*', he said. The *Tonight's the Night* songs had more spirit, more feeling, and though their subject matter was equally depressing, the overall effect of the music was close to inspirational. He decided to put it out instead of *Homegrown*.

This raises one obvious question. Young admitted that putting *Tonight's the Night* out was 'almost an experiment'. He expected bad reviews. So why did Reprise now agree to release it? The album was no more tuneful, no more commercial, than it had been a year earlier.

Perhaps the record company judged that Young's stint with CSN&Y the previous summer had boosted his falling popularity enough to make any album saleable. Perhaps Young pushed a little harder this time. Or perhaps he promised them something much more accessible next time around.

The release of *Tonight's the Night* in June 1975 was marked by a launch party and the phenomenon of Young making himself available for interviews. He claimed that it was the first record he'd ever made that he could party and interview to, but such a rare display of accessibility must also have owed something to an increasingly benign state of mind.

As far as he was concerned the whole 'teen idol' business was over, and he was free to do whatever he wanted. Releasing *Tonight's the Night*, like touring with CSN&Y, just showed how open he was, and how unpredictable. He felt he'd escaped the trap of others' expectations, or at least learned to recognise it in time to take evasive action. He conceded that he'd become obsessive about not making polished records, but maintained that the greater danger had lain in his becoming another John Denver. As he told John Rockwell two years later, 'I was standing on the cliff there. I coulda gone.' He had no apologies for the albums he'd made since *Harvest*. He realised they'd been 'a certain way', that he'd got 'a lot of bad publicity for them', but that was part of the game. If he hadn't thought they were 'valid' he wouldn't have released them.

The relative failure of *Journey through the Past* had neither dimmed his enthusiasm for making movies nor noticeably dented his confidence in his ability to make more. He had all the equipment he needed, and lots of footage already in the can. Movie-making remained 'more than just a hobby', it was 'an obsession'.

He had no specific plans, however. In fact, his life seemed blissfully devoid of such things. He admitted that being out of a relationship had a lot to do with how free and open he felt, 'more open than I have in a long while'. It was the first time he could remember ending one relationship and having no desire to find another. Living the single life in Zuma Beach was a much more social business than living the 'married life' on the ranch: he was 'coming out and speaking to a lot of people'.

Musically he was, like many others at the time, both heartened and inspired by Dylan's return to form, as evidenced by both the 1974 tour with the Band and the early-1975 album *Blood on the Tracks*. Young thought Dylan had shown 'that a major performer can live with his people'. What exactly he meant by this is unclear, but Dylan's ability to bounce back after several years of making albums principally to please himself must have struck Young as a particularly happy omen. The old troubadours could, it seemed, survive. Young was fond of citing Muhammad Ali as a role model – he 'always comes back so strong, just as you thought he'd lost whatever he had originally' – but the same could have been said of Dylan. 'A performer like me is like a racehorse,' Young told Ray Coleman, 'except I don't eat hay.'

He appeared to be almost bursting with confidence. One contributing factor must have been the sense of achievement that went with the release of an album like *Tonight's the Night*. In retrospect the album would be considered one of his best, but at the time its release must have seemed – and indeed was – something of a risk. But Young knew that not taking such risks would, in the long run at least, prove even more risky. In his business he needed to grow artistically not only to stay sane, but to survive as a commercial force.

A second source of confidence lay in the songs he'd written over the eighteen months since the Tonight's the Night tour. For one thing there were a lot of them; for another, he felt he was breaking new ground: he seemed *excited* about the songs he was writing. Some of them were 'long instrumental guitar things', and many concerned the Aztecs and the Incas, though not in any straightforward manner. Time travel within and between the songs was part of it; in one of them Marlon Brando, John Erlichman and Pocahontas all made guest appearances. It was 'like being in another civilisation . . . a lost sort of soul form that switches from history scene to history scene trying to find itself, man, in this maze. I've got it all written and the songs are learned. Tomorrow we start cutting them.'

And who was he cutting them with? That was the third reason for Young's new-found confidence. It was five years since Danny Whitten's descent into addiction had rendered Crazy Horse incapable of providing Young with the platform he needed to play electric guitar. At last, they and he had found a replacement.

Crazy Horse bassist Billy Talbot had met Frank 'Poncho' Sampedro through a mutual friend in 1974. They'd taken a vacation in Mexico together, bought a couple of cheap guitars while they were south of the border, and enjoyed playing together. Although Sampedro, now around twenty-four, hadn't played in a band since high school, Talbot reckoned he had a real feeling for jamming and playing rhythm guitar. Back in the States an opportunity soon arose to find out just how good he was. 'We got back to my house and Ralph [Molina] was there. We had the drums set up and George Whitsell had been staying with his old lady, so George, Ralph, Frank and I, and anybody who would come around – John Blanton, Van Dyke Parks, whoever – would get together and jam. Then eventually George split with most of his friends and Ralph, Frank and I were left and we kept playing together.'

When Young asked Crazy Horse to come to Chicago (probably in November or December 1974) and help out on a couple of the tracks intended for *Homegrown*, Talbot asked if he could bring Sampedro along. Young agreed and was evidently impressed. Early in the new year, after the collapse of the CSN&Y project, he turned up at Talbot's Silver Lake home for some jam sessions, and stayed on for a week, playing and writing several of the songs that would appear on *Zuma*. Crazy Horse had been reborn.

At around the same time, and right on cue, Young recovered the black Les Paul guitar he'd played on *Everybody Knows This Is Nowhere*, and which had been missing for several years.

The band began recording the new album at David Briggs's house in Zuma Beach. During the recording of a new guitar epic called 'Cortez the Killer' one of the house's two electric circuits blew, stopping the tapes. The band played on oblivious, and an entire verse was lost while the power was out. As he emerged with what seemed like a perfect take, Young was told of the loss. He asked which verse, shrugged, and said he'd never liked that one anyway.

Zuma proved to be Young's most accessible album since *Harvest*, for two obvious reasons: the songs were all built around a universal theme – emergence from a broken relationship – and the musical styles they employed encompassed his entire repertoire, from driving electric rock through bouncy country rock to pure folk acoustic.

The lyrics on *Zuma* give the impression of being more crafted, more edited, than on the preceding three albums. The imagery is occasionally leaden, but the proportion of perceptive lines and beautifully dovetailed rhymes seems greater, and the album as a whole more thematically organised than is usual with Young – a concept album in all but name. With each song offering a different slant on the overall theme, each can play off against all the others, creating a whole far in excess of the sum of its parts.

The opening 'Don't Cry No Tears', with Winnipeg-vintage melody and lyrics, sets the tone: it's over, and there's nothing he can do about it. There's no point in crying over a spilt relationship, and he knows it. The feeling of the song goes beyond simple acceptance of the fact, coming close to a sense of liberation. This, of course, is only part of the story. In 'Stupid Girl' he accuses, in 'Pardon My Heart' he wonders, in 'Looking for a Love' he hopes he does it better next time. In 'Barstool Blues' he sits there hoping for something to 'burn off all the fog and let the sun through to the snow', takes another metaphorical slug of whatever it is he's drinking, and bitterly remembers a 'friend' who 'trusted in a woman' and 'died a thousand deaths'.

In each of these songs the lyric seems perfectly matched by its music. The acoustic ache of 'Pardon My Heart' segues into the wistful pop of 'Looking for a Love', and that into the metallic clang of 'Barstool Blues'. On 'Stupid Girl' his voice is double-tracked to great effect, with a cold, matter-of-fact voice out front and a pained inner voice in the background.

For all that *Zuma* is a hard rock album, Young lets his lead guitar loose on only two of the tracks. Lou Reed commented that the playing on 'Danger Bird' was the best he'd ever heard, and though that perhaps overstates the case, it's certainly a remarkable performance. It is as if Young is playing almost in slow motion, straining and stretching notes to produce a venomous intensity. 'Though these wings have turned to stone,' he sings, 'I can fly, fly, fly away,' and as you feel the weight of the damn things you also know deep down that somehow or other this ponderous juggernaut is going to make it back up into the air.

'Cortez the Killer' is less obviously dramatic, more lyrical, and a definite contender for Young's finest song. Musically it consists of a simple verse repeated over and over with slow-burning, gathering intensity, the guitar handling the lead for the first three minutes, the vocal for most of the remaining four. The story the voice tells is of Cortez's arrival in the New World, of the Aztec civilisation he found there, at once innocent and savage, advanced and doomed. Young makes no attempt to teach history: he has no interest in the real past, only in its transmutation into the different truths of myth and legend.

'I think romance is a quest,' Young said of 'Cortez the Killer', and this connection is the key to an appreciation of the song's power. The sudden switch of focus from a civilisation on the brink of destruction to a relationship in the here and now – 'And I know she's living there/And she loves me to this day/I still can't still remember when or how I lost my way' – is neither whim nor accident. Like Cortez dancing into the Aztec Eden, Young has come, as we all come, into another's life as explorer and destroyer, both enchanted and enraged by the new and the different.

On the album's last song, 'Through My Sails' – the 'Sailboat Song' of the abortive CSN&Y sessions – the same theme is pursued, with Young journeying on, away from the glaring city lights and into some oceanic paradise. Though confused and disillusioned he is still learning, and with the wind blowing through his sails he's heading on towards the next human port of call.

A tour with Crazy Horse was originally planned for the autumn of 1975, but it was put back to early 1976, most probably because Young needed an operation on his throat. This was successfully carried out in October, and by the end of November he was on stage again, guesting with Stills at Stanford University on the 22nd and with Dylan at the SNACK (Students Need Athletics, Culture and Kicks) benefit on the 23rd.

Dylan had already been touring for a month when this gig took place, but it wasn't the usual sort of tour. The Rolling Thunder Revue had started out in deepest Massachusetts, with Dylan hiring small halls and clubs, then turning up unheralded with a changing roster of famous friends. Young obviously liked the idea. With *Zuma* released, he and Crazy Horse prepared for their upcoming new-year tour by playing a series of unannounced gigs in towns like Cotati and Marshall in northern California. Young would call a club, ask to speak to the owner and offer to pay off the regular band if he and Crazy Horse could play instead.

Their set was composed mainly of songs from *Zuma* and Crazy Horse's *Crazy Moon*. Three-year-old Zeke Young sometimes opened on drums, before being put to bed in the camper outside. Neil's father remembered sharing a beer in the parking lot with friends, ready to reassure the sleeping child if he woke, listening to the band's music 'bulging the walls' of the roadhouse.

After playing their set the band would simply join the drinkers at the bar. For Young, Rolling Zuma must have been a far cry from playing to 400,000 'shaking hands that grab at the sky'; more like a return to his distant Canadian days with the Squires.

In the same period, just before Christmas 1975, Young got involved in community politics. A local tycoon rancher, Monte Stern, had been trying for some time to obtain planning permission for the staging of a string of outdoor concerts. One of the many neighbours appalled at the prospect was Young. The Broken Arrow ranch was still his sanctuary, and he had no desire to see it overrun by autograph hunters and voyeurs.

This was an understandable reaction, if hardly the moral high ground for someone who'd advanced a career at least in part through playing such concerts. His opposition made him popular in the area, though, because that very experience of outdoor festivals gave his stated objections an authority the average farmer couldn't muster. Turning up at a San Mateo Planning Commission meeting, Young told the assembled regulators that the planned concerts would not be safe: the local roads were too narrow for handling fire or medical emergencies.

One of the promoter's lawyers said he would have a hard time listening to 'Sugar Mountain' any more, but the rest of the local population breathed a sigh of relief. Young was even asked to become a director of the San Mateo Historical Society a couple of years later. He attended one meeting in an observer's capacity, then respectfully declined.

After spending much of February in Miami, recording with Stephen Stills at Criteria Studios, Young set out with Crazy Horse on their planned tour. It featured seven dates in four Japanese cities, ten dates on the European mainland and five in Britain, four of them at London's Hammersmith Odeon.

It was Young's first visit to Japan, and he was surprised to see that many in the audience had even copied the way he dressed, down to the patched jeans. That sort of imitation was one thing in Western countries; when it happened 'among people of a different culture, whose whole background is so different from the West's', he thought it 'nothing less than staggering'.

It was just as hard to get a fix on Europe. The halls were all a blur, the people backstage talked in a different language each night, and everyone thought they were crazy (which of course they were). At least in Britain they shared the same language – well, almost – and the same cultural references. Young would have understood one critic's description of him as having 'the general demeanour of a thoroughly wasted, disorientated James Stewart, ambling wide-eyed, his concentration slipping in and out of focus continually'.

There seemed no danger of the music slipping out of focus. On this tour Young and Crazy Horse managed to reach heights they would rarely scale again, at least until 1991's Smell the Horse tour. Billy Talbot called it 'an idyllic time. Neil was just *sparkling*. We had a band again. I heard us playing like I knew nobody else could play.'

One striking fact about the set-list, which didn't greatly change between the first concert in Nagoya and the last in Glasgow, was how many chapters of his musical career Young now seemed to feel comfortable with, both in their own right and as part of a coherent whole. 'On the Way Home' came from Buffalo Springfield/CSN&Y days, while his first solo album provided acoustic opener 'The Old Laughing Lady' and, in Hamburg only, an electric version of 'Last Trip to Tulsa'. *Everybody Knows This Is Nowhere, After the Goldrush* and *Harvest* each provided several songs, both acoustic and electric, including a solo piano version of 'A Man Needs a Maid' which carried all the raw sadness missing from the recorded version. 'Mellow My Mind' from *Tonight's the Night* was given an in-tune treatment, and the recently-released *Zuma* was generously represented in the electric set, usually by 'Don't Cry No Tears', 'Driveback' and 'Cortez the Killer'.

And then there were the new songs. 'Too Far Gone', another song about being wasted, and the simply affecting 'Country Home' would both later emerge less starkly arranged on, respectively, *Freedom* and *Ragged Glory*. 'Let It Shine' and 'Midnight on the Bay' may well have already been recorded with Stills in February, and would surface much sooner, on the Stills-Young collaboration *Long May You Run*. The ballad 'Day and Night We Walk These Aisles' opened with an easy parallel between movies and relationships – 'Day and night we walk these aisles in the same old movie show/And look to someone to feel for for a while' – but saved itself from mere romantic melancholy with the protagonist's insistence on being put out of his misery – 'Don't make me wait/Stab something through me . . .'

The three remaining tunes were among Young's best, evidence that here was an artist working at the height of his powers. The soaring 'Like a Hurricane', which would be released on *American Stars 'n Bars* the following year, provided the high point of most concerts on the tour. An enormous electric fan stood on one side of the stage, offering a precursor of the props used on the 1978 Rust Never Sleeps tour, blowing Young's past-shoulder-length hair out in a horizontal stream.

'Stringman' would also eventually be released, but the public would have to wait seventeen years, until Young resurrected the song for his *Unplugged* performance and album. Allegedly a song about Stephen Stills, it works as a heartfelt plea for anyone with 'a head where chaos reigns' and a heart that can't make peace with it.

The last song, variously called 'Don't Say You Win, Don't Say You Lose' and 'No One Seems to Know', is a strong candidate for Young's best unreleased song. The first lines seem to say it all: 'Once I was in love/Now it seems that time is better spent in searching than in finding.' In love there's no winning, no losing; the partnered life, like the single life, creates new emotional problems for each of the old ones it solves. Played solo on the piano, the song had a beautiful lilting melody, the voice sad but strong, coming to terms with what it means to be human. 'When you're down you gather strength to leave the ground/When you're high it makes you weak and you fall back down . . .'

Despite, or because of, his new-found satisfaction at the rebirth of Crazy Horse, every so often during 1975 Young found the time to join Stephen Stills on stage. It happened at the Greek Theater in July, and again at Berkeley in the same month. There was the already-mentioned Stanford gig in November, and on New Year's Eve the two old partners could be found playing together for free at a local nightclub.

At one gig, the two of them did acoustic versions of 'Long May You Run', 'Human Highway', 'Everybody's Talkin'' and 'Do for the Others' together, and then several electric numbers with Stills's regular band. At another, the state of Young's throat was such that he was unable to sing, reducing him, in effect, to Stills's back-up man. Stills admitted to enjoying the experience: 'Neil Young backs me up better than anyone in the world. He understands what I'm going for. Neil allows me to explore my chops.' Stills sang several of Young's songs – 'The Loner', 'On the Beach' and 'New Mama' – and promised the audience that there would be one on each of his future albums. He also had a suggestion to make. 'What I want to do is make an album with Neil,' he said. 'We'd terrorise the industry.'

Young, for reasons that remain obscure, decided to go along with this idea. Nash later guessed that the primary motivation was his love for Stills, whose professional and personal lives both looked as though they might be heading into a tailspin. The words of 'Stringman', first aired and presumably written around this time, would certainly appear to confirm the depth of Young's affection for his old partner, and it's hard to believe that he thought he needed such a collaborative album to support his own career.

The pair of them began recording in Miami's Criteria Studios in February 1976, and managed to lay down five or six tracks before Young had to leave for Japan with Crazy Horse. At this stage everything seems to have been going well, so well in fact that when Stills asked Young to go out on tour with him that summer, Young agreed to postpone the American tour he'd already planned with Crazy Horse.

They obviously enjoyed playing guitar with each other. Stills insisted that they improved each other's playing, quoting with approval Robbie Robertson's theory that, left to their own devices, Young always played too slow and Stills too fast. But it was more than just a matter of getting the speed right. 'Whenever we play together,' Stills said in April, 'I teach Neil a little more about being polished. He teaches me a little more about being real.'

The extent to which their mutual regard could be translated into real collaboration was something else entirely. The two were getting on together, but the band was Stills's, each had his own songs, and on his own songs each man expected the other to do what he was told. There were no songs written together, and there wouldn't be much sign on the record of any real musical interaction. Basically they were simply taking turns at being each other's star back-up musician. This shouldn't have come as a great surprise to anyone: it had been the way of things in the studio since Young's first departure from Buffalo Springfield in the summer of 1967.

For the moment none of this seemed to matter, at least to Stills. When Young left for his tour with Crazy Horse everything seemed to be on course. Then a strange thing happened. In Japan, Young decided to call Graham Nash and, according to the latter, told him that he and Stills had been making an album in Miami, had 'great lead tracks and great lead vocals', but lacked 'that special sound'. Or in other words, as Nash was not slow to surmise, him and Crosby.

Why Young took this decision – apparently on his own – to involve the other two is hard to fathom. It might well have been, as Nash suggested, that he felt Crosby and Nash would turn his project with Stills into something better. It's also possible that Young was feeling the weight and intensity of dealing one-to-one with Stills, and had a regressive hankering for the days when he could take a back seat in the foursome. Whatever his reasons, it would prove an unfortunate blunder.

Crosby and Nash had not been idle since the second failure to make a second CSN&Y album at the beginning of 1975. Using many of the songs they'd saved for that abandoned project the twosome had made *Wind in the Water*, an album that, in terms of songs and musicianship, rivalled the best either had achieved in any of their various musical pasts – and which, incidentally, had outsold anything Stills or Young had put out over the last three years. They were busy cutting its alliterative successor *Whistling down the Wire* when Young's call came through from Tokyo.

They might have been wiser to ignore it. But, in Nash's words, 'he said he had these great things, and David and I are not fools'. Young eventually arrived at Nash's house in San Francisco with a tape of what he and Stills had already put down, and played it for him and Crosby.

They must have been impressed, because they left for Miami first thing the next morning.

For a couple of weeks the foursome worked together, with Crosby and Nash embellishing songs Stills and Young had already recorded, and Stills and Young joining in on new recordings of songs Crosby and Nash had been working on in California. At this stage it appears as if Crosby and Nash were willing to pool the two albums – why else would they have been re-recording 'Taken at All' and 'Mutiny', both of which would eventually appear on *Whistling down the Wire*? – but if so, it's hard to understand their insistence on returning to California to finish that album before completing the one with Stills and Young. According to Nash they had come up with only seven songs in Miami, and needed a couple more from Crosby. 'So what we wanted to do was finish all the stuff in Miami that we'd written, finish mixing our album, hope that David would write a couple of songs, go back to Miami, cut those songs, and finish the album.'

So Crosby and Nash departed, leaving Stills and Young with a half-finished album, the promise of their returning at some unspecified date, and the vague hope that Crosby would write a couple more songs in double-quick time. This can hardly have been good news to Stills and Young, particularly since Crosby had never, at any stage in his career, been a prolific writer. What should they do?

It seems that Stills, at least, was of the opinion that they should scrap the CSN&Y project and go back to what they'd intended in the first place. He came up with several reasons, one minute claiming the need for haste in finishing the album – 'we had to get on with it . . . we couldn't wait' – the next claiming some sort of existential imperative in his relationship with Young – 'we just had to do it ourselves this time . . . no Richie Furay, no David and Graham, nobody between us'.

Either reason would have done, but Stills did himself no service when he and his manager alleged that it was all Crosby and Nash's fault – they hadn't been 'hungry enough'. Stills would also maintain that the next logical step in disentangling the two projects – the removal of Crosby and Nash's vocals from the songs intended for the Stills-Young album – had been Young's idea. It may well have been, but it's hard to see how this step was avoidable once the primary decision to abandon the CSN&Y album had been taken. Safe copies of the foursome's versions were kept, though you'd never have guessed it from the virulence of Nash's reaction.

He, and presumably Crosby, saw it as musical vandalism. 'Fuck 'em,' Nash succinctly told *Crawdaddy*. 'They're not in it for the right reasons. They're in it for the bucks ... I will not work with them again. The reason they fucking wiped our voices had nothing to do with music. It had to do with whether they could have an album in time to support their tour.' Both Stills's and Young's careers were going downhill, Nash claimed in another interview, and they were desperate.

It's possible that there was an element of desperation in Stills's behaviour. Watching Crosby and Nash disappear, he may have feared, quite understandably, that not only would the CSN&Y project collapse, but it would carry the Stills-Young project down with it. Forced to choose between offending Crosby and Nash and losing Young, he chose the former.

If this was the case, Crosby and Nash probably shared whatever blame was going. After all, had their rush back to San Francisco been solely a matter of music? Couldn't their album have waited? Maybe there were important reasons why it couldn't – reasons that had nothing to do with money. It's impossible to know. What really strikes the outside observer in all this is how little communication there apparently was between four musicians whose music together had trumpeted the virtues of exactly that. As usual, the chief concern all four seemed to share was a fear of being taken advantage of by the others, either singly or in combination.

The Stills-Young tour got under way on 23rd June, at the first of the specially-selected medium-size venues in Clarkston, Michigan. The music was somewhat ragged at the beginning, but things rapidly improved, reaching the point where Stills thought 'we were tight enough so we could really cut loose'.

The order of play was similar to that on the 1974 reunion tour, with electric, solo acoustic and joint acoustic sets followed by another electric set. Stills reportedly wanted to keep with the same set-list, at least until they and the band were all sure of what they were doing, but Young, as ever, wanted to keep things more spontaneous, and to throw in new material if and when he felt like it.

The atmosphere deteriorated as the tour worked its way around the US north-east. Young claims he was having a good time, but was aware that Stills was becoming increasingly unhinged by a combination of factors. Critics, given their first ever opportunity to review Young and

Stills head-to-head, were not surprisingly treating the concerts more like contests than as musical collaborations, and awarding Young all the victories. For Stills – who has always, one suspects, tried to consider Young an equal – this must have been deeply wounding.

He could hardly blame Young, who was doing the tour at least partly as a favour to him. Almost out of necessity, Stills seems to have sought out scapegoats. According to Young, 'Stephen started thinking that other people on the tour were against him, trying to make him look bad to the audience. It just got real personal. Stephen did some things on stage, yelling at people and stuff, that I just didn't want to be part of. I made the decision to leave after the Charlotte concert: he'd been yelling on stage and there'd been a big fight afterwards. Not Stephen and me, Stephen and others.'

The manner of Young's leaving was typical, an exasperating mixture of the selfish and the hilarious. Allegedly, he and Elliot Roberts were driving the bus towards the next gig when Young suggested a right turn. When Roberts told him they needed to turn left to reach the gig, Young told him to turn right anyway. He then sent each member of the band a telegram, the one to Stills reading: 'Dear Stephen, funny how some things that start spontaneously end that way. Eat a peach, Neil.'

At the time, the official reason given for Young's sudden departure was that his throat needed rest, and Stills was at least half ready to accept this explanation. He may even have been relieved. In any event he lost no time in mending his bridges with Crosby and Nash, and early the following year he and they gathered to make their first album as a threesome since the début release in 1969. The location, once again, was Miami, and one evening, as the session was ending, a tall man with a hat was seen loitering outside in the bushes. It was Young, having a piss before coming in to say hello.

'It was great,' Nash said; 'you see, we never hold any grudges.' Or, an unkind voice might have added, ever learn from your mistakes.

The Stills-Young album that had caused all the fuss was released that summer to no great acclaim. It would be outsold by the album Crosby and Nash had left on hold in California, and not for any reasons of deficient public taste: *Long May You Run* proved devoid of excitement, devoid of any real collaboration and almost devoid of good songs.

The title track is the only really memorable cut. Ostensibly Young's tribute to his first hearse – the date of Mort's collision with universal entropy has been altered from 1965 to 1962 – the song manages to encompass the wider special feeling humans have for things that last in a changing world. In one verse Young even seems to be taking a dig at the transience of pop – the Beach Boys and their 'empty ocean road' – although such an interpretation may simply reflect my own prejudices.

His other four songs range from the vaguely charming 'Midnight on the Bay' to the acutely dreadful 'Let It Shine', on which both he and Stills sound in imminent danger of keeling over. 'Ocean Girl' is notable only for Stills's wah-wah guitar, 'Fontainebleau' an enjoyable rant about the good life in Florida. Young is honest enough to admit that 'The reason I'm so scared of it/Is I stayed there once and I almost fit', and his guitar-playing well expresses his rage at the realisation.

Stills later claimed that Young had written all his songs for *Long May You Run* on the spot, 'as if he didn't want to waste anything special', and, 'Long May You Run' apart, this may have been true. But they were still a cut above the four Stills himself contributed, all of which seemed like bland retreads of his earlier work.

The short twelve-date Crazy Horse tour that had been postponed in Stills's favour finally went ahead in early November. Six days after its conclusion, Young was one of the star guests chosen by the Band for their farewell Last Waltz concert at San Francisco's Winterland. It was a once-in-a-generation show, with the cream of that generation's music – Dylan, Van Morrison, Eric Clapton, the Band, Joni Mitchell and Young – all sharing the stage.

Young fully deserved the company he was keeping that night, but it must nevertheless have been a proud moment, at least in anticipation and in retrospect. On the night itself he arrived exhausted, happily accepted some proffered cocaine as he headed for the stage, and spent the rest of the evening with a wide, inane grin on his face and a wodge of coke hanging out of his nose.

During the same month Young was in the throes of deciding on his next album. *Decade*, a three-record retrospective of his career, was ready to ship, but Young wasn't convinced that the time was right. It wasn't 'time to look back yet', he told Cameron Crowe between gigs on the Crazy Horse tour and, apparently decided, he rang up Elliot Roberts to announce his decision.

Roberts told Warners, who dispatched two executives to see Young. He played them most of a new album with the working title *Chrome*

Dreams, whereupon they agreed to put *Decade* back a year. Young then spent much of the winter tinkering with the new album, before throwing half of it aside in favour of other, even newer songs.

In the early 1990s an acetate of *Chrome Dreams* surfaced in Germany bearing the date 16th March 1977. The acetate included the whole of the future *American Stars'n Bars* Side 2 – 'Star of Bethlehem', 'Will to Love', 'Like a Hurricane' and 'Homegrown' – albeit in a different order. The versions of 'Look Out for My Love' and 'Captain Kennedy' that would appear on *Comes a Time* and *Hawks and Doves* were included, as was the *Rust Never Sleeps* 'Pocahontas', minus the vocal overdubs. The other five songs would also all be released eventually, but in different versions and mostly in radically different forms.

The first of these, 'Too Far Gone' (eventually released on *Freedom*), was here performed as an acoustic duet, with Young on guitar and Frank Sampedro on mandolin. Like the live performances during the previous year's Crazy Horse tour, this version captured the song's wry desperation better than the later release.

'Powderfinger', the electric-guitar highlight of 1979's *Rust Never Sleeps*, was here done acoustically, giving the song a thoroughly spooky feel, much in the manner of the Cowboy Junkies' interpretation on their 1989 album *The Caution Horses*.

'Hold Back the Tears' was just Young and guitar, more intense and more real than the countrified version that would appear on *American Stars'n Bars*. It also had an extra verse – 'I call her name out in the night/I feel for someone but still something isn't right/Ah, those streets I hesitate to use/Look better when life brings on the blues' – which suggested that the protagonist was considering a resort to prostitutes.

'Sedan Delivery' was done at half the speed of its eventual released version (on *Rust Never Sleeps*) and, like the previous song, communicated a greater intensity than its later rendition. It too had an extra verse, and generally conjured up Young's description of his life during this period, often 'getting loose in bars'.

The version of 'Stringman' was not so different to the one released seventeen years later on *Unplugged*. It had probably been taken live from one of the Hammersmith Odeon gigs in March 1976, with the faint electric-guitar overdub added at a later date.

All in all this would surely have been a wonderful album, but Young wasn't satisfied with it. Perhaps it was too downbeat for his current state of mind, or perhaps he had, temporarily, gone off some of the songs.

Whatever the reasons, the nature of the album changed, and the title was switched to reflect this. *American Stars'n Bars* would have one side of songs dealing with American folk heroes and history, the other side offering social comment – the kind that could be overheard in American bars. Unfortunately, the need to research the second side put paid to the first: 'drunk on his ass in bars', Young claims to have forgotten the history part.

It's not known which songs Young originally intended placing on *American Stars'n Bars*. Pocahontas and the posthumous protagonist of 'Powderfinger' and Captain Kennedy could all have been 'American stars', while the singer of 'Too Far Gone' had obviously propped up a few bars, but not one of these four songs actually appeared on the new album. Although the new title was retained, both stars and bars became conspicuous by their absence. In their place Young offered a ragbag of unused tunes and five slices of countrified pop.

The initial impression of *American Stars'n Bars* is of a thoroughly uneven album, with its two sides differing wildly in both style and quality. The side of countrified songs performed by Young, Crazy Horse and the Bullets – Linda Ronstadt and friend Nicolette Larson – is full of energy and enthusiasm, but the songs are relentlessly ordinary, with lyrics and melodies that sound as though they've been recycled once too often.

'The Old Country Waltz' is a pleasantly maudlin tale of loss in love, 'Saddle Up the Palomino' an up-tempo, mildly witty tale of adulterous desires, 'Hey Babe' a pretty throwaway. The starkly-drawn 'Hold Back the Tears' of the *Chrome Dreams* acetate has been at once depersonalised and turned into standard country fodder, proof that Young was capable of becoming another Randy Travis, if anyone had wanted one.

'Bite the Bullet', with its 'walking love machine' and desire to 'hear her scream', is at best tastelessly adolescent, at worst downright offensive. All five songs call on the blander, less incisive side of country music and, though arranged and performed competently enough, simply lack any real edge. Why Young chose to fill an album side with such music is hard to fathom, particularly when it involved dragging him into such dubious lyrical territory as that of 'Bite the Bullet'.

Side 1 was certainly not a good advert for Side 2, but then which Young fan back from the record store would have played anything else before 'Like a Hurricane'? This, the song that had really stood out on his 1976 live tours, was the one everyone had been waiting for. 'Once

I thought I saw you,' it begins, and Young goes on to offer a *Great Gatsby*ish hint of some perfect, unobtainable lover before turning the tables. It seems that it's the love, not the lover, that's beyond his grasp. 'You could have been anyone to me,' he sings; it wouldn't have made any difference – he would still be blown away by love. With a beautiful, yearning melody that even the later pump-organ version on *Unplugged* couldn't quite destroy, 'Like a Hurricane' could have been a great acoustic song in its own right; instead it was used as a basis for the most lyrical electric-guitar playing Young had ever put on record.

What makes the playing so beautiful and so evocative for so many people is difficult to pinpoint. Some people listening to the extended instrumental passages see a hurricane in their mind's eye, but this would seem to suggest violence and speed, and the playing is not notable for either. Interviewed by Mary Turner for a promotional disc, Young had this to say about the song: 'I never play anything fast. And all it is is four notes on the bass, just keeps going down. Billy plays a few extra notes now and then, and the drum beat's the same all the way through. It's like a trance we get into . . . Sometimes, it does sound like we're playing fast but we're not. It's just everything starts swimming round in circles, and everything just starts elevating and it transcends the point of playing fast or slow or anything like that – luckily for us because we can't play fast.'

To me, the electric-guitar passages on 'Like a Hurricane' always suggest a particular landscape, a huge flat world of lakes and reeds, with big birds flying across the sky, making loud croaking noises in the twilight air. I have no real explanation as to why: the guitar occasionally sounds like a crying bird, but I think it's more likely that the senses of beauty and desolation, which Young has intertwined in the music, find my visual meeting point in such a landscape.

The other three songs on Side 2 are all different, both from 'Like a Hurricane' and from each other. 'Star of Bethlehem' offers a graceful melody and what appears a ruthlessly realistic view of love – 'All your dreams and your lovers won't protect you . . . They'll leave you stripped of all that they can get to . . .' – until the last verse affords the most ordinary image of eternal hope, a still-shining light bulb on down the hall. 'Maybe the Star of Bethlehem wasn't a star at all,' Young concludes enigmatically, tying together the searches for God and love, both apparently hopeless, but equally impossible to give up.

The same theme inspires 'Will to Love', seven minutes of acoustic rambling with a background of logs cracking on a fire. The lyrics pursue an extended – some would say overextended – metaphor, using a salmon's instinctive journey upstream to reflect on the similarly inexorable human pursuit of artistic truth and of romantic love. One of Young's more obviously stream-of-consciousness songs, it also reflects on the twinned realities of individualism and isolation. With its fishy subtext of 'fins aching from the strain' and 'belly scraping on the rocks', 'Will to Love' is one of those Young songs that tend to draw extreme reactions. Some find it hysterically funny, others truly sublime.

The album's final song, 'Homegrown', is unfortunately neither. While doubtless a treat for all those concert-going morons who whoop with joy whenever dope gets mentioned in a lyric, its loud-mouthed, boorish country rock seems an utterly inappropriate conclusion to Side 2's otherwise triumphant progress.

But perhaps it wasn't such an inappropriate conclusion to the album as a whole. In 1977 *Stars'n Bars* felt directionless, as if Young was freewheeling, dabbling, waiting for something to grab him, either in life or in music or in both. In this it fairly accurately mirrored the large part of the rock scene that had originated in the sixties and was now showing signs of running short on energy and ideas.

Young's lifestyle at this time seems to have been an enviable mixture of the creative and the carefree. Whereas most people with time lack money, and most with money lack time, he had plenty of both.

One of his favourite ways of spending them was on an expanding collection of antique cars. By 1977 he had about ten, including two of the ten seven-passenger Cadillacs built by General Motors in 1940. One of them had belonged to a South American dictator, and featured the necessary bullet-proof windows. At first Young's cars were housed in a convenient barn on the ranch, but eventually the collection would get too large and be moved into storage nearby. The 'car barn' would become the 'train barn', and home to Young's model-railroad empire.

And then there were boats. While recording with Stills in Miami in February 1976, Young had taken to hanging out at the Coconut Grove, a club frequented by many sailing enthusiasts. An already existing interest was fanned, and he decided to buy a boat of his own, an all-wooden 1920-vintage motor yacht which he rechristened the *Evening Coconut*. Whenever he had the time that summer, Young and his friend Mazzeo would go sailing round Florida's inland waterways.

135

The *Evening Coconut*, with its rotting hull and unreliable engine, was neither a sound investment nor a faithful servant, and during one of its frequent periods out of service Young was persuaded to check out a possible replacement – an old Danish bulk carrier which had been converted into a yacht and somehow ended up in Grenada. Young had the boat collected, found it was in appalling condition, loved it anyway, and decided to restore it to its former glory. This job, which involved stripping the boat to its hull, kept him, several friends and various contingents of hired help busy for much of the next two years. In the process he learned what made the boat tick – and probably a few things about himself besides. It would eventually be renamed the *W.N.Ragland*, after his maternal grandfather.

The carefree lifestyle also carried over into his music. In the summer of 1977, in the nearby town of Santa Cruz his old friend Jeff Blackburn was playing in a band with ex-Grape bassist Bob Mosley, drummer Johnny C. Craviotto and an unknown lead guitarist. The latter disappeared during one of Young's visits, and the resulting temptation proved irresistible. On Young's condition that they play only within the Santa Cruz city limits, the band – now managed by Mazzeo and rechristened the Ducks – started playing the town's bars for a percentage of the evening take.

The group's name came from a local legend. Some years before, a surfer with the unlikely name of Pussinger had cut through a flock of ducks, killing seven, and had been duly sentenced to seven days in jail – one per duck. However, an old and wise duck named Master Mallard had deemed this example of the dispensation of human justice overlenient, and placed a curse on the town. It could be lifted only if and when the entire population gathered under one roof quacking like ducks. Hence every Ducks concert began with massed duck calls from the audience.

Musically, the band played straightforward rock'n'roll. Some of the songs were Young's (including the never-released instrumental 'Windward Passage'), but the band weren't too particular. Any songs celebrating the all-American male trinity of booze, sex and the road seemed fair game.

Young enjoyed playing without the weight of audience expectations. He realised the other members of the band hadn't had the same chance to satisfy their musical ambitions that he'd had, but that was just the way things were. 'Sure they want to go out and do something,' he said, 'but all I want to do is play some music right now, and not go out and do anything. You see, I haven't lived in a town for eight years. I stayed on my ranch for four years and then I just started travelling all over, never really staying anywhere. Moving into Santa Cruz is like my re-emergence back into civilisation. I like this town. If the situation remains cool, we can do this all summer long.'

It didn't, of course. The word got out, and crowds of people started arriving from out of town. A writer from *Rolling Stone* turned up, even record-company scouts. The house the band were sharing was burgled. As he had said he would, Young split. If the other Ducks were left contemplating what might have been, then they hadn't been listening.

Pursuing a pattern that was rapidly becoming familiar, Young followed this orgy of straight-ahead rock'n'roll with a plunge into its opposite – acoustic folkiness. The new album that began to emerge over the next couple of months would be a folkier version of the *Harvest* style, with all the accessibility of that album.

During the Ducks episode he'd joined Crosby and Nash on stage at the Santa Cruz Civic Auditorium for an acoustic benefit evening, playing the still-unreleased 'Human Highway', 'New Mama', 'Sugar Mountain' and 'Only Love Can Break Your Heart'. This last song, he told the audience, had originally been written for Nash. 'I would have written it for Crosby,' Young said, 'but he was just too happy.'

Early in the autumn he set out across country in the bus with his son Zeke, who had just turned five. They don't seem to have had any fixed itinerary, and Young probably got a good deal of writing done during the long hours on the road. By the time he and Zeke had reached Nashville, Young felt he had an album. The summons went out to the musicians who were gradually coming to form the core of his folk-country music: Tim Drummond, Ben Keith, Karl Himmel, Spooner Oldham and Rufus Thibodeaux. This time around, having decided to augment the sound further, Young brought in another thirty or so musicians, including eight acoustic guitarists and a sixteen-strong string section. This collectivity, which Young dubbed the Gone with the Wind Orchestra, would help give the provisionally-titled *Give to the Wind* its deep warm sound. Nicolette Larson was invited along to sing harmony.

Between album sessions the ensemble performed one live gig, before a crowd of 125,000 on Young's birthday, 12th November. The occasion was a benefit for children's hospitals in the Miami Beach area, and was musically interesting for a first and rare performance of 'Lady Wingshot', a song apparently about a young boy's half-sexual fascination with a circus artist. For an encore Young performed a brief rendition of Lynyrd Skynyrd's 'Sweet Home Alabama', the song Ronnie Van Zant had written in reply to his own 'Southern Man'. The two men had since expressed their admiration for each other, but now Van Zant was gone, killed with three other members of Lynyrd Skynyrd's tour party in a plane crash two weeks before. Young dedicated the song to 'a couple of friends in the sky'.

Young's three-record retrospective *Decade* was finally released in October 1977. To those expecting a wilfully controversial choice of material, the set came as a disappointment: all the acknowledged classics, in all his various styles, had been included, along with five previously unreleased tracks.

He had written 'Campaigner' after watching a haggard ex-President Nixon emerge from the hospital that housed his stricken wife. 'Even Richard Nixon has got soul,' the song's refrain declares: the man whom Young named as a murderer in 'Ohio', and who did indeed sustain a murderous war, is apparently also a human being. The world isn't divided quite as neatly into good guys and bad guys as the sixties led us all to believe. This makes action more problematic, but it doesn't take away the need to try. The song's first verse – 'I am a lonely visitor/I came too late to cause a stir/Though I campaign all my life towards that goal' – is also its last.

Young's growing up is much in evidence: the youthful author of the *Stampede*-vintage 'Down to the Wire', with its paranoid fears of manipulative women, seems far removed from the knowing lover of 'Love Is a Rose'. The latter, although musically slight, contains a beautifully concise statement of the perils of possessiveness in love: 'Love is a rose but you'd better not pick it/It only grows when it's on the vine/A handful of thorns and you'll know you missed it/You lose your love when you say the word "mine".'

'Winterlong' was now almost a decade old, though this recording was probably made in 1974. The Spector influence is still audible, however, and Young's voice is at its yearning best, both here and on the deeply enigmatic 'Deep Forbidden Lake'. The latter, featuring keening fiddle and pedal steel, together with visual but opaque lyrics, sounds like *Harvest* with the melancholy button turned up.

On the album sleeve Young appended little word-pictures of each track, sometimes explaining a song's genesis, sometimes trying to place it in a wider context. Of the album as a whole, he said, 'I think it tells a story. This could be the record that defines my influence on the music world for the past ten years.'

Comes a Time was the first album Young had made for more than five years that was immediately easy to listen to. The music lacked sound and fury, the lyrics – on first hearing, at least – any threatening edge.

The overall sound of massed acoustic guitars, occasionally supported by warm waves of strings, is lulling, almost serene, creating a mood that Young's voice, more obviously tuneful than usual – and further sweetened by Nicolette Larson's support – does nothing to dispel. The musical consistency is matched by the lyrics, with five of the songs – 'Look Out for My Love', 'Lotta Love', 'Peace of Mind', 'Already One' and 'Field of Opportunity' – tackling variations on the theme of getting it right in relationships. Several of them stress the protagonist's vulnerability, all of them acknowledge that it's hard work, but there's no doubting his ultimate willingness to take the plunge once more. Some of these songs have a deal less to offer than others, but in the context of such a homogenous-sounding album this doesn't greatly matter: each functions as an aspect of the wider picture.

The two 'family' songs – 'Comes a Time' and 'Already One' – deserve a separate mention. New life has rarely been given a more joyous welcome than in the former, and the child's place in a broken relationship rarely been evoked to better effect than in the latter. 'We're already one – our little son won't let us forget,' the refrain insists; the couple's boy is a constant reminder – of their relationship with each other, of love's mysterious inclination to vanish, of the need to do better next time.

On this, as on several of the album's songs, a darker undertow can be detected beneath the placid surface. The dream/time-travel lyric of 'Goin' Back' goes all the way back to the moment of creation before evoking past worlds of nomadic simplicity. But there's no chance of turning back the clock, and it's only in the fringes of today's world, high up a mountain or deep in a city, that such innocence can still hope to flourish. In 'Look Out for My Love', as the musical gears shift up from acoustic to electric, the lyrics abandon their inner musing to offer a paranoid snapshot of the real world, while 'Human Highway', for all its jaunty melody and wry humour, keeps coming back to the line "Take my eyes from what they've seen". Young's habitual fear and loathing are far from absent on this album, merely muted or held at bay.

The last two tracks seem to stand outside the general flow. 'Motorcycle Mama' is sung – screeched might be a more apt word – by Nicolette Larson, and almost manages to destroy the mood carefully created over the preceding thirty minutes. 'Four Strong Winds', the Ian Tyson song that closes the album, is as beautiful as its predecessor is appalling. A favourite of Young's since 4-D days, it is given a faultless treatment. The acoustic guitars ring, the pedal steel keens, and Young's voice has never sounded more seductively plaintive.

The renewal of his musical relationship with Nicolette Larson sparked something more: when Cameron Crowe visited the singer at his Zuma house he found the floppy-sweatered pair playing what the journalist called 'Pa and Ma Kettle', singing along to the *Comes a Time* tape in front of an open fire. The romance was short-lived, however. Plans to spend at least some of the Christmas vacation with either her parents in Kansas City or his father in Toronto were suddenly abandoned. Instead they retreated to the ranch, not quite sure where they were with each other.

One day, not long before Christmas, they and Tim Mulligan called in on neighbour Pegi Morton. Young had first met her almost exactly three years earlier, and they had gone out together a few times before deciding that, for the moment at least, friendship seemed a better bet than romance. In Young's words, 'We both still had a lot of travelling to do.'

Now both of them were ready for a deeper, more lasting commitment, and that particular evening's visit in December 1977 seems to have provided the moment of realisation. Within a few days Nicolette was living in Young's Zuma house, while he and Pegi were at the ranch, taking the first tentative steps towards turning a friendship into a love relationship.

Over the next few months the couple spent a lot of time together, with Young effectively reoccupying his ranch. Zeke was often there at weekends, giving his father the perfect excuse to indulge his love of model railroads. An already large Lionel layout was beginning to spread itself around the old 'car barn'.

In February he and Pegi went to Florida to check progress on the new boat, and six months later had their honeymoon aboard the *W.N.Ragland* as it made its maiden voyage to the Bahamas. For Young, 1978 was turning into a year of endings and beginnings.

In the case of *Comes a Time* there was at least one false start. Somewhere between recording and pressing, the master tape had been damaged, although not so badly that the flaw was obvious to a casual listener. Young initially thought something was wrong, but, unable to work out what, decided he must be imagining things, and okayed the production run. A week later, listening to a tape taken from the original master, he realised that some of the higher-register frequencies had disappeared. He phoned Reprise and told them what had happened, and no doubt took a deep breath before agreeing to cover the $200,000 costs already incurred. 'I don't like throwing money around,' he told his father, 'but I wasn't going to have this album circulating around the world in bad quality.'

The faulty copies were brought to the storage building that housed part of his growing antique-car collection, and a rifle shot sent through each caseload to prevent their ever being sold. According to Rogan, Young also changed the track listing to prevent Reprise from cheating on him.

When *Comes a Time* came out at the end of the year, Young said, 'It's in the middle of a soft place . . . I hear it on the radio and it sounds nice . . . But I'm somewhere else now. I'm into rock'n'roll.' He was not alone. Something had begun changing in American music over the first half of 1978, as the ripples of the British punk explosion, the so-called New Wave, came spilling across America's shores.

Young's first intimations of this change had come during the European leg of the 1976 tour with Crazy Horse. There was a new music in the air, and a new attitude. Or rather, it was a revival of old attitudes. 'Kids were tired of the rock stars and the limousines and the abusing of stage privileges as stars,' Young thought, and their music reflected these and other resentments in ways that can only be described as direct. Everything he heard about the punk movement, everything he read about it in magazines, or saw of it on TV, strengthened Young's belief that here was something he could not to afford to ignore.

The fact that his fellow musicians from the sixties appeared to be immune to punk's appeal seemed to him significant. 'As soon as I heard my contemporaries saying, "God, what the fuck is *this* . . . This is going to be over in three months," I knew it was a sure sign right there that they're going to bite it if they don't watch out. And a lot of them are biting it this year. People are not going to come back to see the same thing over and over again. It's got to change.'

It wasn't any form of linear progress that punk offered, but a revitalisation, a return to basics in the search for new energy. Punk wasn't breaking any new ground, it was just attacking the old ground with renewed intensity. The name of the game, as Young knew well, was still rock'n'roll. Punk was just 'the latest incarnation . . . it was Buffalo Springfield all over again, it was the Doors all over again'.

It was a revitalisation that suited him down to the ground. While his contemporaries had spent years polishing their sound, creating, in Young's elegant phrase, 'the produced, overdubbed, layered bullshit that came out of LA for so many years', he had devoted as much effort to roughening his music up. Punk was almost a musical reference for him, a statement that he'd been right all along.

It suited Young's character too. Punk was conservative, even reactionary, in its attitude towards the musical basics of rock'n'roll and the process of recording it. It was also extremely radical, because the establishments it was rebelling against, whether musical or political, exemplified the shallow progressivism that had been born in the fire of the sixties, and had been mostly petrified by success or fear in the seventies. For Jimmy Carter read Crosby, Stills and Nash; for the Labour government of the late seventies read Elton John.

Rock was getting stiff in the joints, a bit soft in the head. It was time for another shake-down, and Young wanted to be one of the shakers, not one of the shaken.

In addition, he had started work on another movie, *Human Highway*, which *Rolling Stone* described as 'a documentary-style modern western'. Dean Stockwell, of *After the Goldrush* fame, was also involved in the writing/directing side, and two reasonably well-known actors – Dennis Hopper and Sally Kirkland – had taken parts.

At this stage the general nature of the film seemed depressingly familiar. It would include both concert footage and (mostly outdoor) semi-dramatic footage. Young would be talking to the camera again, both on stage and walking down the road. Perhaps under freeways too. An attack on his tour bus sounded like an idea whose time had already come and gone, probably on a stoned afternoon. Expectations were not heightened by the news that the same producer and chief cinematographer who had worked on *Journey through the Past* would be working on *Human Highway*.

But new elements were also promised. Pursuing his interest in the New Wave, Young had come to hear about Devo, an American band who claimed their music was based on the sound of things falling apart. He asked them to do a concert sequence for *Human Highway*, performing songs of his such as 'After the Goldrush' – complete with customised lyrics ('I was sitting in a burning basement when a pinhead knocked on the door . . . evolution is on the run in 1984') – and the then unreleased 'Out of the Blue', in front of a safety-pinned audience at the San Francisco punk club Mabuhay Gardens. Young himself stumbled across the stage during the show, and was introduced as Grandpa Granola.

Looking at the rushes a few days later Young noticed Devo's back-up vocals for the first time: they were chanting the phrase 'Rust never sleeps' over and over. He called the band, and was told that two of them had devised the slogan years before when working on a Rustoleum account for an ad agency. The phrase struck a creative chord in Young, neatly summarising, as he felt it did, the endless struggle any artist is engaged in to avoid trapping himself in certain styles and attitudes, in the cumulative coils of his own past.

It took Young a few months to come up with an idea for translating this need for self-renewal into a stage show. In the meantime he did what he chose to call his 1978 World Tour – a five-night, ten-performance run at San Francisco's 292-seat Boarding House theatre.

For these concerts, at least some of which were recorded for use in *Human Highway*, he wore a specially-designed microphone that allowed him to roam the stage as he sang. The audiences were treated mostly to unreleased songs, some from the *Chrome Dreams* acetate, some from the upcoming *Comes a Time*, some from the future *Rust Never Sleeps*. In fact nearly all of the best songs he would release over the next five years had already been written by this time – 'Out of the Blue', 'Thrasher', 'Pocahontas', 'Ride My Llama', 'Powderfinger', 'Sail Away' and 'Sedan Delivery' from *Rust Never Sleeps*, even 'Shots' from the distant *Re·ac·tor*, here performed, like all the others, in solo acoustic fashion.

But for his next major tour Young had no intention of playing the folkie, even one with a microphone that allowed him to wander the stage like a demented lumberjack. He wanted to throw his hat into the ring for rock'n'roll, its history and its enduring vitality. For that he needed Crazy Horse, and something more – an idea.

It came to him on his honeymoon, out on the ocean. He scribbled it down on a piece of paper, deciding they had enough time – barely – to build the sets, make the costumes and rehearse before the tour's opening gig on 18th September.

Probably one of the hardest jobs was explaining the concept to his regular road crew. They would be completely covered in hoods, and were expected to 'wave themselves goodbye for a few hours, then move with fervour and purpose'. He would understand, Young told the assembled crew, if any of them didn't feel like signing aboard for this one, but in the event there were no defections. 'He's the only guy I would wear this goddam hood for,' one roadie admitted, before adding, 'He's the only guy that would *ask*.'

The Rust Never Sleeps stage show, which Young had decided would also be a movie (directed by himself, under the pseudonym Bernard Shakey), began with Hendrix's 'Star-Spangled Banner' playing, and small hooded figures – who looked very like the 'jawas' of the *Star Wars* trilogy – scurrying around on the dark stage, their bright eyes flashing in the gloom. As the Beatles' 'A Day in the Life' played, a bunch of these 'road-eyes' struggled to erect a microphone twice the height of a man. The stage thus set, Young appeared, first sitting, then kneeling, looking no bigger than a child on top of one of the grossly oversize amplifiers. He played 'Sugar Mountain' on his twelve-string, then descended the stairs, carrying a giant harmonica, before singing 'I Am a Child'.

As Young explained it, 'He's a little kid, so everything's bigger than life – all of the gear is so huge. So he's asleep on top of this big amplifier, and he wakes up and sings a couple of acoustic songs about being young. Then he comes down off the amp and starts walking around, getting more knowledge, thinking about more worldly things.'

He would then complete the acoustic set, put himself to bed on stage, and be wheeled off by the busy jawas. The electric set followed, featuring a dancing bishop, an explanation of 'rust-o-vision' – 'Has your band begun to rust? After nine years of research in rust development we have decided all bands rust' – and announcements from Woodstock. The last-named were included to imbue the child with a sense of rock's history, to give an extramusical context for the majestic electric music Young and Crazy Horse were playing.

Some critics thought the theatrics got in the way of the music. John

Rockwell, a noted fan of Young's, admitted they were clever, but also considered them 'a little silly and self-conscious'. This seems a harsh judgement: after all, most of the touches were essentially cosmetic; they took nothing away from the music, but did add something to the whole experience. The scuttling jawas, in particular, managed to be vaguely sinister, almost touching and utterly ludicrous all at the same time. They were *entertaining*, in the best sense of the word.

As was usual with Young, the more serious he got, the more his sense of humour showed through. He enjoyed explaining the new technology of 'rust-o-vision': 'It enables the audience to see . . . certain people in the audience, mind you, not everyone can see this . . . but everyone should put on the glasses and give it a shot as far I can tell . . . You have to be in the right frame of mind to see rust particles . . . It's a very high-tech thing. Few people understand it actually, but you put on these glasses, and at certain points, especially in the older songs, you can see it and you can tell where the band starts to falter . . . With the glasses on while I'm playing, if you're tuned in you can see it falling all over the floor of the stage, running down the cord on my guitar . . .'

During the tour he had another idea, which he confided to Cameron Crowe. Instead of coming out and waiting for everyone to be quiet before he played, he would disguise himself as a popcorn vendor and shout out his wares to the crowd. Then an announcement would be made that Neil Young would not come out until everyone was quiet and the popcorn vendor had gone. The vendor would then keep on shouting until the audience got really angry with him, whereupon he would reveal his true identity.

It was a typical piece of Young humour, from its conception right through to the sting in the tail.

Ends and beginnings. On 23rd October Young's Zuma Beach house was consumed by a forest fire, down to its stone fireplace. The following month Pegi gave birth to a son, Ben.

Rust Never Sleeps opens with the acoustic 'My My, Hey Hey (Out of the Blue)' and closes with its electric variation 'Hey Hey, My My (Into the Black)'. Written in the shadow of Elvis Presley's death, and with punk avatar Johnny Rotten much in mind, the song characterises rock'n'roll as a music and an attitude kept alive and vibrant by a form of human sacrifice: the willingness of its practitioners to burn out rather than fade away.

Of course, even an Aztec who believed in the real thing might have been reluctant to put his own head on the block. Young was really giving himself three choices, not two: he could fade away, burn out before the audience's eyes, or prove himself worthy of rock'n'roll's present by coming up with a great album.

Not all the tracks match up. On the acoustic side 'Ride My Llama' is a surrealist fragment, musically slight but charming, while 'Sail Away' is an uninspiring out-take from *Comes a Time*. On the electric side both 'Welfare Mothers' and 'Sedan Delivery' are in some respects disappointing. The former, though witty enough, lacks the kinetic energy it would acquire in later years, while the latter's alternation of slow and fast sections is irritating until it ceases, at which point the repetitiveness of the fast section's flailing beat becomes simply boring.

The other three tracks, however, are good enough to lift the whole album into greatness. 'Thrasher' is the most obviously personal song on the album, at least insofar as it gives as much attention to the world within as to the one without. It's hardly simple or direct, though, and like most of the songs on the album it relies on a flow of suggestive, dream-like images rather than on any confessional simplicity. With its evocative visuals and thought-provoking lines, 'Thrasher' seems to encompass just about everything: an interweaving of personal and social history, the acceptance of mystery and the baring of souls, the pulls of the past and the search for eroded belief, even intimations of mortality. 'Thrasher' may be only Young, his twelve-string and his harmonica, but it cradles a world.

Young said he wrote 'Pocahontas' after watching Sasheen Littlefeather collect Marlon Brando's Oscar for *The Godfather*, and a concern for past wrongs is certainly one element in the song's lyric. But it's not the only one, and there's a sense in which Young is much more interested in the Native American experience – and, for that matter, the Aztec and Inca experiences – as a paradigm of life before the descent into civilisation. The 'homeland we've never seen' is one we never can see: it's America before the European settlement, the America that could only be destroyed by that settlement. But such inaccessibility renders the homeland no less real, and in fact the more corrupt the culture, the greater the emotional pulling power of Arcadian innocence becomes. So we satisfy it with 'an Indian rug and a pipe to share', and fantasies of sleeping with Pocahontas.

The protagonists of 'Powderfinger' occupy a later space in real history, albeit an undefined one, and much the same space in the realm of myth. The hero watches an armed boat heading upriver towards him, and is still trying to decide what to do when the 'first shot hits the dock'. He returns fire, is killed, and then sings a posthumous verse lamenting his death 'so young' and a world in thrall to 'the powder and the finger'. He's one American man, and also everyman. It's one moment in American history, and also everymoment. The music offers the perfect complement, doleful as the young man's predicament, relentless as the river. Young's brief guitar solos are as elegiac as their longer cousins on 'Like a Hurricane'.

Six months after the release of *Rust Never Sleeps* Young released a double album of live recordings from the Rust Never Sleeps tour. There was not a single new song on *Live Rust*, something for which Young faced a certain amount of criticism. He claimed, accurately enough, that anyone who didn't want new versions of the old songs could get all the new songs on *Rust Never Sleeps*, but would have been better advised to rely on two simpler arguments. First, if people didn't want something they were under no obligation to buy it, and second, *Live Rust* was an album worth having in its own right, particularly for its reworking of the electric numbers.

He was probably feeling secure enough in his profession to ignore the critics. The tour and album had finished the job of restoring his career, a job that had begun with the CSN&Y tour in 1974, and continued through a series of excellent albums. Of the musician-writers who had come to prominence in the 1960s he now stood virtually alone as a continuing creative force in the mainstream of American rock music. Hendrix was dead, Dylan had got religion, Paul Simon had marginalised himself, Lennon had gone into hiding, CS&N and the Stones had succumbed to a mixture of smugness and other dangerous habits. New pretenders like Springsteen couldn't begin to approach Young's acoustic-electric range.

It was no great surprise when the *Village Voice* voted Young their Artist of the Decade for the 1970s. During those ten years he'd delivered (not counting *Decade* and *Live Rust*) nine solo albums, each remarkably different from all the others, each informed by an intelligence that was often infuriating but always alive. No one else could make a comparable claim for the same period.

Not unjustifiably he was full of confidence as the decade drew to its close. Not to say arrogance. Asked about a possible CSN&Y reunion he simply asked, 'Who cares?' It was better for their fans 'to remember it the way it was' than to keep harking back. That was 'why Muhammad Ali isn't fighting any more'. As for his own fans, he liked it when they enjoyed what he was doing, but he sure as hell wasn't going to do anything purely for the prospect of pleasing them. In fact, he admitted, 'I sometimes really like aggravating people with what I do. I think it's good for them.'

This sense of great confidence spilled over into his film-making. *Human Highway* had apparently been completed, and tentatively set for a spring release in 1979. Finished or not, it was gazumped by the *Rust Never Sleeps* movie, and its release indefinitely postponed. Young still wanted to make more films, and without changing his basic approach. Script-writing didn't appeal to him, and nor did script-reading; in both cases he claimed that he rarely got past page two. 'I'm still of the school of try to make it up,' he said, 'keep it spontaneous as you go along. You might want a list – a one-page list might be good – with improvising characters. That's the way I would do it. Many people have done it that way and met with an incredible amount of failure. But that's the way I would do it.'

Whatever he did, it would be because he wanted to do it. Young was into having a good time, not taking himself so seriously. That was how the punk bands approached life (Young obviously hadn't met the Clash or Paul Weller), and it was why the old bands were losing it – they had no sense of fun. His advice was that his contemporaries should 'not take yourself too seriously, and just try to have a good time and not try to hold up what you've done as being right and try to stand behind it, I don't think that's the right thing to do . . .'.

Was he serious about not being serious? Maybe. He was also confused. 'People want a star to be flashy and they want something . . . that they don't have to relate to as being human. Things that are human . . . you have your moment, then you go away, but stars are supposed to represent something else I guess – a sort of a super quality of . . . it's great . . . and once it isn't great, people don't want to hear about it because that doesn't satisfy their illusion. They want something to be bigger than life . . . that's where that came from – it's better to burn out than to fade away or rust . . . because it makes a bigger flash in the sky.'

What was he saying here – that musicians who expressed their humanness would have only a short time in the spotlight of popularity? He'd just proved the opposite, being voted artist of a *decade* for being *himself*, on record and on stage, in just such a way that enabled millions of other humans to gain greater enjoyment and understanding of their feelings and their own selves. What people loved about Neil Young in the seventies was precisely that he was *not* larger than life.

In this light, looking back, one can see *Rust Never Sleeps* as not only the end of a great period but the beginning of a lesser one. Young's invocation to his roadies to 'wave themselves goodbye for a few hours' would be applied to himself, only in his case it would prove to be for a matter of years rather than hours. The desire to be 'bigger than life', originally conceived as a reaction to almost fifteen years of being himself in public, would also fuel a growing willingness to shroud his true self in customised roles.

This lesser period might have been as short-lived as most previous phases of Young's career, had all other things been equal. They were not. The discovery, during 1979, that his son Ben was seriously afflicted with cerebral palsy would not only turn Young's and his family's life upside down, but also turn an existing inclination to leave himself out of his music into an emotional imperative.

6

MUSIC FROM ANOTHER WORLD

Ben Young's birth in November 1978 had been a month premature. His face had been badly bruised, his eyes swollen, and he cried a lot. Almost from the beginning Pegi was convinced something was wrong, and nothing happened to change her mind, no matter how many times the people around kept telling her, no, he's fine, don't worry. After two months he still wasn't doing what one-month-old babies were supposed to do, and he never seemed to smile. In fact, it became increasingly clear that he was often in pain.

With what must have been sinking hearts, the Youngs took their baby to Stanford Hospital in nearby Palo Alto for tests. Mustering all that sensitivity for which highly-paid physicians are so renowned, two doctors discussed their diagnosis in front of, but not with, the waiting Neil and Pegi. Ben had cerebral palsy. He was a spastic, quadriplegic, non-oral child.

'It was too big a picture to comprehend,' Young remembered ten years later. 'Pegi's heartbroken, we're both shocked. I couldn't believe it. There were two different mothers. It couldn't have happened twice. Somehow we made it out to the car. I remember looking at the sky, looking for a sign, wondering, "What the fuck is going on? Why are the kids in this situation? What the hell caused this? What did I do? There must be something wrong with *me*."'

There wasn't, doctors told him; it was simply an appalling coincidence. Seven out of every hundred thousand children born in the US had cerebral palsy, and Young now had two of them.

Once they had absorbed the shock, the Youngs began to look into what could be done to help Ben. Later in 1979 a friend brought them clippings from the *National Enquirer* about a Philadelphia-based organisation – the Institutes for Achievement of Human Potential – that specialised in helping parents to help their children to overcome at least part of their handicap. From what they could judge, the level of commitment required from both parents was likely to be prodigious, an impression that was confirmed by a meeting with friends of David Cline who were already involved.

Essentially the child would need active supervision twelve hours a day, seven days a week. The Institutes Program involved, in Pegi's words, 'patterning the child to crawl, teaching him words and numbers and simple bits of information, doing all kinds of tasks to make him use and develop what his mind and body *can* do, rewarding him with stories several times a day while he rests for the next thing on the Program'.

She, at least, soon got the chance to see the whole process at work. While the whole family was in LA for a couple of months early in 1980 – Young was working on *Human Highway* – Pegi helped another couple with a handicapped child who had signed up for the Program. Hearing of the Youngs' interest the Institutes started sending them information and invitations to apply. Still unsure as to whether they could cope, Neil and Pegi found themselves on a short list for acceptance.

It was at this point, in the spring of 1980, that Pegi suddenly started having terrible headaches. She was told that she had an arteriovenous malformation, and that she needed brain surgery, otherwise sudden death was a distinct possibility. Even with the operation there was only a fifty per cent chance of complete recovery.

She must have been petrified, and Young can't have felt much better. He must have wondered what purpose it served to have been voted Artist of the Decade and to be a multimillionaire when his wife was in imminent danger of death and his second son, like his first only considerably more so, had been born with a rare and cruel handicap. The days between Pegi's diagnosis and her one hundred per cent successful operation in early May must have been dreadful for both of them.

She convalesced through June and July, and then the whole family took to the Pacific for two months in the *W.N. Ragland*, visiting several of the Society Islands – Tahiti, Moorea and Huahine. Returning at the end of September, they went straight to Philadelphia where, with other similarly-placed parents, Neil and Pegi attended a one-week, ten-hour-a-day course at the Institutes.

Their doubts as to whether they *could* do it may have persisted, but any doubts as to whether they *should* do it disappeared. According to Pegi, seeing the 'patterning' system at work, understanding the processes involved, made all the difference. 'Once you understand *why* you're doing it – to try to give your child a chance in life that he wouldn't otherwise have – it becomes crystal clear. There was no way you could go home and not do it. Or at least try it.'

Her husband was also won over: it was 'the first time I've heard something that makes sense to me', he said, 'everybody pushing to the limit to make a child try both physically and mentally'.

Ben was enrolled on the Program in early October 1980. For both parents, for the next eighteen months, it would be more than the dominating factor in their lives; it would be almost the only factor. As Young said years later, 'I made up my mind. I was going to take care of Pegi, take care of the kids. I closed down so much that my soul was completely encased. I didn't even consider that I needed a soul to make my music. I shut the door on my music.'

Hawks and Doves, recorded and released in this year of extreme emotional stress, divides itself neatly into two musically different sides, the one reflective acoustic, the other loud-mouthed country rock. The first side offers four songs: 'Little Wing', a lovely but inconsequential fragment originally intended for *Homegrown*; 'The Old Homestead', also written around 1974; the apparently new 'Lost in Space'; and 'Captain Kennedy', a survivor from the *Chrome Dreams* project.

It's been claimed that 'The Old Homestead' is a coded history of CSN&Y, but if so, Young's failure to include any key to the code turned it into one of his most pointless pieces of work, whose only purpose is to amplify the deep sense of disenchantment that dominates this side of the album. 'Lost in Space', though undeniably attractive, is equally infuriating. Are the 'infinity board' and 'magic pen' shorthand for sixties values? What are the 'unknown dangers on the ocean floor'? These may be the ramblings of a man in pain – they certainly *feel* as if they are – but not enough artistry has been applied to the shaping of the emotional raw material, and the only real art on display appears to be the art of concealment.

'Captain Kennedy', while hardly straightforward, is at least coherent. The song's protagonist is the good Captain's son, whom we meet aboard ship and on his way to war, both revelling in the simple joys of life – like sails in the wind and water on wood – and worrying that he may lack the necessary aptitude when it comes to killing his fellow human beings. Three other verses tell the father's more ordinary tale, but at the end the first is repeated, leaving the listener with its potent picture of a humanity at home in the world yet distant from itself.

Alter egos – leader of the doomed Shocking Pinks . . .

. . . and Shaky Deal.

Farm Aid – announcing the event with Willie Nelson . . .

. . . and performing at the first concert, September 1985.

Mandela Day, 16th April 1988.

With Pegi.

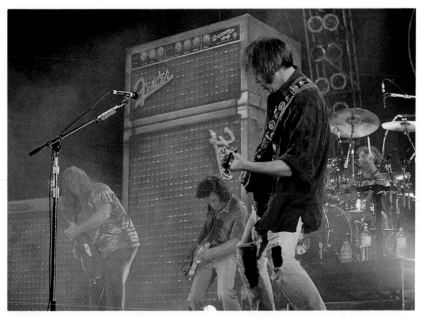

With Crazy Horse during the Smell the Horse tour, 1991.

With Booker T and the MGs, Finsbury Park, 1993.

Cut!

Blowin' in the wind . . . The Smell the Horse tour, 1991.

The second side of the album could hardly be more unlike the first. With his personal emotions on hold, Young had written five new songs about life and politics in America. The lyrics are clear and aggressively so; the music – country rock with a prominent role for Rufus Thibodeaux's fiddle – is just as combative and, after a while, annoyingly repetitive. A sense of unfocused resentment seems, perhaps understandably, to have worked its way into the general tone.

'Stayin' Power' and 'Coastline' both affirm the strength of a relationship, presumably Young's with Pegi, and offer commitments for the future which, though not mentioned as such, must have had as much to do with their son's problems as with their love for each other. A decade later Young would claim that this album was about survival, about 'hanging in there no matter what'; on these two tracks that feeling comes across with an almost violent intensity.

'Union Man', by contrast, is a two-minute satire on unions in the music business. It has the catchiest tune on the album, which perhaps explains why Young uses it again on 'Comin' Apart at Every Nail'. In the latter song, however, the lyrics are not so funny, with Young torn between 'this country sure looks good to me' and the fact that it's 'comin' apart at every nail'. In the first verse he laments the condition of America's ordinary Joe, unemployed and caught between 'the government and the mob', while in the second he bewails the depleted state of America's defences.

This populist equation of organised politics with organised crime was bad enough as a sign of things to come, and the notion that the working man's interests could be furthered by increased military spending was little short of outrageous from a man and an artist supposedly committed to a more humane world. But for anyone wanting to believe that this was all sarcasm or satire – good ol' Neil taking the piss – the last song, 'Hawks and Doves', must have been a great disappointment.

On this song Young pulls all the patriotic strings – from his wife being able to 'dance another free day' to an endless refrain of 'U-S-A' – while shaking his fist at some unnamed enemy. 'Don't push too hard, my friend' sounds more like a threat – and a patronising one at that – than like a friendly warning. 'If you hate us, you don't know what you're saying' is nothing more nor less than the bleat of any bar-stool xenophobe. 'Hawks and Doves' is an ugly song, born in that narrow-minded place most of us sometimes get to visit.

It was a fitting end to an album short on thought and limited in music. For all those of Young's fans who knew nothing of his personal problems, and who'd been expecting a worthy studio successor to the outstanding *Rust Never Sleeps*, the album was a terrible let-down.

Young had also been asked to do the soundtrack for the film *Where the Buffalo Roam*, a 'comedy' based on the life of gonzo journalist Hunter S. Thompson. The resulting album featured music by Hendrix, Dylan, the Four Tops, the Temptations and Credence Clearwater Revival – a fair reflection of Young's taste in mainstream rock. It also included a masterclass in possible arrangements of 'Home on the Range', with Young throwing brass band, strings, fuzz guitar and even an a cappella vocal at the old standard. The latter collision, it must be said, proves strangely moving.

The Young family, meanwhile, was completely immersed in the Program. At first Pegi and Neil bore most of the load alone, but after a few months they started increasing the volunteer input, working out a shift system. Three people were permanently 'on duty', led by either Pegi or Neil through a six a.m. to six p.m. day. On top of this there was the preparation, which filled the evenings – making cards with words and pictures and numbers for the mental-exercise sections of the next day's schedule.

The living room had been rearranged to provide the clear floor areas needed for Ben's crawling exercises, and there was a slanted ladder for him to practise the use of feet and hands for balance and grasping. For two minutes each hour he would wear a plastic mask, which rendered ordinary breathing difficult and thereby encouraged him to take deeper breaths.

Day in, day out, the Program proceeded, and week in, week out. The strain on all the family must have been incredible. Obviously the focus of concern, the one in real pain, was Ben, but this is a book about a man and his music, and the effect of the Program on Young himself – and on his work – has to be considered.

The first striking change was that Young, who had always been free just to take off when he felt like it, sometimes for months on end, no longer had any such outlet. Now a few hours were the most he could hope for, and he generally spent these working on the *Human Highway* movie or in the ranch recording studio. In the past he had usually chosen to record at night, but now the studio could be used only between two and six in the afternoon. And of course there was no prospect whatsoever of his taking his music out on the road.

Young must have felt considerably restricted by all this. And something more. For the first time for a very long time, since at least the signing of his contract with Reprise in 1968, he was not in command of his own destiny. He was not in charge, not alone at the wheel. He was putting others before himself, something that many men, and not a few women, never get around to doing.

If such things can be measured, all of this probably made a better person of him. He thought so, and it certainly seems to have brought him and Pegi closer together. The sad part was that Ben continued to make less progress than they had hoped for. Mentally he appeared to be responding well, but physically there was often no discernible improvement.

With this lack of progress came renewed doubts. Was it all worth it, they wondered, what they were putting themselves through, what they were putting him through? Later on, Young would display great bitterness, calling it 'an almost Nazi kind of programme', policed by guilt. 'You manipulate the kid through a crawling pattern. He's crawling down the hallways, he's banging his head trying to crawl. But he *can't* crawl, and these people have told us that if he didn't make it, it was gonna be our fault, that we didn't do the Program right.' Ben was crying almost all day, it was so hard for him, but they kept going. 'You're brainwashed to think the only thing you can do that's gonna save your kid is the Program, and they have you so scared that if they call and you're not at home, you're off the Program, forget it. You've ruined it for your kid. We lasted eighteen months. Eighteen months of not going out. Eighteen months of not doing anything.' In another interview he said that it was 'the most difficult thing I've ever done'.

Re·ac·tor was made, exclusively on the ranch, during those eighteen months. Around the time Young maintained that the music itself was heavily, even directly, influenced by the Program. The latter was 'driving, implacable, repetitive . . . very strong, very strongly motivated', and so, he thought, was the record.

This, although perhaps true on a superficial level, didn't come anywhere near as close to the heart of the matter as did his comments in later years. Then, comparing music to therapy, he claimed that he had always used the former in the way some people used the latter, as a way of 'getting parts of yourself out'. But over the nightmare years of Pegi's illness and Ben's Program he'd simply shut down his emotions, and 'did things that were more on the surface level, because it was safer'.

* * *

155

Re·ac·tor was the first Young album since *Comes a Time* not clearly split into two halves, and marked a sooner than usual reunion with Crazy Horse. For fans of his *Everybody Knows This Is Nowhere* style, the omens were promising.

And, unfortunately, utterly misleading. *Re·ac·tor* is noisy guitar rock, but there the parallel ends. There is little passion here, little feeling of any kind, unless a general sense of surly restlessness counts as feeling. There is certainly no tenderness or love, and where *Hawks and Doves* was actively, even aggressively upbeat, *Re·ac·tor*, for all its surface sound and fury, is passive and despairing.

On three of the eight songs – 'T-Bone', 'Get Back On It' and 'Rapid Transit' – it seems as if Young has thrown his lyrical towel into the ring. 'T-Bone', which was conceived and recorded in one take, boasts the two immortal lines 'Got mashed potatoes/Ain't got no T-bone' repeated *ad nauseam*, and the other two songs offer little more in the way of ideas. A further three – 'Opera Star', 'Surfer Joe and Moe the Sleaze' and 'Motor City' – have recognisable themes, but these are not so much explored as simply presented. 'Opera Star' suggests 'some things stay the way they are', while 'Surfer Joe' offers 'women and booze' as a universal panacea, and on both songs Young sounds more like a drunk than like a Zen sage. The patriotic fervour is back in 'Motor City', with Young bemoaning the number of 'Datsuns in this town'. His Army jeep is still going strong, despite its lack of a digital clock. Basic is best, and American basic is best of all. Why it's more acceptable for Americans to buy Canadian music than to buy Japanese cars is not explained.

'Get Back On It' is a simple rolling blues number, but the other five of these songs are all guitar-centred hard rock. Despite the presence of Crazy Horse behind him, Young refuses to stretch out on lead guitar, preferring to chop away like a manic rhythm guitarist. The complete lack of lyricism in his playing is presumably intentional, but the resulting sound – harsh, metallic, industrial – only emphasises the emptiness of the lyrics.

So far, so ordinary. Unlike *Hawks and Doves*, however, *Re·ac·tor* had a good new song and an exceptional reworking of an old one. 'Southern Pacific', with its railroad rhythm and subject matter, was the former. Young weaves his love of railways, his sense of things lost – including, perhaps, an idealised America – into the story of an old worker who's been retired and left to 'roll down the long decline'. This version – surprisingly, considering the presence of Crazy Horse, less so considering the rest of the album – lacks the energy that later live versions with the International Harvesters would generate.

The last and best track on the album is 'Shots', reworked from acoustic to electric, and in the process transformed into something extraordinary. The order of verses has been changed since 1978, and the one containing the vow of romantic commitment – 'And so, if you give your heart to me/I promise to you, whatever we do/That I will always be true' – has been expunged by the darkness of the rest.

If 'Southern Pacific' has the comfortable canter of a train, 'Shots' arrives like a horseman of the Apocalypse, propelled by Molina's galloping drums, surrounded by fuzz-tone and buzz-saw guitars and screeches of feedback. Young's quavering vocal spews images of decay and despair, of lives ruled by uncontrollable lusts and fears, out into the dreadful night. This isn't America 'comin' apart at every nail', it's the fleshy mask of civilisation coming away in his hands.

'Shots' may be *Re·ac·tor*'s only artistic *raison d'être*, but throughout the new decade other guitarists and bands would be struggling to find even a quarter of the appalling intensity Young had packed into its seven and a half minutes.

Young seems to have found it easier to work on his movie *Human Highway* than on his music during the spare hours and minutes allowed by the Program, most probably because the film was finished in essentials, needing only the final touches before it could be unveiled for the public. It was finally premièred on 16th August 1982, and received an immediate thumbs-down from the American trade paper *Variety*. A succession of one-off previews followed, but Young had no more success getting a wide distribution deal than he'd had with *Journey through the Past*.

The film is set in a small town with a neighbouring nuclear-power plant, in the near future. Young plays Lionel, a motor mechanic who gets hit on the head early on and drifts off into a fantasy of being a rock star. Not a lot happens in terms of plot, and while Young the co-director manages to indulge his wry black humour and his love of fifties B movies, he does so without ever creating any real laughs or suspense. Lionel was not only 'kind of like Laurel and Hardy rolled into one', but also another side of Young himself, the side he felt the public never appreciated.

Human Highway was arguably a slight improvement on *Journey through the Past* – it didn't carry the burdens of either a soundtrack album or high expectations – but not much more. Young couldn't be criticised for not making a successful commercial film, because that wasn't his intention anyway, or of letting his ego run riot, as Dylan had in *Renaldo and Clara*, but he could be accused of not really having any precise intentions at all. The reasons he gave for making the film were hardly such as to inspire confidence in any sense of overview.

First, he wanted to communicate what was on his mind in whatever way he could, 'so the film was a good way to get away from music for a while so the music would remain fresh'. He also wanted to get away from himself: 'I enjoy being in another character because I'm not Neil Young any more and that's a refreshing situation.' This was all very well – no one could deny that Young had a perfect right to play with other media or other personae as he saw fit – but making a film because it wasn't music, and creating a character because it wasn't him, didn't seem like a very positive or enabling approach. His third reason – 'I got to do some things that I'd wanted to do for a long time' – really tells it all. *Human Highway* is full of ideas, some of them great, which Young had no doubt had for a long time. What they lacked was any coherent context.

The manner in which the movie was made was as significant as Young's reasons for making it. It was, he said, 'made up on the spot by punks, potheads and former alcoholics right there on the stage. It's us, the people who made the movie. We had a story line and a storyboard . . . with little things we wanted to have happening to different characters, and every night my co-director Dean Stockwell and I would get together and plan what we were going to do the next day, and then we would write the dialogue with Russ Tamblyn and give everybody their parts the next morning.'

In other words, they'd more or less improvised it, sacrificing structure and a coherent exploration of ideas on the altar of spontaneity. An image was worth a thousand arguments. Craft was out, art was supposedly in. It worked for him in music, so why not in movies?

The answer was the old one – Salvador Dali could bring the surreal world to life only because he'd learned how to draw the ordinary one. Young had no experience in film-making from the ground up. He was trying to make movies the way he played electric guitar, but there was no mastery of the basic chords, no cinematic Crazy Horse providing the platform from which he could take off and land. So the movies had their nice moments, their nice images, but they never became more than the sum of their parts.

After *Human Highway*, Young himself apparently began to recognise his limitations in this field. In October 1982 he admitted that even the *Rust Never Sleeps* movie had made little money, and that 'film isn't something that comes naturally to me'. 'I tried to paint,' he added, 'but I can't do that. I know I'm not a great film-maker but I have a lot of fun trying.'

And that really says it all. None of Young's films has been great, but none of them has been boring either, which is more than could be said of many a professional film-maker's repertoire. When, in March 1985, an Australian interviewer asked him if he planned to make any more movies, he replied, 'Well, nobody seems to be knocking down my door to get me to make any more films. If I feel like it, and I can shake up the money, I might do it.'

Re·ac·tor sold badly, and this may have been a contributory factor in Young's deciding to leave Reprise. He claimed it was just that both he and the label had had enough of each other after thirteen years, that he 'needed the change'.

He and Pegi had also decided, early in 1982, to leave the Institutes Program. Since at least the latter months of 1981 they'd been trying to balance their own needs with Ben's, wondering whether they were being selfish, wondering just how much improvement in Ben justified just how much disruption of their own lives. It was an impossible equation to work out on their own. At one level they knew, in Young's words, that they 'couldn't take it any more'. At another – how could they do less?

In February 1982 they attended a seminar of the National Academy for Child Development (NACD), an organisation headed by a nephew of the man who'd founded the Philadelphia Institutes, and found many of their doubts and hopes mirrored in what they heard. 'They told us, "Listen, you only need to do this four hours a day. You have to live your life,"' Young said in 1989. They adopted this less rigorous programme, with its greater emphasis on Ben's potential mental progress and, in particular, his communicative skills. Pegi went to work as a volunteer instructor in a local NACD centre, and eighteen months later she and Neil would be named the Academy's Parents of the Year. In the meantime, Young would be taking a new kind of music back on the road.

By 1982 Young's fondness for rust metaphors had given way to a tendency to talk dinosaurs. He liked to say he was one, but only in terms of longevity; his contemporaries were the real dinosaurs, stuck in the past, unable to adapt. They thought the public wanted the same old stuff churned out for ever, but in thinking that they were forgetting how they'd made it in the first place – by offering something new. His own past – the Neil Young of the late sixties and early seventies – was 'like Perry Como'. If he was still taking that stuff seriously, he'd be 'where Crosby, Stills and Nash are today'. No, he was intent on ringing the changes, keeping ahead of the game. 'If you don't experiment,' he would assert in late 1982, 'you're dead! I couldn't keep turning out the same things . . . It's like flogging a dead horse.'

A strong element in the mix was a continuing weariness with his perceived public persona. 'I've been Neil Young for years,' he told one reporter, who wasn't at all surprised. This desire to be someone else – almost anyone else, it seemed at times – would mark several of the interviews he gave during this year of his emergence from the virtual seclusion of the Program.

Still, whatever the motivation, Young's willingness to take chances could only be applauded in a world and an industry where so many chose to play safe. Which direction would he take this time? There were several reasons for taking the high-tech route, for a whole-hearted embracing of the new computer technology. One, no doubt, was sheer perversity – it's not hard to imagine Young's glee at the prospect of confounding his die-hard fans with such a radical image shift: the rustic hippie uncle getting obsessive about shiny machines, with all that distasteful precision.

For the man behind the image it wasn't such a departure. Contrary to the oft-perceived view of him, Young had always been fascinated with the growing impact of computer technology, both on life in general and on his own industry in particular. He'd also always found new music interesting and, for someone fond of claiming he never made any effort to keep abreast of developments, always seemed remarkably aware of what was happening out on the frontiers of the music business. One such development, in 1981, had been Kraftwerk's breakthrough into the American market with their album *Computer World*. Young had been impressed by it, and by the obvious possibilities available to anyone else who shared Kraftwerk's willingness to experiment.

In the late summer of 1981, feeling less than completely satisfied with some of the vocals he'd put down on *Re·ac·tor*, Young went out and bought himself a piece of this brave new world – a vocoder. This was a small machine that computerised sound, allowing someone like Young to 'vocode' (i.e. feed into the computer) any voice – his own, Bing Crosby's, Lou Reed's, anyone's. He would then have four octaves to play with in that voice, could hit any note he wanted, chart its course and tone. He could use his own voice in bass mode, Bing's in falsetto. With a vocoder even Lou Reed could hit a note on the nail.

That autumn, taking advantage of the studio upgrading he'd ordered with the Program's restrictions in mind, Young wrote and recorded two songs he'd written for vocoded vocals around the theme of a computerised world – 'Sample and Hold' and 'Computer Cowboy'. He seems to have been both excited and stimulated by the possibilities of this new music. 'I've always loved machines,' he said later that year. 'I feel that with all the new digital and computerised equipment I can get my hands on now, I can do things I could never do before . . . I know this is just the beginning for me . . . '

Like everyone else he was impressed by the perfect timing of computerised music, but unlike many he didn't also consider it to be a drawback. There was something strangely fascinating, almost unearthly, about such perfection. It wasn't soulless; on the contrary, the '*manipulation*' of machines could be 'very soulful', and in this regard he picked out one new song, 'Transformer Man', as his best for ten years. He admitted to being in 'a very primitive stage of development with all this stuff', but remained in awe of the possibilities. He saw no danger of bypassing the human spirit, only another channel for its expression. After all, he insisted to the many doubters, 'It's still my melodies, my enunciation, my feeling. It just lifts a restriction – why should I *have* to sing with my own voice in 1982, when I can stretch out in different directions?'

Some notion of the range of possibilities he perceived can be gathered from the ideas he had for a video to accompany the *Trans* album. Different characters were created to go with each vocoded voice, including one called Tabulon, with a keypad face he kept hitting. This image, at once funny, visionary and somehow infinitely sad, offered a clue to the third reason for Young's turn in this musical direction – his relationship with his younger son.

Trans, he would say later, 'is about communication, about not getting through. And that's what my son is. You can't understand the words on *Trans*, and I can't understand my son's words.' Throughout the songs he was now writing – prolifically, as if in some great hurry to

161

express what was in his heart – there were references to life lived via a computer. '*Trans* was about all these robot-humanoid people working in this hospital and the *one* thing they were trying to do was teach this little baby to push a button . . . *Trans* is the beginning of my search for communication with a severely handicapped non-oral person.'

On the surface, it would be hard to think of an album theme with greater potential emotional range, or anyone better suited to making such an album than Young, whose reputation in large part rested on an ability to evoke primary emotions like sadness, pain and hope without descending into sentimentality. But with hindsight it's clear he was in no state to make an album worthy of his subject. His stated feeling that this was a part of his life that no one could relate to might seem misplaced – it's not necessary to have experienced disability at first hand to be moved by the struggle to accept or overcome it – but it did serve to rationalise a deep and understandable sense that there were some things he simply didn't want to share with the public. He didn't *want* the message of these songs to be clear or direct. As he said, this was hard enough to talk about, let alone spread across an album. And if he placed his thoughts and emotions out there in the public domain, he also had his children's feelings to consider.

So, he admitted, he 'started hiding in styles, just putting little clues in there as to what was really on my mind'. The desire to express his deeper feelings was overwhelmed by a combination of other factors: the parallel desire to suppress them, an already existing inclination to hide himself in roles (to 'stop being Neil Young'), and the concealing of his true voice in computerised vocals. In such a way, much of the potential power of this music and theme would be lost. Young couldn't let himself be direct, but nothing else – nothing *less* – would really work. He could say that he 'dumped the load on *Trans* . . . told the whole fucking story right there', but he also had to admit that 'it was so well disguised that only I knew what it was'.

In 1992 he went further, identifying *Trans* as 'the beginning of another era, where I was indecipherable and no one could understand what I was saying. That whole era, there's always something wrong. There's always something between me and what I'm trying to say. The invisible shield.'

The adoption of a less rigorous programme for Ben offered Young the chance to take this new music out on the road, and in the spring of 1982, while on vacation in Hawaii, he assembled a band with both this and an album-recording in mind. Those chosen offered an unfamiliar mixture of familiar faces: Ben Keith, Ralph Molina, Joe Lala, Nils Lofgren and Bruce Palmer. The two other members of Crazy Horse – Billy Talbot and Frank Sampedro – would be present on some of the album's tracks, but not on the tour.

Young hadn't played with Lofgren since the Tonight's the Night tour almost a decade earlier, a fact not without significance in that the Trans tour would be Young's most theatrical since those days, and Lofgren would have an important role to play in the theatrics.

Young and Bruce Palmer hadn't played together for even longer, since Palmer's brief stint with CSN&Y in the summer of 1969. In the intervening years Palmer had been surviving on Buffalo Springfield royalties, living with a Sikh sect, playing only the sitar and cultivating a drink problem. Boredom had set in, and earlier that year he had set about trying to persuade his former partners in Buffalo Springfield that a reunion was in order. Perhaps surprisingly, the others had all agreed. More predictably, two agreed dates had since been postponed to accommodate first Young and then Stills. Perhaps partly by way of compensation, Young subsequently asked Palmer to come to Hawaii.

The kind gesture, if that is what it was, nearly backfired. The band cut eight or nine tracks in Hawaii, four of which would appear on Trans and one of which, 'Island in the Sun', remains, in Ben Keith's opinion, an unreleased classic. On their return to the mainland for some warm-up gigs, Palmer was fired, apparently for drink-related unreliability. It seems to have been his good fortune that the only replacements Young could find were musically inadequate. Palmer was re-enlisted on condition that he stay off the sauce.

The album was completed that summer, but would not be released until the end of the year. Trans has nine tracks, and on five of them Young uses the vocoder to effect an electronic distortion of his voice, rendering it unrecognisable to anyone not in the know. Each of these five songs deals in a theme appropriate to its computerised setting. 'Computer Age', 'We R in Control' and 'Sample and Hold' all explore, with neither blind optimism nor blind pessimism, ways in which humans and computers might relate to each other in the future. The protagonist of 'Computer Cowboy' is, in Young's words, 'a twenty-first-century outlaw'. The cowboy gig, which comes with numbered cattle in floodlit fields, is just a front; as Young told his father, 'Late at night he goes into the city and robs computer databanks of memory systems and leaves his alias, Syscrusher, printed over the information he's lifted.' The vocoded 'Come a ky ky yippee yi ay' proved that Young hadn't lost his sense of humour.

'Transformer Man' is Ben, still learning how to 'direct the action with a push of the button', with a look in his eyes that 'electrifies' Young each morning. For someone unfamiliar with Young or his son's handicap there would be no way of knowing this; the song could be interpreted as the story of a young Frankenstein, or simply as some obscure sci-fi fragment. Once you do know what it's about, the song is – no pun intended – transformed. The computerised heartbeat sounds so alone, while the vocoded voices seem to be swimming out of some unimaginable ether, infinitely sad and strange.

In this light the other songs also gather emotional resonance. The vocoded voice on 'Computer Age', for example, begins to sound decidedly ghostly, as if it's trapped in another dimension.

The new version of 'Mr Soul', last recorded with Buffalo Springfield fifteen years before, is a halfway house between the computerised songs and the others. Young's normal voice sings a duet with its computerised cousin, providing in the process a more fatalistic slant on his ode to the disorientating effects of fame. 'Little Thing Called Love' and 'Hold On to Your Love', which open the album's two sides, are both sung in his normal voice, though the latter sets it amid swirling synthesisers. Neither has lyrics worth mentioning kindly, but the former is catchy, and certainly moves more convincingly than most of *Re·ac·tor*, with the electric guitar dancing happily along above the acoustic strumming.

If the bouncy 'Little Thing Called Love' ill prepares the listener for the rest of *Trans*, the rest hardly serves as a suitable entrée to the closing, eight-minute 'Like an Inca'. The song features a continuously repeated eight-note synth riff over a brisk beat, and a lead guitar that simmers without ever boiling over. There are echoes both of the Latinish rhythm Young had adopted for live performances of 'Cortez the Killer' and of the chord progression in Dylan's 'All Along the Watchtower'.

The lyrics also share the two songs' apocalyptic bent, with the rest of the world doomed shortly to follow Atlantis down the proverbial chute. Nuclear annihilation is on the cards, and Young is understandably angry about it: 'Why should we care about a little button/Being pushed by someone we don't even know?' He has two suggestions to make: retreat into a mythical Aztec/Inca past and an apparently contradictory determination to see things as they really are, and act accordingly – 'If you want to get high build a strong foundation/Sink those pylons deep and reach for the sky.'

This is not so much time travel as time-warping, but despite the lack of any rational thread the song still makes some strange sort of sense. As he sings the final lines – 'I feel sad but I feel happy as I'm coming back to home/There's a bridge across the river that I have to cross alone/Like a skipping rolling stone, like an Inca' – there's a sense of liberation, which, though partly explicable in pure musical terms, also derives from a definite feeling that something has been learned and accepted, that somewhere in the song one of the steeper steps on life's long flight has been successfully clambered up.

Like the rest of *Trans*, 'Like an Inca' is different, challenging, brimming with ideas that are either half thought out or half hidden, or both. Young the jungle explorer might have been far from home, even – to judge by the letters he was sending – a little crazy in the head, but he was still out there, and probably eyeing his own reflection in the mirror with much the same look of half-recognition as worn by the hitch-hiking hippie on the album's cover, who stares bemusedly across the highway at the robot trying to bum a lift on the other side.

The so-called Transband's only tour, Young's first for four years, began on 31st August in the French town of Annecy and ended in Berlin's Deutschlandhalle seven weeks later, on 17th October. Young's stated reason for choosing Europe over the US was the debt he owed his fans there after the non-appearance of the Rust Never Sleeps tour, but he may also have reasoned that the kind of show he was offering – experimental, even downright strange – would go down better with European audiences. Computerised music had, after all, originated in that continent, and American audiences were inclined to be more conservative.

There were bound to be some unfavourable comparisons with Young's last visit – the wonderful 1976 tour with Crazy Horse – and indeed there were, but generally it was recognised that this was a different kind of a show: more a 'presentation', less an explosion of self-expression.

One reason the criticism was muted was doubtless that Young chose not to repeat the kamikaze style of his last 'presentation' – the Tonight's the Night tour. The new computerised music was not served up *en bloc*, but scattered through a set designed to appease most of his fans, with electric classics like 'Hurricane' and 'Southern Man' rubbing shoulders with old acoustic chestnuts such as 'Old Man' and 'Comes a Time'. An intimation of what Young now thought of his two most recent albums – *Hawks and Doves* and *Re·ac·tor* – could be found in the fact that throughout the tour, songs from both were conspicuous by their absence.

His appearance was also a matter of note. Both the long-haired lunatic lumberjack of the 1976 tour and the check-shirted, short-haired country farmer of the Rust Never Sleeps extravaganza had vanished, giving way to a man sporting the 'Mafia gameshow host' look: bright green jacket, black shirt, white tie and shades. This strange outfit looked even stranger next to Nils Lofgren, with his gypsy headband flying every which way as he whirled around the stage like a dervish on uppers.

During the tour there were complaints that Young was playing too loud, one reproach being that his guitar was drowning out Lofgren's. Despite this, the two men seem to have worked well together. In several of the *Trans* numbers the pair of them, both wearing vocoders and shades, would strike strange poses and weave patterns in the air with their arms as they swapped computerised vocals. Lofgren, asked whether the movements were rehearsed or ad libbed, simply laughed. 'Neil and I acted so outrageous that those aren't the kind of moves you rehearse – you know what I mean? You don't get in front of a mirror and do weird stuff like that!'

But he was the first to agree that the theatrics were effective, that they gave the audience an access to the pathos of the songs – particularly 'Transformer Man' – which the music alone could not have provided half so well. In Lofgren's words, 'It just put us in this strange place, and it was like being an actor, in a different part, like you were somebody else. And it was great, it just kinda made us both these characters that came alive through music.'

Four of the new songs introduced on the tour would appear neither on *Trans* nor on any subsequent release to date. 'If You Got Love' got the closest, even featuring on some promotional copies of *Trans* before being removed from the official release. A pleasant throwaway with a nothing lyric, it wasn't exactly missed.

'Love Hotel' was played just once, in Birmingham, and even there the band didn't appear to know what they were doing. The words revolve around the love-as-a-hotel metaphor – 'don't get stranded by the lift' – and sound overcontrived. 'Soul of Woman', by contrast, is almost undercontrived. It boasts one of Young's neater paradoxical couplings – 'You can't help nobody until you help yourself/Nobody's gonna help you better than somebody else' – but the musical context is ordinary, the kind of rolling piano blues number that a thousand people have done before, and usually better.

'After Berlin' was also played only once, as a farewell to the tour from the stage of the Deutschlandhalle, but proved to be one of Young's finer unreleased songs. (It was later released on video, but never – yet – on record.) A circular guitar motif over synthesiser chords provides the base for alternating verses and lead-guitar infills. The melody is almost offhand; the words are deceptively simple, and function rather in the manner of planks in a fence – they draw your eyes to the cracks between them. There's a sense of fear seeping out of the song, fear of distances, fear of being locked out of both past and future, fear of a cryptic 'final day'. The endless repetition of the phrase 'Help me' at the end somehow manages to be both soothing and a real cry for succour.

For Young the tour must have been a mixed experience. There had been the occasional round of booing, as fans wanting the old hits found themselves watching a couple of weirdos pirouetting around on stage and singing in squeaky voices, but overall the reception had been as warm as any dinosaur could have hoped for. And at least he'd broken the ice after four years off the road. Henceforth he would again tour regularly – sometimes, it seemed, almost incessantly – and not just for the music and the money. He also had to rediscover himself in the wake of the traumas he'd endured. 'I had to keep playing and playing and playing and not take a break,' he said in 1989. 'I felt disconnected . . . Playing live got me back. That was the only way I could do it.'

Since he was now back out in the world, Young was subjected to all sorts of questions about the state of the nation, his and others. His politics, many assumed, had remained true to their sixties crucible: radical, pacifist, at least vaguely leftist, counter-cultural. He was 'one of us', after all.

But was he? Had he ever been? A great deal of this bundle of assumptions had always been sheer projection on the audience's part, and it had been augmented over the last few years by a large dose of wishful thinking. *Hawks and Doves* hadn't sounded how ol' Neil was supposed to sound, so it had to be sarcasm at best, irony at worst. Young's real ambivalence was too hard to take, particularly over issues on which his audience showed a marked propensity for closed minds.

Unfortunately, Young's 'defection' from this cosy consensus could be ignored only as long as he had the decency not to be too blatant. Yet as the 1980s progressed he grew more, not less, inclined to question some of the assumptions of the – for want of a better phrase – counter-cultural left. Often, I would argue, he did so out of ignorance, at other times out of a sense of white maleness which was obviously a very real part of who he had always been. And sometimes he hit the nail on the head, using his native intelligence and imagination to throw light on matters too long obscured by pseudo-ideological fog.

Of course everyone wanted to hear him condemn Ronald Reagan, the old champion of the right and now the new President. Young preferred to condemn his predecessor Jimmy Carter, for what he considered the serious mistakes of sanctioning a weakening of American military power and, in particular, returning the Panama Canal for no better reason than out of a sense of guilt. Reagan, on the other hand, with what Young called his 'original concept of big government and federal programmes fading away so that communities could handle their own programmes like day care', spoke more directly to the artist's current concern with family matters. 'I thought the idea was good. I thought it would bring people together,' he would say later.

In 1982 he was quite prepared to say that he thought things had improved since Reagan's election, that the American people were 'becoming proud to be a part of it again, on the grandest scale'. As for himself, he told a French reporter with a laugh, he was 'more American than the majority of Americans! A true capitalist pig!'

Young was scornful of those who involved their music in good causes, maintaining that the current anti-nuclear festivals were 'a desperate attempt to return to the sixties'. He was not going to use his art 'to make money for any old cause'; he wouldn't sell himself 'to the world for nothing', whatever that meant. Like Crosby before him, he thought music lasted whereas political issues came and went, but unlike Crosby he was not prepared to condemn nuclear energy out of hand. 'We don't have it down,' he admitted, 'and we don't know what to do with the waste. But how are we going to get to other planets? We need nuclear power to discover what's out there and discover another power source.' In another interview he declared that 'to refuse nuclear energy today is like preferring the horse to the car before'.

Such views, though not inconsistent *per se* with a leftist or even environmentally-minded perspective, were not likely to be popular among Young's natural constituency. And when added to support for Reagan, no matter how partial or focused that support might be, they opened Young up to charges that he had abandoned the ideals of the generation with which he was associated.

If so, Young showed no sign of repentance. At the end of 1982 he might well have retorted, 'You ain't seen nothing yet.'

Once back from Europe, Young decided to dispense with the Transband, preferring to tackle a tour of the US in early 1983 as a solo performer. The first three-quarters of the concert would feature just him on guitar or piano; in the final quarter new technology would be enlisted to fill in for the Transband.

What made the first section of the show interesting was Young's choice of material. For once there were only a few new songs, but audiences were offered ample compensation in Young's new readings of old favourites. 'Revolution Blues' and 'Ohio' were both given intense renditions, with the former sounding more possessed of demonic energy than the electric version on *On the Beach*. 'The Old Laughing Lady' and 'Don't Let It Bring You Down' were also featured; it was as if Young – perhaps deliberately, perhaps unconsciously – was reaching back for those of his songs that focused on the sicknesses of contemporary society. Even on the one outstanding new song, the sad, almost fatalistic 'Are There Any More Real Cowboys?', Young was letting the anger show through in his performances. Despite his recent political comments, he was not sounding like someone enamoured of the status quo.

The sense of doom and gloom was not allowed to dominate the proceedings completely. During the intermission a giant TV-video screen offered Young's sense of humour in the form of a character called Dan Clear, an urbane newsreader and interviewer played by actor Newell Alexander. Dan was wont to give the audience useful information – the location of the nearest fallout shelter, for example – and to offer exclusive backstage interviews with those involved in the show, Young included. 'I started out strong, had some trouble, but finished real well,' the star told him during the intermission in LA.

The final quarter of the show was devoted to material from *Trans*, and here Young used backing tapes and video footage to sing computerised harmonies with himself. Without the band, alone on stage with only his own image to keep him company, Young made the strange soulfulness of songs like 'Transformer Man' even more striking.

Overall the tour was proving an impressive demonstration of how an artist could, to use Young's words about Dylan in 1974, 'live with his people'. He was not only bringing something new and different to the stage, but also offering an imaginative reworking of his past. On this tour Young seems to have had more than his usual strong awareness of his own musical history: the different songs and different eras and different concerns were allowed to interact, to acquire new meanings and shades from each other.

At the end of February the tour was extended for a further five weeks, perhaps unwisely in view of Young's health. He had suffered a dizzy spell on stage early in the tour, and had then fallen victim to a particularly persistent flu virus. As the tour continued, and as the prescribed medications, steroids included, built up in his body, he felt progressively worse.

The night of 4th March was no exception, but Young, despite having a combination of the shivers and the sweats, refused more medication before going on stage in Louisville, Kentucky. At the end of a lacklustre seventy-five-minute set he half stumbled off the stage, bumped into a stagehand, mumbled, 'There's really something wrong with me,' and collapsed.

He later described the scene to his father: 'I remember lying face down on the floor and seeing the carpet very clearly. My eyes were open and I was looking right into the carpet. I couldn't move. Then it was as if I was seeing the whole scene, myself lying on the carpet, the doctor leaning over me, Pegi with her hand on my back just telling me to stay aware, stay there, everything was going to be okay. Meanwhile I was up there, up at the ceiling, watching.'

As the ever sympathetic fans reacted to the concert's cancellation by flinging folding chairs at the stage, the Jefferson County Coroner(!) arrived. He pronounced Young exhausted, gave him Gatorade and chemicals to increase his blood sugar level, and advised him to take a complete rest. About an hour after his collapse Young was able to walk to his bus. He'd been prescribed a course of Halcyon pills, and told to take one a night – but the first proved one too many. He slept for fourteen hours and suffered horrible nightmares, which kept recurring throughout most of the succeeding week. 'For days back at the ranch I was groggy, walking funny ... It took about three weeks for me to get straight, to get back to the point where I could think straight.'

Having recuperated, he set about putting the final touches to his latest record, intended as the follow-up to *Trans*. The latter had been reasonably successful – it would be his last Top Forty album for seven years – but he had no intention of pursuing the same line any further. Over the last six months the feeling expressed in 1982 – that he had only begun to scratch the surface of the possibilities in computerised music – had yielded to his perennial love of switching horses in midstream.

The new album he was finishing represented a return to folk country. The provisional title was *Old Ways*, but exactly how many, if any, of the songs that later surfaced on the 1985 *Old Ways* were included is impossible to tell. 'Are There Any More Real Cowboys?' and 'My Boy' had certainly been written and performed by this time, but there's no evidence that the other seven Young compositions on the later album were yet in existence. Both the old 'Dance Dance Dance' and 'Soul of a Woman' had been played on the solo tour, and were obvious candidates. So was 'The Ways of Love', which eventually turned up on *Freedom*. 'Depression Blues', which later appeared on *Lucky Thirteen*, may conceivably have been written early enough in 1983 to qualify.

If the selection of songs remains unknown, the style of their presentation has never been a mystery. This *Old Ways* was basically *Harvest* revisited. Young had used musicians who'd appeared on either *Harvest* or *Comes a Time*, as well as the former's producer, Elliot Mazer. Like most of *Harvest* it had been recorded over a few Nashville sessions.

Young was pleased with the results – 'so stoked up about that record', as he told James Henke in 1988. He sent the record company a tape with eight songs on it, and waited for the feedback. None came. Eventually, he called them. 'They said, "Well, frankly Neil, this record scares us a lot. We don't think this is the right direction for you to be going in."' It was not Young's first problem with Geffen Records, nor would it be his last.

He'd signed with Geffen after the relative failure of his last Reprise album *Re·ac·tor*, but from the beginning there seems to have been a non-meeting of minds. According to Young, the company had told him that they didn't want to put out the first album he offered them, a collection provisionally titled *Island in the Sun*. It had included two songs later released on *Trans* ('Little Thing Called Love' and 'Hold On to Your Love'), the last-minute exclusion from that album 'If You

Got Love', and the as yet unreleased title track, 'Island in the Sun'.

If the lyrical content of the first three songs was typical of the whole, then the company's rejection may have been a blessing in disguise. This, though, was not their reason for disliking *Island in the Sun*. According to Young, the company's policy was to follow musical fashion: 'The techno-pop thing was happening, and they had Peter Gabriel, and they were totally into that kind of trip . . . They didn't look at me as an artist, they looked at me as a product, and this product didn't fit in with their marketing scheme . . .'

At the time, he had decided to give Geffen and his record company the benefit of the doubt, and for a while this faith appeared to be justified. They were willing to put out *Trans*, which although hardly 'characteristic of Neil Young' – to coin a later phrase – would be easy to promote as a cutting-edge-of-rock product. The first *Old Ways*, however, would not. It was the old hippie with his acoustic guitar again, and Geffen thought that Young was making a mistake. According to the latter, several recording sessions were cancelled without good reason, something he claimed had never happened during his years with Warner Brothers.

Facing a growing feeling that he was being manipulated, Young decided to fight back. If they wanted rock'n'roll, then they could have it. The real thing. As he told the *Village Voice* in 1989, 'I almost vindictively gave them *Everybody's Rockin'*.' The fact that he loved the album – was indeed already half immersed in the new Shocking Pinks persona – was apparently a happy coincidence. He could tweak Geffen's nose and have fun at the same time.

Years later, Young would contend that *Everybody's Rockin'* was one of his best records. 'That record and *Tonight's the Night* are two of my favourites and they're very similar as far as I'm concerned except one is extremely light and the other is extremely heavy . . .'

Or, to put it another way, one is extremely full and the other . . . well, it's empty. *Everybody's Rockin'* comprises ten slices of derivative rockabilly, featuring a couple of vaguely witty lyrics and one attractive melody, all in less than thirty minutes of playing time. The cover – which pictures a slicked-back Neil in a white suit, bathed in pink light – is worth a quick laugh, but this is music that has been done better by others, many times and long ago.

The interesting lyrics belong to 'Payola Blues' – a hymn to fifties DJ Alan Freed with a witty 'cash-a-wad-a-wad-a' refrain – and 'Kinda Fonda

Wanda', in which Young, after admitting to having 'screwed Runaround Sue', claims that 'she wasn't as good as Wanda'. The attractive melody is 'Wonderin'', one of Young's unreleased songs from the late sixties. Though hardly improved, it does suit the rockabilly style and, with a nice guitar line added behind the catchy chorus, sounds good enough to have been a fifties hit.

Unfortunately, that's more than can be said for the other nine tracks. Anyone who liked this sort of material already had more than enough to choose from, sung and performed by people whose heart was in the genre, and who had taken the time and trouble to learn how to make creative use of its limitations. Young, by contrast, seems trapped by them. Too many songs have a similar pace and feel, and his voice doesn't suit the style. The opportunity to try his hand at a few James Burton-style guitar solos has simply been spurned. Instead he bangs happily away at the piano while Ben Keith performs the guitar duties with almost complete anonymity.

There's no doubt that the character and the music featured on the album offered Young a useful disguise and a good basis for part of a live show. *Everybody's Rockin'* may have been fun to make – and even more fun to leave in Geffen's mailbox. But none of this added up to an artistic case for putting the album out. One line from 'Payola Blues' – 'I never hear my record on the radio' – sounded almost too ironic to be true in the context of *Everybody's Rockin'*. It was Young's first, and to date last, boring record.

The Shocking Pinks tour, which criss-crossed America in the summer of 1983, picked up where the winter tour had left off. The Dan Clear character was still dispensing useful advice on the video screen – telling people to keep their heads down if there was a nuclear attack. Before each concert he'd tell the waiting audience they were now going to Young's dressing room, where the singer was being fitted with his wireless mike. Young would appear on screen, together with the roadie who was coiling endless loops of heavy-duty extension cord round and round his neck.

This time, though, Young had a band with him, and a large one at that. Tim Drummond on bass, Ben Keith on a variety of instruments and Karl Himmel on drums were all old Young hands, and in addition there was a trio of Nashville writers/session musicians – Anthony Crawford, Larry Byrom and Rick Palombi – whom Young had dubbed the Redwood Boys, and whose primary function was to provide vocal back-up. Drummond and Keith had also brought their lawyer along, but not for legal reasons: Craig Hayes was having fun playing horn, singing and playing a gangster in the video sequences. In general, this band seems to have contained more musical Jacks-of-all-trades than most of Young's assemblages.

The first two-thirds of the concert followed traditional lines, with Young reinventing both his acoustic and his electric catalogues, and occasionally introducing a new song in his folk-country style. Then, after announcing that he'd like to roll back the years, he would sing 'Sugar Mountain' in front of a video screen showing the current year, 1983. At the song's end he would motion towards the screen with his guitar, and as he disappeared backstage and the numbers slowly rolled backwards, the crew would get on with resetting the stage, bringing on old-fashioned instruments and microphones. When the figures reached 1957, Young would re-emerge in his latest incarnation, as the slicked-back frontman of fifties rockabilly band the Shocking Pinks.

Wearing a white suit, black shirt and pink tie, Young would frenziedly pump the white piano while Tim Drummond played upright bass and Ben Keith tried to look as laid back as Scotty Moore or Hank Marvin. A male vocal group sang back-up, and the Pinkettes kick-danced. (Those in the know would realise that the latter often included the star's wife.)

The show would end with the band leaving the stage and reappearing on the video screen, climbing into a vintage Cadillac. Young would then lean out of the window and do his Presley snarl: 'This leavin' ya just don't *move* me. I wanta play one more song.'

The band's repertoire expanded as the tour went on, with Young playing more guitar than he had on *Everybody's Rockin'* and, surprisingly to many people, offering brass a more prominent role in his music than ever before, with Ben Keith (alto sax), Craig Hayes (baritone sax) and Larry Byrom (trumpet) all involved. In this, the live Shocking Pinks were more than a step ahead of their only album, musically almost a cross between that album's sound and the later live Bluenotes. The proof of this could be heard in the performance of one of the new songs, 'Don't Take Your Love Away from Me', a live recording of which eventually found its way onto 1993's *Lucky Thirteen* compilation. There's a depth, almost a majesty, to the band's music on this track, with Young laying searing guitar lines across waves of brass and cascading drums.

The Shocking Pinks even came complete with a history, as documented in the song 'Get Gone', a live version of which also turned up on *Lucky Thirteen*. It was the old story – hope, more fun than money, too little success and too many drugs. The fictional band's final collective act, sad to say, was to climb aboard a plane 'a little low on fuel'.

And of course the short life of the Shocking Pinks offered Young yet another persona to hide in, yet another parallel existence to embrace. 'I got *way* into that guy,' he said later; 'I was that guy for months. He was out there.'

While Young was 'out there', David Geffen was trying to run a business, and *Everybody's Rockin'* made about as much commercial sense as becoming a Buddhist. Young could see Geffen's point of view – 'he wanted to make a million dollars, and I was in another world' – but such understanding went only so far. The company, according to Young, had 'buried *Everybody's Rockin'*. They did less than nothing. They decided, "That record's not going to get noticed. We're going to press as few of those as possible and not do anything."'

He no doubt complained, perhaps offered Geffen another chance to put out the first *Old Ways*. Geffen's response, when it came, was as ludicrous as it was unexpected. 'A guy came and banged down my door,' Young would later remember, 'and slapped this thing in my face.'

'This thing' was a lawsuit. Young was being sued to the tune of $3 million, for not being 'commercial', for turning in albums that were not 'characteristic of Neil Young'. Once he'd got over the immediate shock, Young must have had trouble keeping the tears of laughter out of his eyes. At last he could tell everyone he'd achieved his greatest ambition – he wasn't himself any more.

Any such euphoria probably faded as fast as the initial surprise. The idea that he could be sued for not being himself might appear ridiculous, but Geffen was also claiming that Young had accepted advances without signing a proper contract. And whatever the merits of the case, who in their right mind would want to get involved in a protracted legal battle with a corporation, particularly when that corporation had ultimate control over the release of their future musical output?

Young also had other causes for concern around this time, some professional, some personal. The Shocking Pinks tour, although in retrospect an important stepping-stone in Young's musical development, had not been an unmitigated success. Audiences had enjoyed the performances' humorous trappings, but the response to the music had been decidedly mixed, especially where the newer rockabilly material was concerned. It seems likely that Young lacked the confidence in this particular musical direction to pursue it any further, at least in the short term.

But what other directions were open to him? He'd only just abandoned computerised music, and Geffen had made it clear that they didn't want the acoustic hippie back. One obvious option was a reunion with Crazy Horse, and it was this that Young decided to try, despite the less than satisfactory outcome of their last work together on *Re·ac·tor*. The band rehearsed in private, then played live gigs at the Catalyst in Santa Cruz on 6th and 7th February 1984.

These performances, which have since been widely bootlegged, featured the usual stalwart choices – 'Cortez the Killer', 'Cinnamon Girl', 'Powderfinger' et al – and several new songs which wouldn't be released for more than two years, if at all. Renditions of 'Touch the Night', 'Violent Side' and 'I've Got a Problem' would all eventually surface on the Crazy Horse-less *Landing on Water*, while 'So Tired', 'We're Gonna Rock Forever', 'Your Love' and 'Stand By Me' remain unreleased.

The mood of all these last four was subdued, vaguely menacing, as if the protagonist was staring out at life through a rain-covered window. The man who's 'gonna rock forever' makes it sound more like a life sentence than a joy to behold, while the man imploring someone to 'stand by me' also knows that he has to 'fall', that there's 'blood on the streets', that he's 'incomplete'. Billy Talbot was given the vocals on this one, perhaps because Young wanted to distance himself from the lyric. As for the music, it seemed like an uglier variant of their usual sound, retaining the power and the rhythm, but lacking the lyricism which normally offered such a potent counterpoint.

Young was satisfied enough to take the band into the studio. Once there, however, nothing went right. He tried to bring in a couple of more 'technically advanced' musicians to help out, but the mix didn't gel, and Crazy Horse were resentful. The sessions, in Young's word, 'sucked' and, after several weeks' work had failed to deliver a single track, were abandoned.

This failure to make music with his faithful old stand-bys must have added to Young's worries, the chief of which had for some time now been Pegi's pregnancy. Understandably enough, the two of them had found it hard to face the prospect of bringing another handicapped child into the world, but Young had had himself checked, and had been told once more that it was pure coincidence that he had two children with cerebral palsy.

Such reassurances notwithstanding, the long wait between conception and birth must have been agonising for both parents. But it was more than worthwhile. Amber Jean, Young's 'beautiful little girl', was born on 15th May 1984.

Geffen might be able to stop Young making records, but they couldn't keep him off the road. In later years he would say that the company's refusal to accept the folk-country *Old Ways* simply made him all the more determined to make such an album. Indeed, the more they resisted, the more country it became.

There were other good reasons for Young's self-immersion in country music over the next eighteen months. On the negative side, 1980s rock music struck him as increasingly devoid of substance, 'more concerned with fashion and image', less concerned with the ordinary lives of anyone over twenty-one. For someone now approaching forty this was not only an aesthetic issue; it was almost like a professional death sentence. It might be better to burn out than to fade away, but Young wasn't ready to go just yet. How could a rock musician grow old gracefully, he wondered aloud in interviews. He still had the urge to 'jump around' out there on stage playing rock'n'roll, but he couldn't help noticing how young the audience was, and somehow it seemed as if he was straining to be something he wasn't.

The sense of community felt by many rock musicians in the sixties and early seventies also appeared to have vanished; it was a manager-eat-agent world out there, where art was spelt with a capital $. Country music wasn't exactly a cottage industry either, but it did seem to Young to have preserved a sense of community among its practitioners and its audience. 'I see country music, I see people who take care of their own,' he told Adam Sweeting in 1985. 'You got seventy-five-year-old guys on the road. That's what I was put here to do, you know. So I wanna make sure I surround myself with people who are gonna take care of me. Because I'm in it for the long run.'

The audiences also appealed to him. Out on the road that summer with the International Harvesters he played a lot of state fairs, whole-day events for the family with sideshows, competitions and picnicking, where everyone stayed on for the evening's concert. For Young, who'd spent much of the last five years completely absorbed in the joys and traumas of his own family, such events must have served as an affirmation, not only of his own priorities in life, but of a whole set of values. This was an

America he could believe in, one apparently far removed from 'fashion and image', one where family life was central, where 'community' was more than the wishful thinking of sociologists, where simple verities still held sway. It was a world still in touch with the rhythms of nature, a world where the worship of God still competed, at least nominally, with worship of the dollar.

It was also a world far removed from urban problems, a world that distrusted intellectual complexity, a world that prized individualism and feared individuality. Its prejudices were also overwhelmingly white, male and heterosexual.

Young had always kept this world in his head, co-existing with another, more humane, feminine and tolerant world, and much of his sharpness as an artist had come from the interplay between the two. For him fully to embrace one at the other's expense would be dangerous indeed.

During the two years of touring with the International Harvesters, Young wrote and performed a number of songs that have not, as yet, been officially released. 'Silver and Gold' and 'Amber Jean' offered simple paeans to his wife and daughter respectively, but 'Razor Love', by contrast, was one of his more enigmatic compositions. It begins, 'I got to bet that your old man/Became fascinated with his own plans,' but the identity of the 'old man' is never made clear.

'Good Phone' is just a clever throwaway, while 'Grey Riders', which watches a ghostly line of horsemen go past, has little more to recommend it than a strong dose of atmosphere. Supernatural forces – this time in the person of the devil – also make an appearance in 'Hillbilly Band', but here the lyric cracks open to reveal the Young beneath: 'I'm mad as hell at something that I don't understand/Thank God I'm on the road tonight with this old hillbilly band.'

None of these songs is bad, but the only memorable unreleased song from this period is 'Interstate'. The song's melody would later be part-cannibalised for 'Harvest Moon', but the Harvesters arrangement, with 'Hurricane'-style organ and Spanish guitar solo, is lovelier, more original, and well attuned to Young's recurrent theme of yearning for home.

Absorption in the country-music community may have facilitated Young's move politically to the right, but there's no doubt that he was already leaning that way for reasons of his own. Perhaps being surrounded by similarly-disposed people simply removed the last inhibitions he had about speaking his mind. At any rate, through 1984–5 he seemed to lose at least some of the healthy ambivalence that had characterised his statements in years past.

His most striking volte-face came with the peace issue. Of course he continued to insist, as Reagan and Thatcher always insisted – as the Pentagon insisted! – that peace was the ultimate goal, but now there was also a strident acceptance of the right's traditional assertion that American strength was a prerequisite for any lasting peace.

He was fed up with Americans feeling guilt for past wrongs – 'You know, you can't always feel sorry for everything that you did.' Vietnam and Afghanistan represented polar opposites: while American involvement in the former was just a good turn that went wrong, Soviet involvement in the latter was simply a matter of 'killing people left and right'. This is not the place to argue the pros and cons of either imperial adventure; suffice it to say that Young was exposing nothing so much as his own ignorance. His comments on Reagan's military build-up were similarly unenlightened. As would become obvious in the 1990s, the Soviet Union was not and never had been militarily ahead of the US, as Young and so many Pentagon spokesmen throughout the eighties liked to claim.

In any case, this was hardly the point. Even if the Soviet Union had been ahead in the arms race, even if Soviet aggressions hadn't been mirrored by American aggressions through the seventies and early eighties, could building more and more nuclear weapons – Star Wars et al – be any sort of answer for a man with Young's sensibility and past record to espouse?

He called it playing hardball – the usual macho expression. He admitted he'd seen things differently in 1967, but he was older now, with a family. It might be – in fact it was – 'fucking nuts' to spend billions on weapons, and Young agreed 'idealistically' with anyone who said that America shouldn't. 'Practically', though, he thought that it should. America had to take care of its own, which meant being strong, which meant spending billions on weapons.

When asked if this wasn't an 'every man for himself' philosophy, Young doesn't seem to have been too sure. 'Sort of,' he told Sweeting, 'but . . . I think it's more like every man for his brother than it is every man for himself. That's how I look at it. I think it's real important to be strong.'

This was neither realism nor ambivalence. It was either simple confusion or bad faith.

In a world that seems, in the proverbial phrase, bent on going to hell in a handbasket, any intelligent response must surely include an element of conservatism. As the twentieth century draws to an end, human beings seem to have less and less control over many of the forces that affect their lives, and, like our physical environment, we increasingly need protection from the soulless interplay of technological innovation and market forces.

The tricky questions, of course, are about choosing what we should conserve and how, and about where and when we should be continuing to push for change. Few would deny the importance of the family in any community, but many object to the championing of family values when such sponsorship merely serves as a cover for the dismantling of community provision.

These are not simple issues, and Young should not be taken too seriously to task for failing to make any better sense of the world than most other people. But his idealisation of the country community, and his adoption of the nationalistic values that seem to rub shoulders so easily with such rural romanticism, would have carried more creative force if they had not involved a denial of other worlds less fortunate than rural America. In the last resort, 'every man for his brother' should mean more than every man for his fellow American farmer.

Sometime between September 1984 and March 1985, Young's problems with Geffen were amicably resolved. According to Young, the two parties agreed that 'I would continue to make records as I felt fit and they would continue to release them'. At last he could make and release his country album.

To anyone who'd been listening to Young talking politics over the last year, *Old Ways* must have come as something of a surprise. Far from being a ringing endorsement of the country community and its values, let alone a redneck manifesto, the album proved thoughtful and musically diverse. The vision of America in Young's music was, it seemed, a more tolerant, more true one than the one he dispensed to journalists.

The album opens and closes with songs about restlessness. The country standard 'The Wayward Wind', with its wishful self-portrait of the American male – unable to settle down, scattering broken hearts behind him – is given an earnest reading, complete with wailing harmonica and scudding strings. Like 'Four Strong Winds' it aches with yearning, although here there's a certain smugness seeping through the angst.

The self-satisfaction is up front on 'Get Back to the Country', which opens with fiddle and Jew's harp trading licks, before moving into full banjo hoedown mode. The song paints Young's life and career in urban rock'n'roll as a momentary diversion from the real thing, which, if we can believe the equally exuberant 'California Sunset', is a countryside that doesn't get snowed on.

Things get more serious with 'Are There Any More Real Cowboys?'. The intro, with its thudding bass-and-drum combination, sounds like a *Harvest* out-take, but both harmonica and vocals – with Willie Nelson handling one verse – are more sombre than anything on the earlier album. This is a countryside swathed in dark clouds.

The lyric is less clear than it at first appears, intertwining three separate but related strands: a lament for the cowboy's traditional way of life, a condemnation of the phoney mythologisation of that lifestyle, and a general plea for family farms facing death-by-progress. The melody is memorably sad, the lines are full of evocative images – the 'dusty pick-up', the 'load of feed before the sun gets high', the modern cowboy 'snorting cocaine when the honky-tonks all close' – and as a general lament for something passing, the song works well.

There is another way of looking at it, however. The 'houses creeping up on the land' may be despoiling some rural Arcadia, but they're also needed for the huge number of American homeless. A concern for the latter might lead one to question the intrinsic value of this cowboy way of life. Is it so worthy of saving? Close to nature, yes; simply honourable, maybe; but also macho to the core. Young may not think that real cowboys should be snorting cocaine or wearing sequins, but it's no accident that in live performances of the song the cocaine reference always gets a big cheer from the part of his audience high on testosterone. It is perhaps telling that the fate of the cowboy and the fate of family farms could be so inextricably linked in his mind, as if the romantic male myth of the one could be stretched to cover the other.

The title song shares the same thought-provoking confusion, here set to a rollicking acoustic tune. 'Old ways can be a ball and chain,' he sings, in the context of finding that he's got 'set in his ways'. Old habits can also be hard to get rid of – fortunately, in some cases: Young thinks the 'old ways' of Reaganomics are turning the American economy around. What the song seems to be saying is that the past is always a powerful factor, sometimes for good, sometimes for bad, sometimes for both. It's a pity Young didn't apply this hard-won wisdom to the creation of

'Are There Any More Real Cowboys?', and offer at least some passing acknowledgement that the American cowboy does not represent the final goal of human evolution.

'Once an Angel' is a heartfelt declaration of love for Pegi, a lovely ballad dominated by piano and steel guitar, which accomplishes Young's perennial trick of skirting the banks of sentimentality without ever quite falling in. 'My Boy' uses banjo and fiddle to much the same effect, as Young tackles the universal parental astonishment at the speed with which children grow. Both these songs are near-perfect evocations of common emotions, simple to the point of wisdom.

So much so, in fact, that the transition from each to the song that follows is vaguely disorientating. This is particularly true of 'Misfits', which rears its strange head out of the utter calm bequeathed by 'Once an Angel'. The song recounts three situations – a crew watching videos in a space station, a hooker collapsing in a hotel lobby, a Native American riding down an empty Dakota highway – which, like the three scenes in the earlier 'Broken Arrow', appear unconnected by anything other than a profound sense of dislocation and isolation.

Young said that 'there are a lot of science-fiction overtones, time-travel overtones, in "Misfits"', but then seemed partly to contradict himself by claiming that all three events could be taking place at the same time. He didn't really know, of course: the song had just appeared in his head, and he'd 'jotted it down on a piece of paper'.

Whatever meaning you derive from it – and there is perhaps a clue to something in the Native American's inability to be himself outside past dreams of saloons and rodeos – 'Misfits' is undoubtedly a powerful song, its bizarre lyrics enhanced by their musical setting, with Joe Allen's insistent upright bass and strings in shuddering waves. 'Bound for Glory' (which follows 'My Boy') is more traditional-sounding, a piano-driven rolling ballad with omnipresent harmonica, and country veteran Waylon Jennings on lead vocal for one of the verses. On the surface the lyrics are simpler too, but beneath it the scope for doubt begins to grow. Paul Puterbaugh in *Rolling Stone* thought that the song was a send-up of 'Me and Bobbie McGee', while David Jennings in the *Broken Arrow* fanzine argued that it was a 'decrying of the tendency to romanticise brief affairs'. There's also a case for seeing it as sharing a pop-song pedigree with Gene Pitney's 'Twenty-Four Hours from Tulsa' – a sort of 'Forty-Eight Hours from Winnipeg'.

It's not that the facts are in doubt – a bored trucker picks up a girl who's past caring and they spend the night in his cab – but the value of the protagonists' shared experience. Is the song's title a satire on the travel-is-freedom lifestyle, a sarcastic description of their quick one in the Canadian wilderness, or a statement on love's simple glory? Or all three? In its way, 'Bound for Glory' gets even closer to life's mystery than 'Misfits'.

The closing 'Where Is the Highway Tonight?' echoes 'The Wayward Wind' as a study in male restlessness, but this time thoughtfully, in the context of a real relationship. The hero is happy where he is, but he stills hears the highway call, and knows that there is no simple answer, that whichever path he chooses will both enrich him and cost him dear. It is a man's song, but not one with any proselytising intent. Here, in one of his best songs of the decade, Young is prepared to explore, rather than simply celebrate, the male experience.

Young saw *Old Ways* as coming third in line after *Harvest* and *Comes a Time*. Although it lacks the easy grace of the earlier two albums, there is a case for saying that it possesses more depth, both musically and lyrically, than either of its forebears. At the time of its release, though, it was completely misunderstood. One reviewer of the album, Allan Jones in *Melody Maker*, thought that Young had adopted 'the superficially sentimental posture of bucolic redneck values only to savagely undermine the existing platitudes and potential psychopathy of Reagan's troubled America'. *Old Ways*, according to Jones, was 'a bitterly ironic, violently hilarious record, full of scathing sarcasm'.

This was utter nonsense, as any examination of Young's life and opinions during this period makes absolutely clear. It was also a slur on the album and its author. Sarcasm, as they say, is the lowest form of wit, whereas *Old Ways* is probably Young's most perceptive album of the 1980s. It does explore what could loosely be described as redneck values, but refuses either to condemn or to condone them out of hand.

Young may not have drawn lines where the more liberal members of his following would have liked them drawn, but he had made it clear that the world was not as simple as either they or their country cousins would have liked to believe.

7

THIS FEEDBACK'S FOR YOU

'I refuse to involve my art in a good cause,' Young had stated forcefully in 1982. Music lasted for ever, 'whereas the charity work will be something different each week'.

At the time it hadn't been such an unpopular thing to say. The Reagan/Thatcher era was still bathed in the golden glow of false expectations, and the only rock musicians showing any great desire to help the rest of the world were Young's old cronies from the sixties, dinosaurs one and all. By the middle of 1985, though, things had changed dramatically. Suddenly, over a few months, charity work had become an indispensable item in any mainstream rocker's career. Global concern was in.

Later in the year Young would describe this as part of 'a huge resurgence in the pop culture in the last year'. 'For the last ten years,' he said, 'there was a desert in that area, but now it seems the consciousness of the sixties and the early seventies has come back.' It was 'a more adult version of what we were starting to do in the sixties'. Given his 1982 sentiments, one could be forgiven for wondering if he had felt that way at the beginning of the year.

The spark that ignited the rock community's explosion of concern was one man's reaction to the Ethiopian famine. In late 1984 the Boomtown Rats' Bob Geldof took the lead in the organisation and recording of Band Aid's 'Do They Know It's Christmas?', which became the biggest-selling single ever in the UK, and raised an enormous amount of money for famine relief. An American clone, which was also made with Geldof's involvement, followed in January 1985: USA for Africa's 'We Are the World'.

An American album was also planned, and the man in charge, Quincy Jones, decided he needed a Canadian contribution. Young was one of those invited by producer David Foster to be a part of what was called the Northern Lights for Africa Society, a band put together to record a

184

song for the album. Foster, Bryan Adams and Jim Vallance had written 'Tears Are Not Enough' for the occasion, and the assembled group of Canadian luminaries – which included Joni Mitchell, Gordon Lightfoot, Ronnie Hawkins and Anne Murray – duly gave of their best. Young, informed by Foster that he was a singing a little flat, riposted, 'Hey man, that's my *style!*' The producer must have thanked his lucky stars that Leonard Cohen wasn't there as well.

One good deed led to another. On 13th July 1985 two satellite-linked concerts were held in London and Philadelphia for Live Aid. Crosby, Stills, Nash and Young were one of the acts invited to perform at the American location, and despite his stated reservations about both charity work and playing with CS&N – Crosby was out of jail on an appeal bond at this time – Young agreed to take part.

There's no reason to doubt his or anyone else's motives in this regard. What rock musician, given the chance to help a portion of suffering humanity by performing in front of a global audience – with all the artistic, ego and commercial boosts such exposure would entail – could possibly refuse? Certainly in Young's case the appearance at Live Aid did not apparently indicate any change in political views. A few months later he would be telling the *Washington Post* how he owed almost everything he was to the American system, how patriotic he was, and how he still supported Reagan's arms build-up. Any possible connection between a world awash in weaponry and the economic plight of the countries Live Aid was seeking to help seems to have passed him by.

One of the songs he chose to sing at the concert – one of the few *new* songs sung by anyone – was somehow symbolic of his position. 'Nothing Is Perfect', according to Adam Sweeting, was 'a strikingly forthright declaration of Young's current absorption with family life and an almost gung-ho enthusiasm for Ronald Reagan's America'.

The song's first verse has Young talking about his children and wife and home, and generally acknowledging how much he has to be happy about. The second has him saying much the same about his adopted country, lauding its natural abundance, the mental strength of its soldiers, the community spirit of its workforce. The chorus follows each statement of good fortune with the words 'But nothing is perfect in God's perfect plan/Look in the shadows to see/He only gave us the good things so we'd understand/What life without them would be'.

This notion, that being fortunate should make us more aware of those who are not, clearly makes sense, particularly in the context of Live Aid.

But – not for the first time in Young's career – the sense of the song is belied, indeed almost destroyed, by its tone. He sets these lyrics in one of those sticking-together-through-thick-and-thin country ballads – music that tells its own conservative story. And once he has added a positive reference to 'Stand By Your Man' and thrown in a plug for the 'hostages at the airport', the song begins to reek of self-righteous narrow-mindedness, Middle America-style.

Fortunately for Young – and for those who would benefit from his energy and attention – the following year saw the birth of two charities that he could serve without qualms. He wouldn't sell his art for nothing, he'd said in 1982, but both of these were assuredly something.

Farm Aid was in fact conceived on stage at the Live Aid concert in Philadelphia. Between songs, Bob Dylan – master of the iconoclastic throwaway – had mumbled, 'Maybe they can take one or two million and use it to pay the mortgages on some of the farms.' This remark, reflecting the xenophobia that had occasionally surfaced in Dylan's work over the previous five or six years, did not pass unnoticed. For several reasons. It might run completely contrary to the spirit of Live Aid, but it did touch a chord in two different groups: the America-firsters who wanted to do something to help *Americans*, and the liberals who wanted to do something to stop the corporate carve-up of rural America which Reagan's policies were encouraging. Hell, the small farmer *was* America! The cause of his salvation could unite liberal and redneck under one banner. For Young, still with one foot firmly planted in each camp, it was almost too good a cause to be true.

He'd actually missed Dylan's comment on stage, but Bob was kind enough to repeat it later at the hotel. Young was impressed. 'You see,' he said, 'even before Live Aid was over, everybody was trying to figure out what's next, how we can do something. It worked out that we have a problem in this country that is really something that if you have pro-American feelings, and want to make things right, you could get behind. I can't imagine anyone *not* getting behind it. How can you sit down at the dinner table with your family and say "Pass the corn" without relating to what's going on here?'

A few days later, he and Willie Nelson discussed the matter as they worked on the video for 'Are There Any More Real Cowboys?', and decided to pursue the matter. On 9th August, Nelson met with a golfing buddy, James Thompson, who also happened to be the State Governor of Illinois; the nascent Farm Aid was promised the University of Illinois's football stadium for a concert. John Mellencamp took on the job of filling the concert bill with rock stars, while Nelson gathered in the country contingent. Young, with a thoroughness that did him credit, set about discovering exactly what it was the farmers really needed.

'We started on a purely emotional level,' he admitted, but the further into the problem he got, the more he learned. Young said that at the beginning 'we thought we could help the farmers out, help them buy back their land and straighten it out' but it soon became apparent that throwing money at the farmers, even if enough could be raised, would provide only a short-term fix. What the farmers themselves wanted, as Young discovered in meetings with them, was reform. In the Carter era, many had taken out high-interest loans, and during the Reagan years, as prices for their produce had plummeted, interest rates on the loans had stayed high, creating an unbridgeable gap between income and debts. The problem could not be solved except in Washington. Young conceded that it was ironic, his being involved in politics, but considered it 'a natural progression'.

As luck would have it, a bill the farmers supported was already seeking passage through Congress. Sponsored by Iowa Senator Tom Harkin, the proposed legislation claimed to offer a major rise in the farmers' profit margins, and only a slight accompanying rise in consumer prices, through referenda-agreed production ceilings.

It also threatened to put a few corporate noses out of joint. As soon as it became apparent that Farm Aid was becoming, at least in part, a propaganda vehicle for the Harkin Bill, the organisers started getting phone calls from people eager to explain what a shoddy piece of legislation it would be. Young decided to check things out for himself. He rang Harkin in Washington and went through the list of those who had contacted Farm Aid with criticisms of the bill. To no one's great surprise they all turned out to be representatives of conglomerate agribusiness. Satisfied, Young then went to Washington to get himself thoroughly briefed, not only on the Harkin Bill but on every aspect of the problem. As he listened, Young said, he 'tried to remember the farmers and the looks on their faces'.

The Farm Aid concert – the first in what turned out to be a still unfinished sequence – took place on 22nd September, with Young and Nelson opening the fifteen-hour show at the unearthly hour of 9.45 a.m. Some of those sharing the stage, and the live TV coverage, were Joni Mitchell, Roy Orbison, Bonnie Raitt, Rickie Lee Jones, BB King, John Fogerty, Bob Dylan, Billy Joel, Hall and Oates, X, Johnny Cash, Don Henley, Lou Reed, Foreigner and Tom Petty. A sum of $10 million was raised to be spent on psychiatric counselling – suicides among American farmers were up twenty per cent – and on legal aid for those fighting loan foreclosures on their farms.

There were some niggling doubts about the wonderfulness of it all. For all the talk about this being something that affected all Americans, the musical entertainment was almost exclusively provided by white faces. As for the rest of the world, well, the refrain throughout was 'It's time we did something for us'. Most of those present seemed blissfully unaware that American-controlled institutions like the World Bank and the IMF had been doing something for them at the Third World's expense for several decades. Live Aid had at least had the decency to put humans first, flag-waving second.

Even some of the performers found this distasteful. John Mellencamp admitted to getting a little confused as the bile of national chauvinism oozed out through the liberal crust. 'That's not why I was there,' he said, but he was prepared to put up with it for the sake of the cause – 'you can't go shooting all the dogs cos one's got fleas'.

He may have been right. And keeping Farm Aid within the family, so to speak, also had its advantages. Live Aid was so universal, so holy, that it seemed able to keep itself above politics; Farm Aid didn't have the same safe option. The performers might have been trumpeting 'America first', but many of them went beyond bathing America's farmers in a warm and ultimately empty sense of solidarity, by openly lobbying for specific political legislation, and by asking people to write to their congressional representatives in support of the Harkin Bill. In the last analysis, any concert denounced as 'a carefully orchestrated political event', as this one was by the president of the Illinois Farm Bureau, must have had something good going for it.

Young's second charity of choice was closer to home. His and Pegi's experience with Ben had persuaded them of the need for a school in the San Francisco Bay area that specialised in teaching severely handicapped non-oral children to communicate – '. . . kids that can't make it in normal schools,' Young explained, 'because people think they're dumb, because they can't communicate. We're trying to teach them how to communicate using all kinds of devices and interfaces and computer programs. We're trying to design tools, to make a universal tool that all handicapped people could use, no matter what their handicap . . . We have a long way to go and we're working at it.'

Setting up the Bridge School, which Pegi intended to run on a full-time basis, occupied much of 1985–6. Thereafter the provision of financial support for the school would become one of Young's primary concerns. Limited-edition photographs would be sold to raise money for the school, and what would eventually turn into a series of annual benefit concerts began in November 1986 at the Shoreline Amphitheater in Mountain View, California. Some 17,000 people paid to see Don Henley, Tom Petty, Bruce Springsteen, Robin Williams and CSN&Y.

The latter's reunion, which had been made possible by Crosby's completion of his jail term, featured performances of 'Only Love Can Break Your Heart', 'Change Partners', 'Find the Cost of Freedom', 'Ohio', 'Hungry Heart' (with Bruce Springsteen) and, of course, 'Teach Your Children'. This reunion would also prove the jumping-off point for yet another attempt at the ever elusive second CSN&Y studio album.

Young had been living a fairly reclusive life for much of the last five years, and one of the advantages of doing benefits like Live Aid and Farm Aid was that he could get to meet and talk music with a large number of his fellow musicians. These did not include just his contemporaries in the dinosaur section, but those who had come to prominence in the late seventies and early eighties, many of whom had been influenced by him.

In fact, throughout the eighties Young's status as a musical forebear would seem almost permanently on the rise, as group after group stood up to say how musically influential his earlier albums had been, and how inspiring they had found his whole career as an exercise in artistic integrity. While Young had been abandoning rock for the age-friendly pastures of country, new bands like Green on Red, Jason and the Scorchers, the Dream Syndicate, the Long Ryders, the Beat Farmers and Dinosaur Jr were taking up the torch he had long kept burning with Crazy Horse.

Young was listening to the new music, as he always had. In March 1985 he said that he liked several of the new American country groups, and recognised the quality in U2's work. Less predictably he expressed admiration for the Eurythmics and the Thompson Twins.

Perhaps the exposure to all these different musics made him more aware of how limited country was as a genre; perhaps contact with the likes of Lou Reed gave him reason to believe that it was possible to rock on through his forties without looking or feeling ridiculous. In any case, he had never really given up on rock'n'roll: his performances of 'Down by the River' on the International Harvesters tours might have carried more country trappings than the old Crazy Horse version, but in essence they were still hard-edged rock music.

And, as always with Young, change was its own justification. After two summers with the Harvesters, after finally forcing a country album – and a good one at that – down Geffen's throat, he had simply got bored with country. He wanted to rock again.

But not with Crazy Horse, not yet; the sour taste of the 1984 sessions must still have been rankling. No, it was time for something different, once again. In the spring of 1986, news leaked out that Young was making an album called *Landing on Water*, and that it offered a feast of synthesisers.

The album, when it came, carried on its sleeve the information that Young played guitar, Danny Kortchmar bass, Steve Jordan drums, and all of them played synthesiser. There's no doubting, particularly after *Old Ways*, that *Landing on Water* has a contemporary sound, and that state-of-the-art computerised keyboards were used in its creation. It's an often impressive album, if somewhat unlovable.

Two British groups – the Who and the Police – seem to have left their influential mark. The drums are out front, the bass often carries the melody, and the lead guitar is more often found chopping out chords than playing notes. Both Young's voice and his guitar – when it's being used in a lead role – are buried in the mix, and the consequent flattening of the sound compresses the music. The overall impression is akin to that of meeting someone who is apparently full of passion and energy and enthusiasm – until you look in their eyes, which are brimming with cold anger.

The sound suits the lyrics. On *Old Ways* Young had allowed his life back into his music, but *Landing on Water* is something of a relapse: if the songs on the latter album are self-expressive, then both the self and the expression are well disguised. Young appears to be more interested in tossing around a few ideas than in examining his emotional life – a legitimate enough ambition, but not one that has ever worked particularly well for him.

With their machine-line synth riffs, the first two songs – 'Weight of the

World' and 'Violent Side' – both sound like candidates for the soundtrack of a remade *Metropolis*. The first tells of how repressed the protagonist was before discovering true love; the second seems to agree with Freud that repression is an essential prerequisite of civilisation.

'Hippie Dream', with its ominous bass line and synthesised tremolo, has the most interesting lyric on the album. Allegedly an open letter to David Crosby, it also affords a glimpse of Young's own confusion concerning their mutual heritage. Still in his Freudian groove, he portrays hippie self-indulgence as a slippery slope to violence and addiction – the 'tie-dye sails' become 'the screamin' sheets'. It's not that simple, though. The song's opening admonition – 'Take my advice, don't listen to me' – suggests that Young himself is still a believer. 'Just because it's over for you don't mean it's over for me,' he sings, before claiming that it's still 'a victory for the heart every time the music starts'. In the end it's not so much the hippie dream that has failed as too many of the hippie dreamers.

The lyrics of 'Hippie Dream' offer enough in the way of clues for the listener to create his or her own sense of what it means. Unfortunately, most of the other songs on *Landing on Water* lack such democratic accessibility, leaving only a heavy beat, an often interesting interplay of synthesisers, and the impression of emotional shut-down. 'Touch the Night', with its lyrical feel, evocative lyrics and only half-buried vocal, does somehow stand out, but more, one suspects, because of the lack of such qualities in the other songs than for any great merits of its own.

Whatever the album's merits, the recording of *Landing on Water* seems to have re-energised Young's lifelong love affair with rock'n'roll. And rock'n'roll on the road, to Young, has usually meant Crazy Horse. In July 1986 it was announced that the US north-east would bear witness to their first tour together since Rust Never Sleeps.

This one would have a similar name – the Rusted-Out Garage tour – and, on its American leg at least, a similar musical ferocity. True to Young's inclination over the last decade, it also came complete with theatrical-style context and props. Young and Crazy Horse styled themselves the 'third-best garage band in the world', and the 'rusted-out garage' was the stage. On one side a huge lawnmower leant against a huge amp, on the other a huge spider dangled menacingly. Every now and then a huge mechanical cockroach would scuttle hugely across the floor.

This fictional group also had problems with their own species. A neighbour complained about the noise, a talent scout offered them next to nothing if they'd sign away next to everything, and Neil's 'Mom' gave them encouragement. 'I've heard them practise,' she would confide as she took the washing down, 'and it just ain't happening.'

The music at the centre of the show was garage rock at its loudest and most basic. Young's music with Crazy Horse, always a blend of power, imprecision and passion, was here the rawest it had ever been, all flailing solos, screaming feedback and manic distortion. The country singer with the nice grin from Austin City Limits had become the berserk stomper with the angry scowl. This wasn't family entertainment; it was the music of rage, frustration, resentment and violence. It was male music. It was guitar music. It was also probably the first time in several difficult years that Young had allowed himself the luxury of using his music as a way of letting go.

Whatever it did for him, such music certainly seemed to work for his hard core of devoted fans. For them, the Young-Crazy Horse combination, far from wilting over the years, appeared set on course for some future feedback apocalypse. Their guitar hero was back.

The rest of the world still needed convincing. Leaving a trail of deafened audiences across the American rust belt was all very well, but it would not bring back all those older fans who'd given up on him in the early eighties, nor reach out to all those teenagers who hadn't even been born when *Harvest* was released. Young needed a good album, a good *rock* album, if he wanted to be accepted once more as a prominent artist in the rock mainstream.

Life was not that album, though it did show signs that Young was beginning to recover some of the musical discernment that had made him so successful, both artistically and commercially, in the late sixties and the late seventies. For the first time since *Rust Never Sleeps* he had produced an album of varied musical styles and lyric themes.

To start at the bottom: the three garage-rock numbers – 'Too Lonely', 'Prisoners of Rock'n'Roll' and 'Cryin' Eyes' – are basic to the point of being boring. They demonstrate all of Young and Crazy Horse's weaknesses – sloppy playing, lack of rhythmic imagination, weak vocal back-up – and sound as if they've been recorded in a giant wet sock. The lyrics are as uninspired as the playing.

'Mideast Vacation' and 'Around the World' (both of which Young chose to include on the 1993 'best of Geffen' *Lucky Thirteen* album) sound like tracks from *Landing on Water* with the vocals mixed further forward. 'Around the World', with its satellite-eye view of peasants sweating, submarines sailing and so on, and its childish questioning – 'Why don't we illuminate?' indeed! – is saved from complete vacuity only by its counterpointing of this world with the world of fashion. A musical juggernaut, it lumbers forward with all the dramatic power, and all the subtlety, of a war machine.

Musically, 'Mideast Vacation' is more of the same, but lyrically it's a great deal more interesting, both in itself and for what it says about Young's political state of mind. For a start, the song is apparently torn between taking itself seriously and refusing to do so: although the sentiments being expressed certainly tie in with what Young was saying in interviews, the manner of their expression – the song's protagonist is a CIA renegade, a 'Rambo in the disco, shooting to the beat' – puts a distance between the ideas and the man. On this song Young appears to be stepping back from that complete identification with the standard all-American mind-set that he'd come close to embracing in the mid-eighties. This is still a part of me, he seems to be saying, and I still feel there's a lot of truth in that way of looking at the world, but it's not the sum total of all I think and feel.

The first of the ballads, 'A Long Walk Home', continues the theme, accepting American good intentions while it questions the consequences of American actions. 'Why,' the song asks, in a return to Young's more ambivalent position of the early eighties, 'do we feel that double-edged blade cutting through our hands?' If there is a vocal equivalent of hand-wringing then Young manages it on this song.

'Inca Queen', the third in a series of songs with pre-Columbian themes, lacks the depth of its predecessors 'Cortez the Killer' and 'Like an Inca'. It has a lovelier melody than either, though, and the passages of Spanish-sounding acoustic guitar are as beautiful as they are out of place. In the old Inca capital of Cuzco they still spit at the mention of Spaniards; Young's twisting of legends for his own use has rarely seemed more cavalier. The song, in which an Inca queen inspires the building of a city in the clouds to await an extraterrestrial visit, even manages to place elephants in the Peruvian jungle. Young's vision of Latin America has always been mostly a reflection of his own adopted country, more a matter of what the latter has lost than a world possessed of any reality in its own right, but whereas on songs like 'Cortez the Killer' the dissonance provides depth of meaning, here on 'Inca Queen' it begins rather to smack of a cultural hijacking.

The other two ballads close the album on a high note, albeit a sad one. 'When Your Lonely Heart Breaks' sounds as its title would suggest, with Young's aching vocal set above doom-laden synthesiser chords and drumbeat. 'Don't sit counting your mistakes/ Don't be waiting for love to come back,' he urges, but the mood is too powerful to allow the listener to imagine him doing anything else. 'We Never Danced' is more enigmatic, apparently looking forward to a reunion with a loved one after death, but also concerned with life on earth: 'If you don't really know where you want to go, it makes no difference which road you take.' Jack Nitzche helped with the arrangement and, with Young's high-register vocal, ghostly vocal chorus and tinkling piano, the song's echoes of *Buffalo Springfield Again*'s 'Expecting to Fly' are on the angelic side.

Young hadn't bothered to sing as well as this for a long time, and throughout the album there's a sense – perhaps in hindsight – that he's stretching his musical limbs, starting to try to please others as much as himself. *Life* is by no means a good album, but there are good things on it, and hints of more to come.

If *Life* offered some small encouragement that Young was at least holding his own against the dreaded rust, the European tour with Crazy Horse in the spring of 1987 not only made clear how much lost ground he had to make up, but also came close to destroying the relationship he and Crazy Horse had shared for so long.

Since the Transband tour and *Trans* in late 1982, Young might as well have not existed in Europe. His return in 1987 did little to restore his reputation. 'We sold shit for tickets,' he told *Pulse* magazine in 1991. 'A lot of places had to cancel the shows. It was a disaster.' In one town in France they were stranded for four days, having had two shows cancelled owing to low ticket sales. At that time the band, in Young's words, were at the 'height of our uncoolness'. As far as Europe was concerned 'we were just lost, we were gone, we were nothing then'.

The sense of being 'nothing' can't have done much to repair relationships frayed by months of touring. The music was sometimes good, but Young would later find reasons for criticising the others in the band, particularly as regards their inability to remember arrangements. The looseness that had always been Crazy Horse's glory was beginning to look more and more like simple sloppiness. Over the last eight years Young had got used to playing with technically better musicians.

The members of Crazy Horse no doubt also had their reasons, individual and collective, for harbouring very mixed feelings about Young. No matter how much each of them liked and got on with their old friend, there was no getting away from the fact that theirs was a profoundly unequal relationship. Most of what they'd achieved and earned was down to Young's habit of regularly employing them, so they had good reason to be grateful. But the same time, it can't have been easy not to feel some resentment towards someone who just chose to employ you when the mood so took him. It had, after all, been eight long years since he'd taken the band on tour.

No one could be blamed for any of this – Young had no more obligation to provide Crazy Horse with lifelong employment than he had the Stray Gators or anyone else. But feelings are not often logical, often suppressed, and more likely to surface when the world seems to be going against you. It was an argumentative, sometimes rancorous tour.

This atmosphere at least made for a good video. The latest instalment of Young's obsession with making movies featured two Video-8 cameras, both apparently named Otto, which would be left running more or less permanently wherever the band were. Sometimes someone would talk to an Otto, but mostly the cameras just observed 'a lot of things that really go down on a tour that are not cute or funsy-wunsy . . . There's a lot of guts in it, a lot of feeling.' Young had no hopes for a mainstream cinematic triumph, though. The *Muddy Track* video, as it came to be called, 'could never be released for real'. After all, it wasn't 'HBO or anything like that, thank *God*!'.

There were always Crosby, Stills and Nash. In Australia in March 1985 Young, asked about a possible reunion, told the interviewer that 'my friend Mr Crosby has escaped from his place of keeping where they were straightening him out, so I suppose that now he's a fugitive we won't be getting together'.

Crosby eventually served some time in the Texas State Penitentiary, emerging in 1986 without the freebasing habit that had almost destroyed him. CS&N joined with Young for the first Bridge School benefit in November, and again in February 1987 for an acoustic Greenpeace benefit in Santa Barbara. The latter was more than a matter of a few unrehearsed songs: the foursome performed two ninety-minute sets.

Young, for one, seemed delighted. 'CSN&Y is *alive*,' he said. 'Everybody's here now. Can't be CSN&Y if you don't have Crosby ... He was always the spiritual leader of the group ...' The prospect of a more substantial reunion, involving a tour, an album or both, seemed closer than it had for many years.

There were also obstacles. CS&N already had a summer tour scheduled, and any plans to record were likely to be stymied by David Geffen. Having swallowed a succession of Young albums with the commercial potential of *The Carpenters Sing Kraftwerk* he was understandably reluctant to let Young waltz off to Atlantic with CS&N for an obvious money-spinner. Nash offered the opinion that Geffen would relent – if he didn't, Young might well fill an album with versions of 'My Way' – but as 1987 passed there was no sign of a white flag.

In times past CSN&Y had hardly needed real obstacles to impede their collective plans, but this time around there was enough determination to carry them through almost a year of waiting. One reason, no doubt, was a mellowing of the participants. They had, as Young said, been through a lot together; they knew each other's strengths and weaknesses. Stills and Young had even been playing fairly regularly with each other at informal Buffalo Springfield reunions.

For Young, making music with people he'd known that long and that well was always going to be an interesting challenge, and perhaps the four of them were now mature enough to bring out the best in each other. He admitted to being 'curious'.

There's no doubt, though, that Crosby's triumphal return from the edge of the abyss was the main reason for their keeping the idea of the reunion alive. Young had gone on record as promising to work with the other three if Crosby pulled himself together, and obviously he wanted to honour the commitment, but it was more than that. Crosby's return, Young thought, was an inspiration, and the man himself was 'a really good role model for a lot of people in the same boat'.

In fact the whole band could function in the same way, Young believed, so long as Stills and Crosby could prove themselves as together as he and Nash were. 'We should be physically able to take on the job of setting an example for an entire generation that could be halfway to the fucking grave.' If audiences could see all of CSN&Y come back 'stronger and sharper' than before, then 'no matter what's happened to them in their lives, no matter how many good friends have died, how much shit they've piled on themselves, how many losses they've endured – whatever it is –

if we can be so strong after everything we've endured, it would be like fresh water running over the entire audience'.

Of course they would need good music too, but Young had no doubts as to whether they could deliver it. In fact, early in 1987 he seems to been almost carried away by the possibilities. They could have 'a huge tour', maybe 'a great record'. None of their previous albums, *Déjà Vu* included, had captured what the band could really do: there was 'a lot more depth and rawness and a lot more funk and soul in this band than has ever been heard on record'. As far as he was concerned, the fact that their old audience was still out there meant that CSN&Y were beyond fashion. They could keep coming back every four or five years for the next twenty. 'Who's competing with us?' he asked. 'If the Beatles were playing today, that would be something that we could think about . . .'

CSN&Y had never been short on confidence, and, as it turned out, they would soon have the chance to put their music where their mouths were. Towards the end of 1987 Young reached a series of agreements that took him off Geffen Records and back onto Reprise, and allowed him to record with Crosby, Stills and Nash on Atlantic. At last they could all get on with recording the album.

But they would not, for now, do a tour together. Young, who a year earlier had been predicting 'a huge tour', now decided that 'a CSN&Y tour would be a nostalgia tour to a great degree', and that the four of them weren't yet physically ready to assume the burden of representing their generation. He also had a new interest of his own.

The Bluenotes evolved rather than sprang into being at Young's command. When he and Crazy Horse returned from their acrimonious European tour in the late spring of 1987, they immediately went out on a short American tour. The one major change in the show was the insertion of a mini-set of blues songs between the solo acoustic and electric/Crazy Horse sets. In a mock lounge-bar setting Young played blues guitar, with Frank Sampedro on organ and one of the roadies filling in on saxophone. Listening to the tapes of the shows afterwards, Young, finding little to interest him in the familiar acoustic and Crazy Horse material, focused on the blues numbers, and began to see possibilities. By the autumn of 1987 the Bluenotes had been created, by the addition, first, of six horns to Crazy Horse, and then the replacing of Talbot and Molina with a bassist (Rick Rosas) and a drummer (Chad Cromwell) better suited to the type of material Young wanted to play.

In the spirit of Rolling Zuma and the Ducks, Young chose to take the Bluenotes out on the road without the benefit of his own name. The anonymity didn't last very long, but perhaps he reasoned that people could hardly expect to hear traditional Neil Young music if his name wasn't even on the posters. If they did, hard luck – he was fed up with playing his old hits. The material he did choose to play was a mixture of the newly written and the very old. At least three of the songs featured in the band's late-1987 sets – 'Hello Lonely Woman', 'Find Another Shoulder' and 'Ain't It the Truth' – had been written in Winnipeg or Fort William in 1964. Not surprisingly they relied more on energy and directness than on musical or lyrical complexity.

Young also seemed to be enjoying a change of style on guitar. The feedback and distortion, the emphasis on making an interesting *noise*, had given way to the blues guitarist's liquid purity of tone. And of course he'd given himself another role to play. This time around Bernard Shakey had become Shaky Deal, a vaguely seedy hipster in black fedora, shades and sports jacket. Shaky, like the Shocking Pinks leader, was something of a throwback, hankering not only for music at its basic best, but also for a little old-fashioned integrity. He didn't much like the state of the music business, and he had one particular bee in his bonnet: the sponsorship of musicians.

This was a pet hate that Young, in various guises, had been peddling for several years, but now at last he had found a song that expressed his anger. The lyrics of 'This Note's for You' were not exactly deep – 'Ain't singing for Pepsi/Ain't singing for Coke/I don't sing for nobody/Makes me look like a joke' – but they could scarcely have been more direct.

It turned out he wasn't alone in his prejudice. On the contrary: 'Never in my life have I had a song that people reacted to so instantaneously,' he claimed; 'people just start cheering and singing when we play it.' The song was simply an expression of his relationship to the conglomerates. 'I can't sell my voice and my melodies to some company,' he said, 'and then turn round, sing a song from the bottom of my heart and expect anybody to believe it.' He accepted that he might appear old-fashioned, agreed that 'the majority of people in my business feel differently about it, that it's their chance to score and make a lot of money'. But how, Young asked himself, could he sing a song like 'Ohio' sponsored by a beer company?

He did admit that one particular offer would tempt him. If Budweiser would agree to restore the Mark Twain Zephyr, a classic train built in

1935 and one-time holder of the world speed record, then he would graciously allow the company to sponsor him touring the country in it. Afterwards he would 'give the train away to the Smithsonian or something'.

After the ponderous intensity of *Life*, *This Note's for You* seems both light-headed and positively nimble of foot. Young and the Bluenotes sound as though they're enjoying themselves, and it's infectious. The cover claims that this is 'the dawn of power swing', and whatever its shortcomings, *This Note's for You* certainly gets the toes a-tapping.

The album's one overriding weakness is its songs. There are six real swingers, and four after-hours ballads. Of the former, only three have any distinction: the anti-sponsorship title track, 'Hey Hey' and 'Life in the City'. 'Hey Hey' stands out for its sheer exuberance, but 'Life in the City', with its obvious urban theme, marks something of a turning point for Young. Sure enough, there's a passing reference to farms 'going to seed', but this song surges down the streets of the America that Young appeared to have forgotten. There are 'families livin' under freeways', there is 'murder in the home and crime on the streets'. The guitar line stabs its way across the wailing horns as the drums ignite.

All four ballads feature muted guitar and horns, and touchingly restrained vocals from Young, but only 'Twilight' manages to transcend the generic mood (not to mention its own irritating click track). The simplicity of its yearning-for-home theme is one reason; an astonishing display of blues guitar from Young is the other.

On the six unspecified songs the album's faults tend to outweigh its sense of adventure. The lyrics are mostly nondescript, the guitar often too far back in the mix, while the horn arrangements sound as derivative as they are energetic. In the case of most other artists it would be tempting to categorise such an album as an excellent first attempt at a merger of styles, and hope for more from the next. With Young, of course, waning interest and the fear of stagnation has usually ensured that the first attempt is also the last. It's therefore rather a shame that *This Note's for You* was recorded so early in the Bluenotes' career, and one can only hope that the live material in Young's possession will see the archival light of day before his older fans have left their toe-tapping days behind.

On a more positive note, it did seem as if the roles Young was picking out for himself, the musical styles and personae he was half exploring, half hiding in, were moving closer and closer to home. In this respect *This Note's for You* could perhaps be seen as the last motel night on Young's long journey back to his musical self.

The album, although well received in critical quarters, was not likely to pull Young back into the mainstream. But as fortune would have it, the video made to accompany 'This Note's for You' would provide him with what the record could not – renewed celebrity as a musical maverick.

Julien Temple, who had already worked with Bowie and the Stones, was hired to direct the video, but the basic concept probably originated with Young. For one thing, the visuals were implicit in the song's lyrics; for another, the whole thing reeked of his sense of humour.

The Bluenotes were filmed performing the song at the Continental Club in Hollywood, and this footage was intercut with spoofs of well-known ads featuring rock stars Eric Clapton, Michael Jackson and Whitney Houston. The choice of two black stars to lampoon was unfortunate, and the incineration of the Jackson lookalike's hair more than slightly insensitive, but it was not such racial considerations that formed the basis of MTV's disapproval. There were vague noises from the lawyers about trademark infringements, but the bottom line, as far as the company was concerned, was that they didn't dare offend their sponsors. According to Young, MTV had been shown the script before the video was shot, and had okayed it, but when push came to shove the company had changed its mind. Offers to edit out the spoofs and to indemnify the TV company against lawsuits were refused.

Young claimed he wasn't surprised. The song was what it was all about: it drew 'a line, and we knew people would have to stand one side or the other'. MTV had a rebellious image, but they lacked 'the guts to show something that's not middle-of-the-road'.

In the end, perhaps remembering Lyndon Johnson's old adage that it was better to have your enemy inside the tent pissing out than vice versa, MTV reversed its decision and showed the video. It proved as popular on TV as the song had proved on stage, and many an adolescent who'd never heard of Neil Young could delight in the anti-corporate rebel-rousing of Shaky Deal and his boys. So much so, in fact, that Young and Temple ended up with the MTV Video of the Year Award for 1988, much to the singer's surprise and, dare we hope, the sponsors' chagrin.

To the casual or hopeful observer, Young's various complaints about corporate America – its betrayal of the American farmer, its betrayal of art through sponsorship, its betrayal of the poor and homeless – might all have appeared to spring from a coherent leftist perspective, one built on the ruins of his misplaced faith in Reaganism's empty panaceas. To anyone who bothered to ask Young, however, it became obvious that he had no coherent overview. A reasonably clear idea of what was wrong with the world had not come complete with any clear idea of how to put things right.

When asked whether the social concern he'd expressed in 'Life in the City' would manifest itself outside his songwriting, he simply rambled. Maybe a portion of his concert receipts 'could go to a food-share programme, but then that's like a different form of government. You're walking on shaky ground. We've got this capitalist democratic society, and if we try doing all these things to help the homeless then all of a sudden it's not a free country any more, because you're being told where your money has to go.' Rather than wonder whether that much freedom was worth that many homeless, he chose to cover his confusion with a joke, suggesting that Budweiser should set up a centre for the homeless where people could sleep when it got too cold – with, 'you know, free beer for everybody'.

He offered a similar recipe for the country in election year. He didn't want Reagan's chosen successor Bush, only 'kind of liked' the Democratic challenger Dukakis, and came down in favour of Jesse Jackson as the only candidate offering real change. Jackson, he thought, would be the best bet for helping the homeless. But at the same time he thought Jackson would 'screw up a whole bunch of other things' in providing this help, 'because of the methods he'd have to use'.

An ungenerous reading of all this would be that Young recognised the problem, but wasn't prepared to countenance any diminution of those rights and privileges that Americans above the poverty line tend to hold as self-evident. If a free market couldn't co-exist with a workable welfare system, then that was tough on those needing welfare.

Young claimed to be basically happy with the free world. Everyone knew that it didn't work half the time, but at least we were 'free to correct our mistakes'. He didn't explain why this freedom to make amends was so seldom invoked, but he did continue to paint, with increasing venom, musical pictures of the 'mistakes'.

Throughout 1988 Young continued to revel in his relationship with the Bluenotes. The new range a horn section offered, not to mention the sheer proficiency of the musicians, gave him added incentive to write. As he told James Henke, in an obvious reference to Crazy Horse's limitations, he was no longer waking up thinking, 'Well, if I write this, are the guys gonna be able to play it?'

The songs he was writing – and performing during the summer/ autumn Bluenotes tour – were also more striking than any he had composed for a long time. 'Crime in the City (from Sixty to Zero)' was performed in both acoustic and electric guises by Young and the Bluenotes in 1988, and versions of each are available on bootleg CDs. Running at eighteen and seven minutes respectively, these performances far surpass those later released on *Freedom* and *Weld*. The eleven-verse acoustic version is sadder, and sounds purposeful enough until it is compared with the electric version. This features driving drums and clanging guitar underneath the verses, screaming guitar between them, and a vocal that's more snarled than sung. The lyrics are full of selfishness, stupidity and senseless violence; the different scenes move in and out of focus, through the genocide of the Sioux, the protagonist's broken home, and drug deals on the street. In one verse, a prison warden and guard come across a buck and fawn in their empty prison yard. Let's just keep them here with 'intimidation and fear', the guard suggests, but 'The warden pulled the trigger/And those deer hit the ground/He said nobody'll know the difference/And they both looked around'.

It's 'up against cash', Young sings ominously of some prospective legislation, and in both this song and the twelve-minute 'Ordinary People' there's a sense of a refreshingly crude populism at work. 'Ordinary People' has a grander sound, with horns and blues guitar framing rambling Dylanesque verses, and the drums ticking away like an unexploded bomb, but it carries the same scattergun approach to American reality. In parts it's almost like a 1930s novel set to music: the villains are the familiar pairing of big business and organised crime, both reduced to the classic 'man in the window with a big cigar'. The good guys, on the other hand, are completely depersonalised, like a crowd in an Eisenstein movie. They're 'Ordinary people/They're gonna bring the good things back/Hard-working people/Put the business back on track/Nose-to-the-stone people/I got faith in the regular kind . . .'.

These lines come at the end of a verse recounting the birth of an old railway engine, and throughout the song there's a feeling that Young is retreating back into some mythical time when everything worked the way it was supposed to. His urban world here bears remarkable similarities to his rural one. Such nostalgia can be dangerous – after all, it was from such a populist perspective that Fascism emerged in the 1920s – but in the context of these two songs Young's rampant fury carries all before it. 'They're ordinary people, and they're living in a nightmare,' he rages, and three years on from 'California Sunset' it's hard to do anything but cheer.

None of this new energy and radicalism of Young's surfaced on the record CSN&Y had made in the spring of 1988, and which was finally released in November. But if *American Dream* was something of a disappointment Young could hardly blame the others. The record had been made at his ranch and, according to Nash, mostly under his supervising hand. He'd even had Stills up there a week early to make sure the two of them could co-exist. The recording sessions had been 'insanely tension-free', and the resulting music, according to Young at the time, sounded 'great'.

Young has four solo compositions on the album, and two with Stills. Of the latter, 'Drivin' Thunder' doesn't live up to its title, but 'Night Song' offers one of the album's atmospheric highlights, complete with a great Stills vocal and fine guitar work from him and Young.

The four solo songs are very uneven in quality. 'American Dream's tale of a politician's fall from grace would be utterly forgettable if not for its irritating melody and irritating pipes. The simple acoustic 'Feel Your Love', on the other hand, is one of Young's best ballads of the eighties, and worth the second-hand price of the album on its own. 'I really want the night to end/I really want the sun to rise,' he sings. The key lies in the 'really': it has taken the song's protagonist a lifetime to reach this point, of being *really* able to deal with love and light.

The other two songs seem like a matched pair of pistols. While 'Name of Love' melodically offers a defiant affirmation of those sixties values that have held CSN&Y together through the years, 'This Old House' functions here as an almost macabre reworking of Nash's 'Our House'. It's as if Young is qualifying the reunion, staking out his distance from the rest of them. Two cats in the yard or not, this family is getting evicted for failure to keep up the mortgage.

Nash maintained that the album's songs made good the conceit of its title, that here were a dozen songs about the American Dream *circa* 1988. But the sad truth was that CSN&Y had little to offer in this department: a few rants against familiar bugbears, and a tired and tiresome reliance on an undefined 'love' as the universal panacea. There's no bite to *American Dream*.

The soft-edged semi-acoustic shuffle of *American Dream*, which had been recorded in the midst of the Bluenotes period, bore little relation to the music Young was making by the time of its release. Early in 1989 he toured Australia, New Zealand and Japan with a pared-down version of the Bluenotes, travelling first as Young and the Restless – a pun on the long-running US TV soap opera – and then as the wonderfully-named Lost Dogs.

The music, which Young ironically dubbed 'popular music' and one critic described as 'a big throbbing noise', came with industrial sound effects, roadies in hard hats and an accompanying psychedelic slide show. It was urban in sound, urban in its lyrical concerns, urban in its violence. Most important of all, Shaky Deal, Young's latest alter ego, had given way to . . . Neil Young. And Neil Young was seething with all the fear and loathing he'd been holding inside himself for the last ten years.

Once back in America he started to deal it out in the studio, recording eight or nine songs for an album, first at the Hit Factory in New York, then at the ranch. One provisional title for the album, *Times Square*, gave way to another – *Eldorado*. The songs were mostly electric hard rock, with desperately controlled vocals, scything guitar lines, and seemingly random explosions of feedback.

Young listened to the mastered album and liked what he'd done, but he doubted if his audience would, because, as he put it, 'there was nothing but abrasiveness from end to end'. At any other time in the last ten years this would have been unfortunate, but nothing more. The album would have been released, regardless of Geffen or Warners, regardless of its commercial potential, regardless of anything other than the fact that Young wanted it out.

But recording this album seems to have been different. Perhaps it was just the last stage in a cumulative process of recovering the links between his feelings, his thoughts and his art; perhaps the music he'd been playing on stage and in the studio over the last six months had been truly cathartic. Either way, he now felt strong enough to compromise. The *Eldorado* album, he knew, would not get played on the radio; it was too much of an 'assault'. It might be a fine album, but this time around that wasn't enough: Young wanted to put out something that people would notice, that had an effect.

Still, he liked *Eldorado* too much simply to abandon it, and a five-track EP of its nucleus appeared in Australia and Japan. Young reasoned that while no one could construe this as a major release, those who cared enough about his music would find some way to beg, steal or borrow a copy. In the meantime he went back into the studio to record the songs he would need for the more variegated *Freedom* – some light for the darkness, some love and gentleness to set against the rage. A couple of these songs – 'The Ways of Love' and 'Too Far Gone' – dated back to the seventies. They offered a route back, Young thought, for the many who had liked his music then.

Others, like 'Hangin' on a Limb', were apparently recent compositions. He even had a new anthemic song which, like 'My My, Hey Hey' on *Rust Never Sleeps*, worked as both an acoustic opener and an electric closer. 'Rockin' in the Free World' would also do something for Young's reputation as a prophet, becoming as it did more and more topical as the year of eastern Europe's liberation wore on.

Eventually he had the songs he wanted, and most of him felt pretty good about it. 'It's the first time I've felt like doing an album like this in years,' he said. On his other eighties albums he'd been 'more into style. But I was losing track of what I wanted to do.' Three years later he would go further, saying that with *Freedom* 'I just came out of it, surfaced. It's like trying to get to the top of the water, so you can come into the air. Finally I broke through.'

But there were also reservations, and a sense that he had, in seeking a balance of styles, someone sold out. 'That's where the compromise was made,' he said in 1989, adding that it was 'disappointing – *Freedom* had to be slightly pasteurised'.

After *Eldorado*, anything would sound pasteurised. The EP's 'Cocaine Eyes' opens with a few fuzz-drenched notes, with Young's voice in the background saying 'Let's try one like that', before it swings into the sort of clanging riff that would wake the dead. 'Ain't a day goes by I don't burn a little bit of my soul,' Young sings, and you believe him. There is nothing lazy about this music, nothing relaxed or satisfied: it's taut as high-strung electric wires, and these occasionally snap, spewing sparks all over the neighbourhood. The last thirty seconds of the song sound like a rollercoaster ride in an electric chair.

'Don't Cry' is slower but even tauter. The guitar seems to be dragging chains along the ground while an eerie bell-like clang and Young's straining voice share the sky above. Every now and then the guitar gets

NEIL YOUNG

ambitious, and murky clouds of feedback threaten to engulf everything, before clearing once more to reveal the same rolling chains, same dull clunk, same desperate voice. At the end the voice is left hanging in the air like some disembodied nightmare.

'Heavy Love' offers more axe-swinging rock'n'roll. It has much the same clanging rhythm as 'Cocaine Eyes', but, not surprisingly, fails to match the earlier song's manic drive and guitar pyrotechnics.

'On Broadway', the Drifters' hit from 1963, is given a stately opening, and for the first two-thirds of the song it sounds as if all Young has added is a vocal more in keeping with the bitter desperation of the lyrics. But the drums get more insistent, the guitar starts trying to bury the wailing voice in distortion, and Young emerges from the final explosion of feedback screaming 'Gimme some of that crack!'. The music descends into bedlam, before cutting itself off like a gunshot.

There is silence. And then, rising out of this aural portrait of the American city, a clearly chiming guitar and castanets. With only one – almost playful – screech of the guitar to remind the listener where he's come from, we enter 'Eldorado', Young's fourth excursion into the Latin America of myth and legend, and one of his finest songs.

The first verse sets the scene: the mission church, the villa, 'the riders on the hill . . . the shooting starts . . .'. This is Mexico or somewhere very like it, a hundred or more years ago; lawlessness reigns. The second verse brings the song into the present, but the only thing that appears to have changed is the nature of the bandits, now busy doing a deal in a hotel room, surrounded by women in diamonds and sable. The real Latin America – the mariachi band – is outside, 'beside a garbage heap'. In the third verse the deal is completed, and 'the briefcase snaps goodbye' – to the deal, the dealers, an entire continent. In the final verse, in Eldorado, a white bullfighter dressed in gold lamé offers the possibility of his own death as entertainment for the excited crowd.

'Eldorado' is a song about how, in general, money destroys humanity, and how it has always done so in North America's relationship with its Latin neighbours to the south. Five hundred years on, Cortez the Killer is now a successful drug-runner – so successful, in fact, that he's able to keep the locals supplied with human sacrifice material.

Freedom bears the strengths and weaknesses of what it is – an expansion and dilution of *Eldorado*. It contains three of the latter's songs, and only one of these – 'Don't Cry' – has been weakened in the pursuit of user-friendliness. The six-minute 'Eldorado' remains the brilliant

206

centrepiece, and the decision to include 'On Broadway' in preference to 'Cocaine Eyes', although strange, is not too damaging.

Both 'Crime in the City' and 'Too Far Gone' suffer in comparison with earlier variants. The latter, in particular, is a pale shadow of earlier live performances with both the Bluenotes and the Restless. More than half the verses are gone, and the song's drive has vanished with them. 'Too Far Gone' has been much countrified since its 1976 début, and given the additional burden of a particularly unconvincing vocal from Young.

Although he wrote 'Hangin' on a Limb' and 'The Ways of Love' fifteen years apart from each other, it would be hard to tell which was the earlier simply by listening to them. Each has a lovely melody and attractively ringing acoustic guitar, quavering vocals from Young and nicely understated back-up from Linda Ronstadt. As is so often the case, Young's lyrics straddle the line between childlike innocence and simple mawkishness.

Of the new songs, 'Someday', 'No More' and 'Wrecking Ball' are all fully realised, lyrically interesting and musically different, both from each other and from everything else on *Freedom*. 'Someday' is a rolling ballad which comes complete with pedal steel and brass, chain-gang chorus and lyrics that range from Rommel to the Trans-Alaska Pipeline. 'No More' is a tale of things lost, some for better, some for worse, told over a resigned and beautifully restrained guitar line. 'Wrecking Ball' sounds like the skeletal Springsteen of *The River*, and conjures up the same sense of people trapped in shells.

The one great new song Young brings to *Freedom* is 'Rockin' in the Free World', which – again like 'My My, Hey Hey' – appears in two versions, as both acoustic opener and electric closer. According to Young, 'I wrote that song out on the road ... on my bus, and I thought of the first line and said, "My God, that really says something but it's such a cliché, it's such an obvious thing," so then I knew I had to use it.' The song itself is not so much ambivalent as double-edged. There's no triumphalism here, no suggestion that America or the West has got it right; on the contrary, every line of the verses is a condemnation of the way that world is being run. Against this, he offers only a faith in rock'n'roll, both as the ultimate escape ('try to forget it anyway I can') and as a force for good in its own right. For Young it's still 'a victory for the heart each time the music starts'; although of course he doesn't say so, it's also a victory for the mind each time someone makes an album as perceptive and diverse as *Freedom*.

The real strength of *Freedom* lies in its breadth of vision. The album, whether intended as such or not, takes its place among Young's other 'American' albums, each of them a multi-faceted portrait of the world in which he lives, from his own relationships to the wider social and political realm. It is not a pretty picture he paints in 1989, and the only real consolation to be gathered from *Freedom* resides in the fact that the despair of the opening 'Rockin' in the Free World' has become, by the album's end, the same song's anger.

Late in 1988 Young had been the evening's guest of honour at a Music Therapy Foundation benefit dinner in New York. As the musician father of a severely handicapped child, he was obviously interested in how music could be used to help autistic and retarded children, but he was not directly involved in the Foundation's work. His presence at the dinner was a simple acknowledgement of how much his high profile and fund-raising activities had achieved in heightening public consciousness *vis-à-vis* handicapped children.

Young's involvement with the Bridge School had of course continued on through the past year. The second Bridge benefit had been held in December 1988 at the Oakland Coliseum – an acoustic evening featuring Dylan, Tracy Chapman, Tom Petty, Jerry Garcia and Bob Weir from the Grateful Dead, Billy Idol, Nils Lofgren and, of course, CSN&Y. A third would be held the following October, and a further benefit annually thereafter.

More good news for the school came early in 1989: an album of Young's songs was being recorded by a variety of artists, with most of the profits coming the school's way. The inspiration behind *The Bridge*, as the album would be called, was producer Terry Tolkin. A long-time Young fan, Tolkin had already worked on a compilation of music by alternative bands entitled *God's Favorite Dog* in 1985. He now contacted friends Sonic Youth and Henry Kaiser, who brought in Dinosaur Jr, Victoria Williams and David Lindley, and called up Nick Cave, Loop, the Pixies and Soul Asylum simply on the hunch that their musics showed a workable affinity with Young's.

Tolkin obviously had a good ear. Not only were they all enthusiastic, but each also considered Young a major influence on their own music. The album, which was released around the same time as *Freedom* in late 1989, reflected the exuberance and taste of those concerned, and contained several stunning performances. Young particularly liked Dinosaur

Jr's 'Lotta Love', which was about as far removed from the original as it was possible to get; Nick Cave's 'Helpless' and the Pixies' 'Winterlong', on the other hand, came close to matching their composer's renditions, while Sonic Youth's 'Computer World' surpassed the original.

Young loved the album. 'We put that on in the bus when we were on the road and just blasted it over the speakers and were walking round listening, shaking our heads and everything.' He also liked the 'lot of money' the album's makers were able to donate to the school.

The world was not short of good causes, nor did Young any longer show any reluctance to help out. In November 1989 he headlined a concert at San Francisco's Cow Palace, one of three simultaneous benefits for the victims of the October earthquake in northern California. The finale was a jam featuring him, Carlos Santana and Steve Miller.

Nor did Young appear wary of using his music to express political opinions. Joining CS&N on stage in LA, he dedicated 'Ohio' to the 'students who just got slaughtered in China'. In December, he closed a show at London's Hammersmith Odeon with the same song, same dedication. Here, free of harmonies, the performance was full of anguish, a fitting end to an evening that many Young fans found his most intense in years. Wired for sound, he stalked the chairless, microphoneless, propless stage like a man possessed.

As 1990 unfolded Young seemed almost omnipresent – some achievement for a forty-five-year-old who hadn't had a Top Twenty album in ten years. A re-recorded soundalike version of 'Hey Hey, My My' could even be heard in a TV commercial for Lee jeans, at least until the lawyers caught up with the company. In February he joined the band Alarm on stage in New York for their performance of his 'Rockin' in the Free World'. In March *Freedom* won the *Rolling Stone* Critics' Best Album Award for 1989.

The good-cause benefits showed no sign of abating. On 31st March a benefit concert was held for ex-CSN&Y drummer Dallas Taylor, who was critically ill with a liver disease brought on by drug and alcohol abuse. The need for donors was advertised, and money was raised both for Taylor and a for a drug-education foundation. The next day the same musicians – CSN&Y, Don Henley, the Desert Rose Band – gave another concert, to benefit a local anti-pollution measure, the California Environmental Protection Initiative.

Young, greatly encouraged by the way in which events in eastern Europe had demonstrated the power of ordinary people to influence governments, was hoping that Westerners could bring the same pressure to bear for environmental change. 'We can't wait for the bureaucrats to figure out they're going to do it and make it fit into an economic programme,' he said around this time. 'We have to do it now.'

The fourth Farm Aid concert, which took place at the Hoosier Dome in Indianapolis on 7th April, incorporated a strong environmental theme. Throughout the concert – which featured Young, Nelson, Mellencamp and the usual star-studded cast – speakers pressed the point that loans to farmers were being increasingly tied to the use of agribusiness chemical products. Farm Aid and environmental protection appeared to go hand in hand.

Nelson Mandela had nothing to do with either, but nine days later Young was at Wembley to join the Mandela Day celebrations for the recently-released ANC leader. 'It was important to do that,' he said. 'It represented a feeling of hope.'

Talking about *Ragged Glory* in 1990, Young claimed to have written the last seven songs in a week, in late March of that year. Although this statement failed the accuracy test – 'Farmer John' was written by someone else, 'Day That Used to Be' in 1988 – it did evoke memories of the similarly prodigious songwriting bout in 1969 that had produced the core of *Everybody Knows This Is Nowhere*. Nor did the parallel end there. Both bouts had seen the creation of two songs constructed around simple changes as platforms for extended jamming.

There was only one band Young could get to play these songs. Crazy Horse, two-thirds of whom had, in Young's words, 'something to prove' after the 1987 tour, were summoned to the ranch, probably in late April 1990.

As usual, Young was pleased that they were all back together. No matter where he'd roamed musically over the years he had always come back to Crazy Horse, and the feeling was that he always would, bringing home each time, he hoped, a new ingredient for the pot. The music the four of them made together was a key theme in his musical history, almost a musical anchor. 'Crazy Horse,' he said proudly, 'is a rock band, and we make a great sound. And we sound like no one else.'

In the jamming department there wasn't even any competition. Young thought the spontaneity had gone out of mainstream rock. Players weren't 'reaching out in the instrumental passages and spon-taneously letting them last as long as they can'. This was exactly what he wanted to do, and he could 'only really do it well with one band . . .'.

The promotional video for *Ragged Glory* undeniably suggests a wilful approach to life and music. For one thing, Young can be observed seeking out new sound sensations by shoving his guitar down a toilet bowl; for another, the sight of scantily-clad farm girls shaking their backsides at the band comes across as a deliberate throwback, a little boy's finger raised at all those feminist types out there.

Young admitted that the long feedback fades on most tracks were calculated to get up someone's nose. 'Everything now is concerned with formats,' he said. 'This is, fuck your format.' As for the record's thematic content, he claimed it could all be gleaned from listening to the one track that had been left off the album, but thoughtfully placed on a single, the seven-minutes-plus 'Don't Spook the Horse'. It 'kinda condenses the whole album', he maintained, and it was, as a consequence, ideal for reviewers who didn't like him. Since the song advises a thorough inspection of dogs, horses and pretty little girls to make sure they 'ain't rolled in shit', it must have seemed fair to expect an album as crude as they come, a veritable shit-kickers' manifesto.

Ragged Glory certainly takes few musical hostages. There's little relief from the raw, predictable thump of Talbot and Molina's rhythm section, and Frank Sampedro is rarely allowed to demonstrate more than his usual reliability. But the manifesto really ends there. Across this basic backcloth Young offers a feast of lead-guitar playing, moving through notes and lines and riffs, from pure music to pure noise and back again, through clarity and distortion, from playful to angry and from joyous to sad. Not since *Everybody Knows This Is Nowhere* had he given himself this much space and time to stretch out in.

This in itself is enough to nail any preconceptions of simple crudity, but in addition, the songs themselves gather in depth and subtlety with each hearing. 'Fuckin' Up' is a massive tirade against self-destructiveness, but it also finds time for a rare mixture of poetry and menace, from the woman on the hill, 'curves beneath your flowing gown', to the pack of howling dogs, their 'broken leashes all over the floor', and the 'keys left hanging in a swinging door'.

Both 'Country Home' and 'White Line' are mid-seventies vintage, determinedly slight; 'Over and Over', by contrast, has a captivating riff and Young's hoarse, straining voice pursuing the thread of sexual ecstasy through past and present. The two ten-minute epics – 'Love to Burn' and 'Love and Only Love' – contain his best extended guitar solos since *Live Rust*, and are both heartfelt pleas to 'take a chance on love'. Such advice is rendered all the more poignant by the lovers in the former song, quarrelling in their 'house full of broken windows' and bitterly asking each other, 'Why did you ruin my life, where are you taking the kids?'

'Mansion on the Hill' even dares to state Young's continuing belief in the hippie dream. 'There ain't no way to ever lose love's dream,' he would sing on the live version of the song, and the psychedelic music still filling the air is only a musical reflection of that reality.

'Days That Used to Be' was written on the *W. N. Ragland*, after Young had received the news that MTV had rejected his video for 'This Note's for You'. The rejection made him worry that he was out of touch, and the song was 'sort of like an answer to . . . it was kinda like the way I felt, kinda lost'. It explores the passage of the years and the inevitable loss of innocence; it confronts distances – both the general distance between middle age and youth and the particular distance between Young's middle age and his youth in the idealistic sixties. Together, this song and 'Mansion on the Hill' reflect that balance between loss and renewal which would dominate *Harvest Moon*.

8

AUDIO *VÉRITÉ*

Having just had released, at the grand old age of forty-five, one of the best rock'n'roll albums of his or anyone else's career, Young felt the urge to take it out on the road. A US tour was booked to begin on 22nd January 1991 in Minneapolis, and while Young and Crazy Horse were rehearsing at Prince's Paisley Park studios the gods conspired to provide the perfect context for killer rock'n'roll. The Gulf War broke out.

Young could have ignored it, sidestepped it, used the old cop-out that music had nothing to do with politics. He chose otherwise. 'We couldn't just go out there and be entertainment,' he said; 'it would have been bad taste.'

Instead he decided to reflect the war, to bring it home as an aural experience. From the opening gig onwards, a solo electric version of Dylan's 'Blowin' in the Wind' replaced the planned 'Mother Earth', with Young transforming the song Hendrix-style into an outpouring of anger, anguish and confusion. 'Older songs that I knew people could relate to' – songs of rape and murder such as 'Cortez the Killer' and 'Powderfinger' – were brought in to replace some of the *Ragged Glory* numbers.

The concerts began appropriately enough with Hendrix's 'Star-Spangled Banner', the sounds of Vietnam and the burning ghettos cutting across the Woodstock dawn. On the stage a yellow ribbon was tied round the giant microphone stand; at the rear a huge peace symbol loomed over the band. The juxtaposition of the two could be seen as yet another of Young's muddled attempts to have it both ways – pro-American and anti-war in a primarily American war – but on this occasion his reasoning seemed clear enough.

The yellow ribbon was a straightforward token of recognition that Americans were fighting and dying, and that their relations might well be in the concert hall. And not only Americans or their allies, Young told a radio interviewer: 'Everybody's over there fighting whether they're from Iraq or wherever they are. These people are caught in this thing that's bigger than all of us and they're going to lay down their lives, a lot of them. So let's think about them, you know, that's what the yellow ribbon is. In my mind it doesn't even have a side.'

As for the peace sign, at one level it simply reflected the age-old human hope that there was a less absurd and dangerous way of settling human disputes. At another it stated, quite clearly, that any war was crazy, including the one in question. Feeling concern for those involved didn't make it any less so.

This wasn't a courageous stand on Young's part – as, in the existing American mood, a clearly-stated, outright opposition to the war would have been – but it was an honest stand. He wasn't trying to have it both ways; in this instance he *knew* he was confused. 'That was the feeling,' he said, 'that corrosive mix of emotions and no one kind of knowing what to do. This guy has been calling us a dickhead, poisoning his own people. But idealistically, we shouldn't be doing this. We shouldn't be waging war. But if we're gonna have a war, is this a good one to have?'

He didn't know, and he wasn't alone. In the audience in front of him, peace signs vied with American flags, without any sense that they contradicted each other. In the wider world beyond the concert halls, many of those who had whole-heartedly opposed the American war in Vietnam found it harder to condemn a UN-sanctioned war against a tyrant like Saddam Hussein. Thousands of innocent Iraqis were being killed by air power, but there was always the fear that their unchosen leader was developing a nuclear weapon. Even for a political world increasingly short on simple answers, there were few to be found here.

Meanwhile the latest technology was unleashed on a helpless civilian population in front of a global TV audience. Young and the band would be watching CNN's coverage in their dressing rooms, then going out to play, images of the war transported from the screen into their music. 'When we were playing that stuff,' Young recalled in an interview, 'it was intense. It was *real*. I could see people dying in my mind. I could see bombs falling, buildings collapsing on families.' And the music was *loud*, 'loud in the way a crashing plane is loud, amped up for that war sound . . .'.

Originally known as the Ragged Glory tour, it later adopted the charming sobriquet Smell the Horse. A more appropriate moniker might have been Taste the War.

A double CD of live performances from the tour was released later that year under the name *Weld*. Young admitted that there was 'nothing different' about the album, that there was 'no ground-breaking going on, except in actual energy'. 'Blowin' in the Wind' was the only song on it not previously released by him, and several of the others were making their third or fourth appearance on a Young album. Nevertheless, his claim that many of the new versions were the best ever, that he and Crazy Horse had 'nailed a lot of stuff', proved justified. 'Love and Only Love', 'Welfare Mothers' and 'Tonight's the Night' deserve particular mention, and the yodelling yell that opens 'Fuckin' Up' is alone almost worth the price of the album.

Or the price of the video. This, directed by Young himself under his familiar pseudonym of Bernard Shakey, comprised a more or less straightforward compilation of concert performances – in most cases the same ones as had appeared on the album – with a fair sampling of audience participation. Only in a couple of instances did Young use the video to make the war connection more visually explicit.

After 'Crime in the City' the screen fills with CNN footage of the bombing of Baghdad, which fades around the lone figure of Young, wreathed in smoke and light, playing the opening chords of 'Blowin' in the Wind'. The camera turns to the audience, peace signs and American flags aloft, then back to Young singing Dylan's words, and the billowing yellow ribbon. It's a beautiful visual reflection of American thoughts and feelings about the war, all at war with each other.

Later in the video, footage of a bird doomed by its new coat of oil appears – appropriately enough – between 'Fuckin' Up' and 'Cortez the Killer'. At the end of the latter song, after the final semi-disbelieving 'What a killer!', a series of war shots – a Stealth bomber taking off, a lone GI, allied planes over Iraq – leads into 'Powderfinger', Young's tale of invasion and murder. There's no doubt whom he sees as the victim here: he might just as well have sung 'Look out Mama, here come the smart laser-guided weapons'. Or maybe even 'Tin soldiers and Schwarzkopf's coming'.

Those with a taste for sonic adventure could purchase something extra with their *Weld*: a limited edition of the double CD set came with a third component, *Arc*, a single CD featuring thirty-five minutes of, well, *noise* . . .

The idea went back some time, to 1987 and the *Muddy Track* video of that year's European tour with Crazy Horse. Young had often simply perched a camera on his amp, and this, vibrating madly as it shot past him at the audience, had caught, in Young's words, 'the sound of the entire band being sucked into this little limiter, being compressed and fucking distorted to hell . . .'.

It was the beginnings and ends of the songs that seemed to Young to offer the most, and he started to isolate them from the body of the songs, to regard them as something special in their own right. He showed the video to Sonic Youth's Thurston Moore, complete with the separated, distorted beginnings and endings. Moore was amazed enough to suggest that Young put it out on a record.

And as Young worked on *Weld* he realised how it could be done. 'I took fifty-seven pieces that we called "sparks" . . . took them out, numbered them, and disassociated them from the concerts that they came from. Of those fifty-seven pieces, I chose thirty-seven. I had them all on a database and I had all the keys and the lyrics that were in each piece written down, and the location of the piece so I could tell what hall it was from, so that I could move from one hall to another so the sound wouldn't change so radically.' Spliced together, the pieces became *Arc*.

Weld might be 'nothing different', but Young had great claims for *Arc*. 'If you look at my music over the last thirty years,' he said, 'and want to see where I'm at now, this is it.' But what *was* 'it'? Well, it was 'just sounds. That's the essence of it. It's like New Age metal . . . It has no *genre* or *attitude*; it's not like it's coming from this place or that place. It's just metal. And it's exploding, it's molten, it's happening . . .'

The album's defining characteristic was the lack of a regular rhythm, of a beat. Unlike most contemporary albums, which Young characterised as 'an hour of music with programmed beats, all because somebody dialled it in', *Arc* delivered 'thirty-five minutes without a beat anywhere'. This absence offered freedom. 'You were constrained by the beat. Everybody says that beat is the heart of rock'n'roll and I agree with that, the beat is where it's at. The masses go for the beat. But *Arc* is like being inside a very big thing. I equate *Arc* to that movie *Fantastic Voyage*, it's like a trip through a power chord. The chord may last five or six seconds but it takes thirty-five minutes, at the size we're reducing ourselves to, to go through it. To me *Arc* is more art and expression than anything I've done for a long time. It's elevator music for maniacs. This is white rap. It has no beat and very few words.'

It was, he said, 'like jazz or something'. It defined 'a whole new region of exploration for me and possibly for others'. And it would appeal to 'people on the fucking edge'.

Arc often sounds like a car crash in slow motion. It could provide any number of different soundtracks for any number of TV ads for air safety bags.

Arc sounds like a space movie. And a war movie. The Gulf War, any modern war.

Arc sounds like demented musicians thrashing their instruments. Which is what it is.

Some days *Arc* sounds like a piece of music that's having trouble getting started – for all of its thirty-five minutes. Other days it sounds like a piece of music that's having trouble getting finished – for all of its thirty-five minutes.

Or you can pretend you missed the first fifteen hours and arrived just in time for the thirty-five-minute wind-down.

There are echoes of the Velvet Underground's 'Sister Ray', the only piece of music I know that is guaranteed to give me a headache if I don't keep paying attention. (There's probably a moral there, but I'm not sure what it is.)

After concluding the gruelling Smell the Horse tour on 27th April, Young apparently took things fairly easy for the rest of 1991. He prepared the *Arc/Weld* material for release, and kept his concert appearances down to a few special events like the fifth Bridge benefit and the Bill Graham tribute, both in November. A planned tour of Japanese dates for Amnesty in September was cancelled, at least in part owing to Young's contracting an ear infection. He did have one date in the recording studio, to sing back-up vocal for old friend Robbie Robertson on the song 'Soapbox Preacher'. According to Robertson, Young was even looking like a soapbox preacher that day.

As regards his own music, Young now seemed set on an acoustic course. It was partly a matter of necessity: after *Arc/Weld* he 'couldn't do any more of that. I'd burned out on it – it took so much I had to get away and wait for it to come back. Really, I was just burned to the max.' One particular problem was the damage sustained by his ears during shows performed at warlike volume.

But there were also positive reasons for a return to his folk-country style. He expressed one philosophically: 'What you want is to get away to the quiet, to things that are so small and quiet, but when you get in them, they're huge. It's like under a magnifying glass, instead of something so big that it blows the walls off . . . it's the opposite. I've gone to that extreme now. It's natural. It's a natural progression . . . '

With acoustic music there was more chance to 'open up' the songs, to reach into the heart of what they were about. 'When you play by yourself,' he said in a radio interview, 'you get more involved with the nuance of who you really are, and what you are doing. So, I'm getting in touch with myself this way . . .' He was going back to basics, to 'words and chords and melody and people'. He could afford to now, because he no longer felt he needed somewhere to hide.

Taking his acoustic music out on the road was also a very different experience from touring with Crazy Horse or the Bluenotes. For one thing, different people came. Young reckoned that about half his overall audience would come to see both his soft acoustic and his hard electric personae, but the other halves for each genre were like chalk and cheese. Whereas his electric self tended to attract undefined 'extremists' – one description might be 'youngish white male drunks' – the acoustic performances brought together a whole lot of people who would never meet anywhere else: ordinary family people, between the ages of ten and sixty, of both genders.

It was time to get in touch with them again, to sing them the new songs he'd been writing about his life, and see if they found echoes of their own. Young was fond of describing the upcoming *Harvest Moon* as the calm in the eye of *Arc/Weld*'s hurricane, but it was a lot more than that. It was indeed a return to basics, but not just of the music – of the business of living, too. For the first time in many years, Young was writing and performing songs from the heart about his own life and loves, his own fears and fulfilments, not those of some character created to hide as much as it revealed.

During 1992 he toured intermittently, with chair, semicircle of banjo and guitars, pianos and pump organ, eschewing a set-list in favour of playing what came to heart and mind, alternating short strings of gigs with periods at the ranch. In the intervals he gathered the Stray Gators back together to record the new songs. The album would be called *Harvest Moon*, and would feature most of the band that had played on *Harvest* – but there had been no premeditated intention to produce a sequel. The songs, according to Young, simply suggested the musicians. The rest was coincidence.

Harvest Moon actually sounds less like *Harvest* than like *Comes a Time*. It has all the latter's quietness, lack of aggression and thoughtful demeanour, and none of the former's need to prove itself. The music reflects Young's relaxed state of mind. Above the strummed acoustic guitars and shuffling drums the pedal steel gently keens and the harmonica softly wails. Young's vocals are careful, restrained, full of inner strength, and admirably backed up by a supporting cast that includes Nicolette Larson, Linda Ronstadt and half-sister Astrid Young. Even the vague familiarity of many of the melodies is comforting. It was, he said, 'a more female record than any I've done. I think women who probably didn't like the last two will like it. It's a feminine record and I wanted that element to keep on coming back.'

Three of the songs – 'You and Me', 'Harvest Moon' and 'Such a Woman' – are essentially straightforward celebrations of the depth and longevity of Young's relationship with his wife. Though all are obviously heartfelt, and arguably key elements in the album's overall mosaic, none is particularly special. 'Such a Woman' has been so beautifully dressed by arranger Jack Nitzche that its underlying plainness is only the more apparent.

'Old King', the album's closest brush with a hoedown, is a posthumous tribute to Young's dog Elvis. 'Dreamin' Man' is on first hearing a simple admission of woolly-mindedness, but slowly darkens into the tale of an armed misfit who follows women through shopping malls. Nor is he the only one with 'homeless dreams': the female protagonist of 'Unknown Legend' roams the desert highways of her dreams while 'dressing two kids, looking for that magic kiss'. These are Americans in 1992, filled with a deep sense of loss of they know not what.

Young's own sense of loss forms part of the story on the four remaining tracks. 'One of These Days' has him looking back on, and regretfully accepting, the dispersion of friends, while 'From Hank to Hendrix' offers a more ambitious attempt at understanding the process by which people carry their pasts into their presents. It's about music, and Young's own trip from Hank B. Marvin through to Jimi Hendrix, but it's also about relationships, and finding 'the same smile' in so many places. The possibility of divorce is mentioned, then forgotten; as death is part of life, so divorce is part of marriage: 'You're constantly wondering . . . whether it's gonna last or whether it's going to explode.'

All things must pass, but perhaps they don't need to pass quite as fast as a throwaway culture would like. Some things grow deeper with time, some don't. The way Young saw it, you have to work at avoiding 'the boredom and repetition and eventual demise of the relationship because of those things'. Being in a relationship meant 'keeping things new and staying fresh, not just getting into a mould and doing the same things over and over again, but really trying to discover and feel them for the first time . . .'.

It was now twenty-three years since Young had asked the question 'If so many love you, is it the same?', and *Harvest Moon* finds him in much the same territory. In 1969 he had wondered in song whether multiple relationships offered the soul what it needed; now he expresses the doubts of a middle-aged married man, and wonders how he can grow within a monogamous relationship, particularly one set in the context of a wider culture obsessed by youth and change for its own sake.

The need to preserve, to build on what exists, to resist change for change's sake, is as applicable to the wider environment as it is to two people working on a life together. In 'War of Man' Young presents a slight but charming animal's-eye view of the planet; in 'Natural Beauty' he ties everything together to produce a bona fide work of genius. The song is recorded live, with just Young on guitar and harmonica, what sounds like a synth and vibes behind him, and Nicolette Larson joining him on the high and lilting chorus. The overall effect is a mixture of the sad, the resigned and the determined. The lyric sounds simple at first – but only at first.

The chorus begins, 'A natural beauty should be/Preserved like a monument to nature.' The juxtaposition of 'nature' and 'preserve' is ironic, in that what comes 'naturally' should not need intervention. Unfortunately, thanks to our shortcomings as a species this has become the central irony of our civilisation: we now need worldwide environmental action just to keep things the way they are. The next two lines – 'Don't sell yourself too short my love/Or someday you might find your soul endangered' – establish another connection. By selling the planet short we have put nature in danger, and by selling ourselves short, by applying the same misconceived values to our lives, we put our own true natures in danger.

There are no answers in 'Natural Beauty', just glimpses of connections between human life, the world humans inherited and the world humans live in. The first verse moves ominously from a newborn baby crying to 'an anonymous wall of digital sound'; the second contains the line 'What a lucky man to see the earth before it touched his hand'. It seems logically absurd, but like the 'homeland we've never seen' in 'Pocahontas', that unsullied Earth is carried within us. In the final verse Young is at the rodeo, noting the brand-new Chevrolets, the brand-new seamless pants – all the paraphernalia of our consumer culture – and watching 'the moment of defeat/Played back over on the video screen/Somewhere deep inside of my soul'.

This song encapsulates the central theme of *Harvest Moon* in all its aspects: the need to accept unavoidable loss, whether of age or of innocence or of beauty, and to struggle against avoidable loss, whether of love or of friends or of a habitable environment. The past must be carried into the future as a living thing. For both the individual and the planet, in Young's words, 'The idea is to keep living. Don't snuff yourself out.'

'Feel the years drop away!' Reprise urged consumers in their promotion of *Harvest Moon*. The album's author, though happy to admit that *he* couldn't feel any dropping away, seemed in pretty good shape for anyone approaching their forty-seventh birthday, let alone someone who'd carried a fraught medical history through twenty-five years of rock stardom.

His state of apparent omnipresence continued. 1991's Godfather of Grunge image merged into 1992's Old Acoustic Hippie to produce a kind of generic Elder Statesman of Rock, equally at home with metal and with wood; with his own generation and with the latest batch of teenagers. Even rap received his seal of approval. 'Hey man, this is the coolest shit,' he told a surprised Ice-T, explaining how he often found that the need to *sing* words was limiting. With rap 'you say what the fuck you want to say'. As he'd always said, Young liked *good* music – the genre was secondary.

In January he was invited to induct the Jimi Hendrix Experience into the Rock'n'Roll Hall of Fame. He naturally lauded his favourite guitarist, but he also paid tribute to the other two members of the band. 'It's hard to say if he could have done that without these other two guys,' he remarked in his speech, and perhaps as he did so he cast a thought back to all those who had helped *him* along the way, from the Jades to the Restless.

The benefits kept coming: the fifth Farm Aid concert in March, an LA gig in aid of Massachusetts' Walden Woods in April. Young himself was a beneficiary of another kind in May, returning to Fort William (now nominally part of Thunder Bay) to pick up an honorary doctorate at Lakehead University.

In October he broke off from touring to appear at the Bob Dylan tribute concert in New York – the Bobfest, as Young dubbed the occasion – and provided one of the evening's highlights with passionate versions of 'Just Like Tom Thumb's Blues' and 'All Along the Watchtower'. His appearance immediately followed a hate-filled welcome for Sinead O'Connor, who had defiantly sung Edwin Starr's 'War' at the hostile crowd before leaving in tears. Young showed her no sympathy, either at the time or afterwards, arguing reasonably – but perhaps not very compassionately – that anyone as outspoken as O'Connor should learn how to deal with the inevitable reaction.

Politically, 1992 was yet another Electionfest, and Young, seemingly forever on tour, was frequently asked his opinion of the candidates. He still didn't like Bush, who appeared to offer no hope of the changes needed by a faltering economy, and he wasn't too sure about Clinton. The man himself was a 'fighter', Young thought, but 'the Democratic way of doing things' did not inspire him with optimism.

He rather liked the third candidate. Ross Perot wasn't business as usual; he did seem to offer radical change. 'I'm kind of a radical myself,' Young professed; 'I think if you're gonna stir things up, stir them up hard. Do it, get it done. At the same time I have to warn myself that some things are too big to move too fast, otherwise you'll break them . . . Ross Perot has a sense of genius about him that I find very interesting. I'm not scared by him. A lot of people find him sinister and threatening. But that's because he's so open . . . '

Or then again, it might be that many people found Perot's barely concealed racism and homophobia a tad too close to Fascism for comfort. For someone who considered himself, in environmental matters at least, 'a citizen of Planet Earth first and a citizen of whatever country second', Young's intuitive respect for the maverick was leading him into dangerous territory.

'I don't think,' Young said in 1990, when asked to describe his guitar-playing technique. 'My head has nothing to do with it. I think it's my whole soul. My whole body and my whole soul. Just doing the fucking dance of the pyramids.' In fact, the more mindless his playing, he thought, the better it was. 'My best shows, I can't remember what I did. That's how I know I was probably pretty good . . . '

He has always been the first to admit that he's not the most technically gifted guitarist in the world. His right hand is fast enough, but his left –

like that whole side of his body – is slow. He doesn't know the scales, and is happy to concede that 'a lot of notes I go for are notes that I know aren't there'.

None of this really matters, at least as far as he is concerned. Although willing to be impressed by the technically gifted, he has always found technical precision hard to relate to. The bottom line, as always, is passion: 'If you have feelings that you want to get out through music, that's what matters.' As a guitarist Young has rarely done anything else. According to Frank Sampedro, 'he has a giant soul – there's nothing technical about it'. Billy Talbot considers it 'musical innocence'. Young himself accepts that he is 'a maker of noise – and a melodic noise too, sometimes'.

Young insists that Crazy Horse are due a lot of the credit. 'You can call it a solo,' he says, but 'it's the whole band that's playing. Billy Talbot is a massive bass player who only plays two or three notes. People are still trying to figure out whether it's because he only *knows* two or three notes or whether those are the only notes he wants to play. But when he hits a note, that note speaks for itself. It's a big motherfucking note. Even the soft one is big . . . Frank uses the biggest strings of any guitar player I've ever seen. Frank is probably even more of a crude player than I am, because his lead isn't as developed as mine. But his strings are *so* big! . . . He hits a note and it's a big note . . . Without Crazy Horse playing so big, I sound just normal. But they supply the big so I can float around and sound *huge*. The big is them.'

When playing, Young looks for that magic moment of elevation. Once off the ground, 'when I'm playing or jamming it starts in my head, my nose starts feeling this rush of air and I realise I'm starting to hyperventilate and you just get more and more into it – the endorphins in your body feel it . . . It doesn't always work – sometimes it just sounds like a long time playing the same groove and nothing happens. Other times it's like a euphoric, cosmic orgasm.'

What goes up must come down; afterwards it's all a bit strange. 'When I come off stage I feel a bit disoriented. If I've been playing a good show, I'm really fucking disoriented. I really wanna know, geographically, what's happening. I'm trying not to walk into any walls. Usually I'm hyperventilating. Probably a little bit echoey in the head.'

To paraphrase one of his songs: every solo goes by, he burns a little bit of his soul.

*   *   *

Young's approach to writing leans every bit as heavily on spontaneity as his approach to guitar-playing. 'Sometimes it comes through and sometimes it doesn't. As long as you stay open to it, it keeps happening . . . If it doesn't come for a couple of months, that means you're supposed to take a rest. You don't have to do it all the time. The music would be contrived if you tried to force it. It would be futile. I stay there as long as I can, when I'm writing a song, and then the avenue will simply close up. Sometimes I'll wait a year and a half before the rest of the song comes through.' Since writer's block afflicts only those who sit down to write before the inspiration strikes, Young has never suffered from it.

He finds he has ideas for songs when driving, after waking early in the morning, while out walking; the muse can grab him at any time, and demands instant attention. 'If you're walking down the street,' he told a Canadian TV show on songwriting, 'and you start hearing a song, don't wait. Because you'll forget it. It will never be like it was.'

The process should involve as little conscious thought as possible. 'It's a funny thing about music,' he said in 1989. 'The worst thing you can do is *think*. That's the lowest.' The author should try not to interfere in his own authorship, just be present at the birth.

Post-natal fiddling should also be kept to a minimum. Editing, after all, is a conscious thinking process. Young's notion that the song comes *through* him rather than *from* him imbues him with a sense of responsibility for the purity of its genesis, to the point where he considers editing akin to a 'taking of liberties'. 'My mind is working behind the scenes and puts these things together without me consciously thinking of it, and then when the time is right it all comes out. That's more like, you know, creation in the true sense of the word than it is contrivance. So it doesn't really need to be edited so long as you get it out right, get it out clean, you know, without second-guessing yourself every line thinking, "What are people gonna think of me if I write this?"'

There are obviously no hard and fast rules. Many of Young's songs have changed over the years, both before and after their recording, and there seems no reason to believe that Young never changes one between its conception and its first public airing. At home Pegi hears him try something out, 'then, over a period of days or weeks', she listens to it 'grow and develop'. And 'when he is working on lyrics, he sometimes sings around the house, but softly, little more than a murmur'.

The end result should say something more to the audience than just a take-it-or-leave-it. Young's songs may reflect what is going on in his life, whether inside his heart or out in the world, but he also wants them to offer a way in for the listener, to stimulate his or her mind: 'They don't have to finish the story, but leave whoever's hearing it out there with a sort of canvas to draw his own pictures.'

When Young thinks he has enough such songs, 'I pick the best and try to bring them together around a theme'. If he needs more, or if he feels something different is required to place the overall theme in greater relief, he goes to the vaults for an appropriate song. Once he has some idea of which songs will feature on the next album, then he starts thinking about which musicians seem most suited to what he has in mind. And once that is decided, recording dates are fixed, preferably around the time of a full moon.

Recording is not Young's favourite part of the creative process. On the one hand he admits to lacking the patience necessary for the making of highly crafted records; on the other, he has no interest in making such records anyway. 'I hate recording studios and production, all of it. I don't like the factory assembly-line kind of thing . . . I like recording like I like films. I like *cinéma vérité* films . . . I like audio *vérité*.'

This has been true since the early seventies, when, Young admits, he 'became obsessed with capturing and recording the moment. Everybody I knew was doing more and more in the studio. I considered it a form of suicide to make polished records. The cleaner other records were, the more angry I got about it.' He would rather 'do a performance of the song, where I sing and play, and get the feeling of the song, and it may not be perfect and it may not have the big sound that it needs to get on the radio, and it may not have the perfect beat, or the computer to make everybody feel relaxed . . . I don't have that and I don't want it.'

He does use overdubbing, particularly for backing vocals on live albums, but thinks it should be either kept to a minimum or used only when he has a specific end in mind, such as 'where I was trying to go for a particularly slick sound or I wanted to get something that was completely sterile – which I might want to do sometime'. As a rule, though, he prefers taking musical photographs to painting musical portraits.

Either alone or with a band, Young goes into the studio and does a song two or three times. That's often enough, but if it isn't he'll stop and return to the song in a few days, rather than just keep bashing it out until all the spontaneity is gone.

He has acknowledged that he owes a great deal in the studio to David Briggs. 'Without him,' Young has said, 'we are all wondering if we are doing the right thing.' But he doesn't need technical guidance: for someone so fond of emphasising human spontaneity, Young has a long history not only of understanding the advancing technology of recording, but also of devising his own technological aids. As with cars and trains, he leans towards old, tested and tried equipment, and for mixing prefers a small two-valve board from the early sixties to total reliance on the wonders of contemporary technology. It gives the music a warmer sound, and thus offers a corrective to the harshening effect of digital recording.

Young says that he records everything in digital from the beginning because it all goes digital in the end, and it's better to know what you're dealing with at each step of the recording process. If restricting himself to analogue records and tapes were still a commercially viable proposition he might well do so, because he believes – and seemed to spend most of 1992 telling the world – that digital music is 'torture', 'sensory deprivation', that humanity has entered 'the dark ages of recorded sound'.

He puts up an impressive case. The surface durability and production clarity of CDs is indisputable, but it's not music that's being reproduced: 'You're listening to binary numbers being spat out of a digital converter ... That's code and digits and information and when this little chip sees that, it spits out toners and frequencies that recreate the sound of music . . .'

The erasing of surface hiss might seem like a step forward, but 'along with the hiss went depth of sound and the myriad possibilities of the high end where everything is like the cosmos, exploding stars, echo. From the eighties on, no records contain that kind of quality any more and those are the very things that stimulate the human body into reacting and feeling and enjoying music. Those things are gone now. CDs do not give you the music. They give you a representation of the music. It's like a surface thing – it's not the real deal.'

In interviews in recent years, Young has often drawn parallels with photography. Take a regular camera and one of the new digitals, he said in 1993, take the same shot with each, and pin the blown-up photographs on the wall. From twenty feet away 'the digital one looks a little sharper, and the other one looks beautiful but not as crisp. Then walk up close. The film is beautiful – the closer you get the more detail you see, the more richness. But when you walk up to the digital one you see a bunch of dots. And each dot is just one colour only. There's no detail at all . . .'

It was the same, he felt, with music: 'If you're listening to this digital sound, instead of being encompassed by all the possibilities, and all the richness of the sound, right away you're satisfied. You've heard it. You don't have to hear it again.'

He quoted psychiatrists who'd found that CDs don't relax people the way analogue music does, and predicted that within fifteen years new, molecular computers would again allow music to be recorded through an organic base. Then everything originally recorded on analogue, before about 1981, would be put out yet again, with all the improvements CDs had brought, and without the loss of richness. But all the music recorded digitally between 1980 and 2010 would be unenhanceable.

When asked whether his opinion might be out of step with that of the majority of people working in the music industry, Young replied that in that case 'the entire recording industry is fucking wrong, every one of them, and some of them know it'.

As a coda, it's interesting to note that at Boston's Berklee Music College, the Music Production and Engineering Department's Dave Moulton researched the analogue-digital dispute in general, and Young's allegations in particular. He found the audible differences between the two media 'pretty small' and came down in favour of digital as cheaper and easier to use. But he also referred to recent Japanese research, which showed that digital music's reduction of frequency range lessens both measurable brain activity and the listener's conscious awareness of interest, satisfaction and beauty.

As the eighties turned into the nineties, and Young met with renewed artistic and commercial success, he also seemed more inclined to look back over his career. Perhaps he was being asked questions that encouraged such an inclination by newly eager interviewers; perhaps the past was much in his thoughts as he worked towards the eventual release of his own archive material. Perhaps simple age played a part – forty-eight-year-olds are, after all, more inclined to look back on their lives than twenty-four-year-olds.

His eclipse in the eighties was much on his and interviewers' minds. His explanations, though, were as contradictory as ever. Though quite willing to acknowledge that family traumas had caused him to repress his own emotions, he could still pronounce himself satisfied with what he'd done through the decade. 'Everything I did made sense to me,' he said, and the further he got from the eighties, the more sense everything made. 'I knew what I was doing when I put those records out, and I knew what the reaction would be. I knew what people wanted from me and what they weren't getting. But still I knew that time would go by, and then people would see them like a group of records – almost like a period, if they were paintings. And now, there they are. They're becoming more clear all the time.' After Picasso's blue period, Neil's shocking-pink period.

He had made interesting records in the early eighties – *Trans* and *Old Ways* in particular – but the suspicion persists that he made them almost despite himself. He admitted having removed his soul from his music, admitted having been unwilling to confront his own situation directly in song, thereby denying himself his greatest strengths – passion and honesty. Instead he made a succession of cold-eyed, outward-looking albums which were bound to expose his greatest weaknesses – a refusal to think things through, a lack of knowledge and a distrust of craft.

Young's own sense of the Geffen albums could be gleaned in 1993 from the *Lucky Thirteen* compilation, and a strange sense it was. 'Like an Inca', 'Are There Any Real Cowboys?', 'My Boy', 'Touch the Night', 'Twilight', 'Life in the City' and all the *Life* ballads are conspicuous by their absence. Two songs each have been plucked from *Trans* (one an extended version), *Old Ways*, *Landing on Water* and *Life*, seemingly at random. The album ends with two live Bluenotes performances, neither of which features 'Ordinary People'. The only real interest lies in the two live Shocking Pink performances of 'Get Gone' and 'Don't Take Your Love Away from Me', and the unreleased acoustic 'Depression Blues'. If Young really believed in 1993 that *Lucky Thirteen* offered his best work from the Geffen era, then he didn't have much company.

He was looking back further than the eighties in one of the rare new songs he unveiled in 1992, the clearly autobiographical 'Hitch-hiker'. The song is a litany of drug abuse, from a first try with hash in Toronto, through amphetamines, to Valium in California, then grass in the country and cocaine on the road. 'When I was a hitch-hiker on the road,' the first and last verse goes, 'I had to count on you/But you needed me to ease the load/And for conversation too/Or did you just drive on through.' He could be talking about any or every type of mutual dependency, in his relationships with his bands, his audience, even his unruly self.

He offered a musical retrospective of this whole period in his recorded appearance on MTV's *Unplugged*. Here, the choice of material both matched expectations and made commercial sense. Since the thirteen previously-released songs had appeared on eleven different albums, *Unplugged* would function rather well as a sampler for all the new fans he had gathered over the last few years. Those who already owned all the songs would still need to buy this album for the belated release of the wonderful 'Stringman'.

In the event, the album became an excellent buy in its own right, purely on the strength of Young's singing. Although the musicians, Young included, may well have been content to do no more than recreate the peaceful feel of *Harvest Moon*, his vocal performances were so intense and heartfelt that even a song as old and apparently perfected as 'Helpless' could be brought to new life.

His stage presence, on this show and several others during the period, was as familiar and comforting as an old glove. With his long scraggly thinning hair, checked shirt and face torn between a scowl and a smile, he would wander from instrument to instrument like a tramp checking out park benches.

What does the future hold for him? There have been several reports that his two non-concert movies will appear on video, but as yet they have not done so. Nor has there been news of any fresh movie project. Young has stretched his acting muscles over the last few years, playing cameo roles in (largely unsuccessful) Hollywood movies such as *Made in Heaven* and *Love at Large*, but generally his attention appears to have been fixed on his music.

A huge CD retrospective of his career has been in the works since 1990. It was originally conceived as a series of boxed sets each comprising four CDS; the first set was planned to cover the period 1964–70, and to include recordings by the Squires, Buffalo Springfield and the solo Young. Each CD would contain almost as much previously unreleased as released material, and the boxes were to appear at roughly eighteen-month intervals.

The project has since been expanded still further, with plans to release a complete set of Young's albums, together with fifty or sixty previously unreleased songs. This would be available on special order only, while the shops would carry a series of boxed highlights and a single CD containing the cream of the cream.

As for new music, Young has spoken over the past few years of possible collaborations with Frank Sinatra, Eric Clapton and Lou Reed. The former was invited to work with the Bluenotes but, according to

Young, 'we just didn't seem to get the feedback required to continue down that road'. He shared a dressing room with Clapton at the Bobfest, and thought they had 'played together really well; the guitars blended nicely'. He said in 1992 that he had always wanted to play with Lou – just the two of them on guitar plus bass and drums – and that he 'wouldn't mind going to New York and trying something'.

At the Bobfest, Young, like most of the invited stars, was backed by the almost legendary sixties Stax band Booker T and the MGs. The collaboration worked so well that he asked them to tour Europe and the US with him in the summer of 1993. It proved a wise move: this band offered Young a blend of musical precision and raw passion he had not experienced before. There were few new songs from Young, however, and it seems unlikely that an album of the tour will be released.

Where his recording muse will take him next is anyone's guess. He has never hidden his respect for those who follow their musical inspiration wherever it leads. He has given Linda Ronstadt as one example, Bobby Darin as another. 'I used to get pissed off at Bobby Darin,' he said in 1988, 'because he changed styles so often. Now I look at him, and I think he was a fucking genius.'

On the other hand, Young has also been fond of asserting that everything he has done has been linked by a common thread – himself. Van Morrison is as much of a genius as Darin was, but his music isn't 'that much different now than it was when he started'. It's 'just *him*', Young said in 1991. 'And *me* is what I do.'

Whether he can keep up the innovative pace of recent years is also open to question. Not because of his age – after all, why should songwriters have a shorter lifespan than novelists or poets? – but perhaps because of shifting priorities. 'The real music of my life is my family,' he said in 1993, and in interviews he talks glowingly of going dancing with Pegi, of birthdays with the children and their friends toasting marshmallows round the fire. He has a paradisal ranch, an ocean-going boat, and a model-railroad layout that in spring 1993 made the lead article in a national magazine. He has an electronics development company working on alternatives to the CD, which he refers to half-jokingly as 'the beginning of my life's work'.

He is even designing electronics himself. Acquiring the headswitch with which Ben controls model trains 'made me think of all these things I could do to make life easier for the disabled. I'm working on ways of controlling environments completely with one button.' His knowledge is all self-taught, and he finds such work as therapeutic in its way as music: 'I find it really good for my head to get into this logic. Way into logic. And then just completely leave logic. Go the other way. It works really good.'

Critics have been trying since 1970 to sum up Young's impact on rock music, and there is no reason for them to stop doing so now. His career, like his voice, has always polarised opinion, and nowhere has this been more apparent than in *The Rolling Stone Illustrated History of Rock & Roll*. When this was first published in 1976 it contained a scathing piece on Young by Dave Marsh, which sat uneasily amidst the generally laudatory reviews of other musicians' careers. In more recent editions, Marsh's piece has been replaced by Don McLeese's more generous appreciation.

Marsh is in the main a fine writer – his *The Heart and Soul of Rock'n'Roll* is probably the best available work on singles – but his article on Young was marred by a string of factual errors and a general mean-spiritedness. Few of his attacks were aimed at Young's music; rather he turned his fire on other critics and the artist's 'self-mythologisation', which together had conspired to make Young 'seem more important than he really is'. Marsh's one coherent criticism concerned Young's 'refusal to commit himself to one style and develop it'. His dabbling was 'symptomatic of that refusal ... Instead of a unified body of work, Neil Young has forged only a series of fragments, some relatively inspired, some absolutely awful.'

McLeese, of course, considered this same refusal to lie at the heart of Young's artistic success. Far from lamenting the lack of 'a unified body of work', he noted that 'Young refuses to sell himself short, to resolve the messiness of flesh and blood into a tidy, more marketable package'. McLeese takes it as a given that for Young, 'musical development would defy conventional notions of progression and maturity'.

Both critics are right, and wrong: the dichotomy they present is false. One could ask Marsh what a rock musician's 'unified body of work' would look like after twenty-five years. Like the Rolling Stones' or Springsteen's endless recycling of the same riffs, sounds, themes? Like Lou Reed's peripatetic progress? One could say to McLeese, okay, you've told us which notions of progress and maturity Young would *not* follow – now tell us which, if any, he has.

Young's career certainly follows a pattern, or, more accurately, several patterns. He himself placed *Harvest*, *Comes a Time* and *Old Ways* in one group; *Everybody Knows This Is Nowhere, Zuma, Rust Never Sleeps* and *Ragged Glory* in a second; *Tonight's the Night, Everybody's Rockin'* and *This Note's for You* in a third. The first three are clearly linked by their folk-country sound, the second four by Crazy Horse, the third three by the shaky personae fronting the bands. There are other chains of albums. *After the Goldrush, Zuma, Comes a Time* and *Harvest Moon* are inward-looking, relationship-centred, whereas *On the Beach, Rust Never Sleeps, Hawks and Doves* and *Freedom* all look outwards, at society as a whole.

Whether or not there is any 'progress' within these chains is debatable. Is *Ragged Glory* an advance on *Everybody Knows This Is Nowhere*? Probably not. How could such progress be measured? An increase in maturity, however, seems undeniable. *Neil Young* is the work of a twenty-three-year-old setting out on his first marriage; *Harvest Moon* is that of a forty-six-year-old who has been through several relationships and learned things about himself in the process. Young may have refused to commit himself to the development of one musical style, but he has certainly committed himself to growing up, and that cannot but come through in his music.

Like any artist, he has limitations. And as with most artists, the limitations are also strengths. The confidence to follow his instincts that makes the songs so real is a product of the same part of his make-up that prevents him from developing any particular musical avenue.

Young is rich, white and male, and although such characteristics do not in themselves lead to a narrowing of social vision, they are not so easy to transcend for someone who speaks so clearly, so illuminatingly, from the core of exactly who and what he is.

And this same ability to speak straight from the soul, which sometimes makes his whiteness and maleness so alarmingly apparent, is exactly what allows him to be so unashamedly and revealingly human.

One last word on the artist's evolution. When I saw Young perform at Great Woods near Boston in September 1993, midway through the second instrumental section of 'Like a Hurricane', one particular passage on guitar sounded like an echo of the Shadows and Hank B. Marvin. But if in one sense he was still playing what he had been playing in 1963, in another he could not be. Longevity of career creates its own form of evolution, with or without the artist's intent. Listening to Young's passion spilling out across the arena, I could maybe hear 'Wonderful

Land', but I could also hear the rage of 'Ohio', the lyrical tenderness of 'I Believe in You', the sadness of 'Transformer Man' and the crazy joy of 'Cinnamon Girl'.

The man has enriched the culture we all share, and enriched the personal experience of all those who have followed his wayward progress through the years.

Long may he run.

DISCOGRAPHY: THE ALBUMS

1989 Eldorado (EP)
     Freedom
1990 Ragged Glory
1991 Weld
     Arc
1992 Harvest Moon
1993 Lucky Thirteen
     Unplugged

ACKNOWLEDGEMENTS

During the researching and writing of this book I naturally applied for an interview with its subject. I didn't expect any great revelations – musicians, it seems to me, nearly always do their best talking with their music – but I did want to give Young the chance to confirm or deny some of the more controversial stories that have appeared about his life and music over the years. As it happened, I was simply told that Mr Young was not giving interviews at this time, and that the man himself did not wish to be associated with any biography.

Fair enough. He has given enough interviews down the years, and I have made particular use of those conducted by the following: Elliot Blinder (*Rolling Stone*, 30th April 1970), David Cavanagh (*Select*, November 1990), Ray Coleman (*Melody Maker*, 25th August 1973 and 10th April 1976), Cameron Crowe (*Rolling Stone*, 14th August 1975 and 8th February 1979), David Fricke (*Melody Maker*, 30th November 1991), Robert Greenfield (*Fusion*, 17th April 1970), Richard Harrington (*Washington Post*, 12th September 1985), James Henke (*Rolling Stone*, 2nd June 1988 and 4th October 1990), Allan Jones (*Melody Maker*, 7th November 1992), Ira Kaplan (*Spin*, March 1993), Alan Light (*Rolling Stone*, 21st January 1993), Jimmy McDonough (*Village Voice*, 18th December 1989), Steve Martin (*Pulse*, December 1991), Jas Obrecht (*Guitar Player*, March 1992), John Rockwell (*New York Times*, 27th November 1977), Karen Schoerner (*New York Times*, 25th November 1992), Bud Scoppa (*New Musical Express*, 28th June 1975), Adam Sweeting (*Melody Maker*, 7th and 14th September 1985) and Mary Turner (Warner Brothers promotional disc WBMS107, 1979).

Broken Arrow, the quarterly journal of the Neil Young Appreciation Society, besides being both generally useful and a good read, has also yielded transcriptions of several more interviews: a 1982 interview with the French magazine *Rock & Folk*, translated by Kathryn Wheatley (Issue 8/9); a 1983 US TV interview (Issue 12); Young's March 1985 press

237

conference in Sydney (Issue 21); two unnamed and undated radio programmes dedicated to *Déjà Vu* and *Harvest* (Issue 37); a 1990 *World Première* US radio interview (Issue 41); a November 1991 *Rockline* US radio interview (Issue 46); a 1990 MTV radio transcription (Issue 47); a 1989 BBC Radio 1 interview (Issue 49); a 1992 BBC Radio 1 interview (Issue 50); and a 1992 Greater London Radio interview (Issue 51).

Other articles and interviews used include: Alan Jenkins's interview with Billy Talbot (*Broken Arrow*, Issue 41); Ted Joseph's interview with Graham Nash (*Sounds*, 18th September 1986); Allan R. McDougall's interview with Stephen Stills (*Rolling Stone*, 4th March 1971); Antti Marttinen's interview with Nils Lofgren (*Broken Arrow*, Issue 51); and Bob Young's piece on his brother in *Maclean's*, May 1971.

Other books worth reading include Scott Young's hard-to-get-hold-of *Neil and Me* (McClelland & Stewart, Canada, 1984), which offers a parent's-eye view of Young's childhood; John Einarson's *Don't Be Denied* (Omnibus, UK, 1993), a fascinating account of the singer's Canadian years; and Dave Zimmer's *Crosby, Stills and Nash* (St Martin's Press, USA, 1984), which is an indispensable ally for anyone in pursuit of the gleesome threesome.

On a personal note, I would like to thank Penny, David and Clare at Bloomsbury for their professional assistance, and all the various friends who helped in various ways during the researching of the book. Some of the latter, it must be said, have become better acquainted with Young's music than they either intended or desired. I hope to be forgiven in time.

David Downing
October 1993

INDEX

239